T0103178

THE GREAT DEPRESSION: A DIARY

THE GREAT DEPRESSION

A DIARY

BENJAMIN ROTH

EDITED BY JAMES LEDBETTER AND DANIEL B. ROTH

PublicAffairs | NEW YORK

Copyright © 2009 Diary text by Daniel B. Roth.
Copyright © 2009 Introduction and Editor's commentary by James Ledbetter.

Hardcover first published in 2009 in the United States by PublicAffairs™,
a member of the Perseus Books Group.
Paperback first published in 2010 by PublicAffairs.

All rights reserved.
Printed in the United States of America.
No part of this book may be reproduced in any manner whatsoever without written permission except in the case of brief quotations embodied in critical articles and reviews. For
information, address PublicAffairs, 250 West 57th Street, Suite 1321, New York, NY 10107.

PublicAffairs books are available at special discounts for bulk purchases in the U.S. by
corporations, institutions, and other organizations. For more information, please contact the Special Markets Department at the Perseus Books Group, 2300 Chestnut Street,
Suite 200, Philadelphia, PA 19103, call (800) 810-4145, ext. 5000, or e-mail special.markets
@perseusbooks.com.

Book Design by Jenny Dossin

The Library of Congress has catalogued the hardcover as follows:
Roth, Benjamin, 1894–1978.
The Great Depression : a diary / Benjamin Roth ; edited by James Ledbetter and Daniel
B. Roth.—1st ed.
p. cm.
Includes bibliographical references.
ISBN 978-1-58648-799-7 (hardcover)
1. Depressions—1929—United States. 2. United States—Economic conditions—1918–
1945. 3. Roth, Benjamin, 1894–1978—Diaries. I. Ledbetter, James. II. Roth, Daniel B.,
1929-III. Title.
HB37171929 .R656 2009
330.973'0917—dc22
2009026790

Paperback ISBN: 978-1-58648-901-4

Printing 17, 2023

CONTENTS

When I graduated from law school in 1956, I was fortunate to be able to join my dad, Benjamin Roth, in his Youngstown, Ohio, law practice. By that time he had been a lawyer for thirty-seven years, and following the end of the Depression, he had developed a substantial clientele as a sole practitioner. As a new lawyer, I had no clients of my own and therefore devoted all of my time to working with my father's clients. That is when I first learned that he had maintained a detailed diary of financial issues throughout the 1930s.

As my first assignment, Dad asked me to study the diary so that I could gain insight into the Depression mentality of his clients. He suggested that in order for me to represent them, I had to understand the traumas they had suffered during the Depression and the scars they still bore in the 1950s. I recall attending a meeting with an elderly client and a trust investment officer and listening to the client tell the officer that the only way he would transfer any of his assets into a trust would be if the bank would agree in writing to never invest any of his money in anything other than U.S. government bonds. (Subsequently, the client loosened that restriction, and the bank did very well by building a diversified, conservative portfolio.)

My grandfather Samuel Roth had come to this country in 1877 and settled in Manhattan, where Dad was born in 1894. The family relocated to Youngstown, Ohio, in 1900, and Dad attended the local schools. He then earned his undergraduate and law degrees at what is now known as Case Western Reserve University in Cleveland, Ohio, where he helped pay his college expenses by playing the violin in the orchestra pits of the local silent movie theaters. While in law school, he met my mother, Marion Benjamin, a student at Oberlin College. Immediately following his graduation from law school, Dad was sworn in as a lieutenant in the U.S. Army and joined his three brothers on active duty during World War I. At the end of the war, which coincided with my mother's graduation from Oberlin, my parents were married in Cleveland.

In 1919 my folks settled in Youngstown, where my father opened his law office. A year later my sister, Connie, was born, followed five years later by the birth of my brother, Bob; I entered the family in September 1929 (thereby

ABOVE. *Benjamin Roth gathers with his wife, Marion, and three children, daughter Connie and sons Daniel and Bob, in 1935.*

RIGHT. *Dan Roth plays with his two cousins, Jim (left) and David (right) Elliott, and his dog, Puddles, in Youngstown, Ohio, in 1936.*

ABOVE. *Benjamin Roth hosting Thanksgiving dinner with his family in 1937. Seated at the table (from left to right) are Benjamin's sister-in-law, Roma Elliott; his brother, Morris Roth;, his daughter, Connie; Benjamin himself; his mother-in-law, Irene Benjamin; his father-in-law, Morris Benjamin; and his wife, Marion Roth.*

causing the entire stock market to crash, according to my parents!). I recall little before 1934, though I clearly remember that my parents constantly discussed money problems and "pinched" every penny. When I was six or seven years old, I fell and cut my forehead. As I lay on the sofa, bleeding badly, my mother phoned my father (yes, we had a phone) and asked whether we could afford to have a doctor come to the house (no, we had no car). My father called a doctor who was one of his clients. The doctor made the house call and patched me up—but then refused any payment because of my father's having provided some legal services for him without charging a fee.

I have many fond memories of growing up in the 1930s, even as terrible as those years were. My mother taught piano lessons at home, and on most evenings our family would perform "concerts," gathering around Mom's piano with Dad playing the violin and we three children singing. On warm summer evenings, my parents would open the front door, and many of our neighbors would sit in our living room or on our front porch and join in the fun. Those were the days of simple pleasures; there was no need to spend money or to own a car. In retrospect, I realize that throughout their entire married life, my parents always lived within a short walk of the bus line, and even in his eighties my dad would leave his car in the garage and ride the bus to and from the office. When I first began to work with him, I offered to drive him downtown, but he refused, explaining that he enjoyed getting to know the other passengers, many of whom became his longtime friends.

In 1937 Dad purchased a new car, his first since selling his old one in 1932; my sister, Connie, left for college; and the country entered into a second deep depression. I can clearly recall my parents discussing whether they would be able to afford to keep Connie in college (there were no student loans in those days), and they finally told her to take one semester at a time and they would do their best to keep her in school. Their "best" was good enough, and Connie received her teaching degree and ultimately became a highly respected teacher in Boardman, Ohio.

As I read through this period in the diary, I am amazed by my father's determination to learn as much as possible about economic issues. In fact, in spite of his financial hardships, he frequently writes about how grateful he is for the "post-graduate" education afforded him by the Depression. He often expresses his unquestioned belief in America and our capitalistic system as well as his conviction that conditions would ultimately improve with the result that we would be a stronger nation without changing to a communistic or socialistic society. Most of all, I gained tremendous respect for the strength and endurance displayed by both of my parents during those difficult years.

Dad was not the type to lecture, though. He taught by example. By the time I was in my early teens, Youngstown's steel industry was booming again, and racketeers were getting rich on illegal gambling. Dad and two other men decided to run for city council on a platform of cleaning up the rackets. All three were elected, and they succeeded in driving the illegal gambling out of town (the racketeers simply opened up a gambling resort just outside the city limits called the Jungle Inn, which was ultimately closed by state and federal officials). Immediately after he was elected to office, he received a number of "gifts," including free passes to all of the movie theaters. I was thrilled with this and could hardly believe it when Dad promptly returned all of the "gifts" with polite thank-you notes. When I complained to him that we should keep the movie tickets, he simply explained that honesty and integrity are not matters of degree.

My family survived the Depression and the war that followed. In 1943 Bob began his college education at Oberlin, but then joined a program with the U.S. Navy that resulted in his receiving his bachelor's degree from Harvard. After serving as a naval officer, he earned his law degree from Columbia and became associated with a Manhattan law firm. By 1951 my parents' lives had finally calmed down, and they were beginning to prosper. I had received my bachelor's degree and was serving on active duty as an air force lieutenant during the Korean War when their lives fell apart again. I was called home on an emergency leave to attend my brother's funeral. Even though more than fifty years have passed, I can still remember my parents' grief. It took years for my parents to put their lives back in order, only to then watch my sister, Connie, die at the age of fifty-three.

How my parents coped with these tragedies is beyond my comprehension, but they did—and came out stronger than ever. Mom threw herself into club work and was elected president of every club she joined. She ultimately served as president of the General Federation of Women's Clubs in the state of Ohio. When she died at the age of ninety-seven, there were still clubs bearing her name: the Marion B. Roth Club, a Youngstown-area organization, and a statewide club called the "Marionettes."

Dad's therapy was to increase his workload. He continued practicing law until shortly before his death at the age of eighty-four. It was my great fortune to have been able to work side by side with him for more than twenty-eight years. He was my partner and mentor, and for that I am truly blessed. My parents never left Youngstown; it was their life.

During the time I worked so closely with Dad, he frequently discussed his diary. He looked forward to his retirement, when he planned to edit and publish it. Needless to say, he never retired. In 1978 he gave me the diary, consisting of fourteen handwritten notebooks that included entries from 1931 to 1978 (this volume ends in 1941, as the U.S. entry into World War II finally marked the end of the Depression). He expressed the hope that I would someday fulfill his wish, and I am very proud now to do so.

INTRODUCTION BY JAMES LEDBETTER

As a business editor, it's not often that I read copy that gives me chills.

But then again, October 2008 was a chilling time. In a few turbulent weeks, the nation's economic mood had turned from apprehension to alarm, and giants were dropping all around with an ominous thud. One of the oldest and most prominent Wall Street firms, Lehman Brothers, had declared bankruptcy. Fannie Mae and Freddie Mac had to be taken into government receivership. AIG, a massive insurance company that had been acting like a highly leveraged bank, was bought out by the U.S. government in order to keep it from going under. The stock market, predictably but nonetheless cataclysmically, fell into a tailspin. In a six-week period from September 12 to October 27, the Dow Jones Industrial Average lost more than 28 percent of its value, and it seemed entirely possible that it could fall much further.

During this time I received an e-mail from a Bill Roth at Citigroup, who told me that his grandfather Benjamin had kept a diary during the 1930s. He asked whether my fledgling Web site, The Big Money, online for barely a month, would be interested in publishing parts of the diary, and sent me some sample entries. My eye was drawn to this entry, dated July 30, 1931:

> Magazines and newspapers are full of articles telling people to buy stocks, real estate etc. at present bargain prices. They say that times are sure to get better and that many big fortunes have been built this way. The trouble is that nobody has any money.

This was, of course, exactly what was being said in the media as I was reading it seventy-seven years later.

Another entry, dated August 9, 1931, reads:

> Professional men have been hard hit by the depression. This is particularly true of doctors and dentists. Their overhead is high and collections are impossible. One doctor smoothed a dollar bill out on his desk the other day and said that was all the money he had taken in for a week.

I couldn't stop my mind from jumping to a place I didn't want it to go: Could we be headed for another Great Depression? Immediately, my defenses kicked in: No matter how many leading financial institutions were failing, we weren't yet even in a declared recession. The government had a massive, unprecedented plan to save the banks. We had the Federal Deposit Insurance Corporation (FDIC) and a truly globalized economy, both powerful cushions against what happened in the early thirties. It couldn't get that bad again—could it?

Yet the more I read the diary, the more I realized that no one living in the 1930s had known for certain that they were headed into a depression, either, until they were in its midst. And even then, they constantly scoured the landscape for signs of recovery, as we are doing today.

.   .   .

Benjamin Roth's diary is a remarkable document, spanning fourteen handwritten volumes over five decades. In the early part of Roth's professional career—the years before he began keeping this journal—his law practice grew as part of Youngstown's historic boom. In 1900 the population of Youngstown was 45,000; by 1930 it was 170,000. That explosive growth was almost entirely the result of the rising steel industry. Youngstown possessed that magical combination necessary to produce steel: proximity to coal, limestone, and iron ore, plus capital, from the success of the iron industry in the late nineteenth century. Like the discovery of gold in California a half century before, the production of steel in Youngstown created a genuine boomtown, with ripple effects felt throughout the nation's economy. At the beginning of the twentieth century, the steel industry in and around Youngstown was still embryonic; by 1927 it surpassed Pittsburgh as America's largest steel-producing region.

A burgeoning town—with the need for increased housing and commercial activity—provided a young lawyer with plenty of business. While steelworkers themselves did not make high salaries, the managers of companies like Republic Steel (founded in 1899 and eventually the third-largest steel producer in America), Youngstown Sheet & Tube (founded in 1900, and for Roth the very barometer of local economic conditions), and Truscon Steel (a steel-door manufacturer that was purchased by Republic Steel but continued to do business under the name) prospered, and there was plenty of work to be done in property deeds, insurance, and similar commercial law work.

But not long after the stock market crash of October 1929, much of the region's economic activity went into reverse, a process that Roth set out to understand as a witness at the center of the storm. To this day, historians, journalists, and economists continue to debate the exact forces that caused the worst economic downturn in American history. Like many of his contemporaries, Roth considered the 1929 stock market crash as the start of the Depression. Hordes of people who invested their life savings in the market were wiped out during the punishing "black days" of late October 1929. Stock values had begun to soften in September of that year, but on Thursday, October 24, mass selling caused the prices of the stocks to drop dramatically as brokers couldn't find buyers to keep the stock value afloat. Investors' panic continued on Monday, October 28. Millions more shares were traded, and stock prices continued to plummet. Then on Tuesday, October 29, the market completely collapsed: More than sixteen million shares traded and fifteen billion dollars in assets were lost. By mid-November the market had lost more than a third of its value.

While the gut-wrenching drama that played out in the stock market those October days made an indelible mark on Roth and many Americans, only about 2.5 percent of Americans actually owned stocks in 1929. Many subsequent historians see the crash as more of a catalyst for the Depression than its cause. Still, as economist Joseph Schumpeter put it, Americans of all walks of life "felt that the ground under their feet was giving way." And the crash closed a frenetic era in American economic history, a period in which the stock market became the get-rich equivalent of the previous century's gold rush. The notion that anyone with just fifteen dollars a week could become a millionaire by "playing the market on margin" pervaded American culture during the boom of the 1920s. This helps explain why Roth—who did not own stocks in the period covered by this diary—paid such close attention to the market. (In fact, we have cut many entries where closing stock prices were included with no context or commentary.) The seemingly endless rise in the stock market in the 1920s was exhilarating: Radio, newspapers, and even women's magazines fostered and capitalized on this fascination by running stories daily on the market and ways to get rich on stock "tips." As Roth ruefully noted later, many amateur investors had little to no knowledge about investment fundamentals, or even the specific health of the companies in which they invested; they were speculators, through and through. As the saying goes, they got theirs.

While the Great Crash didn't cause instant mass unemployment or suddenly halt production lines, the events of October 1929 did expose structural

Thousands of panicked Wall Street investors gathered on the streets outside the New York Exchange following the devastating stock market collapse of 1929 that took place over the course of three days: Black Thursday, October 24; Black Monday, October 28; and Black Tuesday, October 29. Benjamin Roth pasted a clipping of this exact newspaper photo in his diary. (© Bettmann/CORBIS)

problems in the 1920s boom economy. And the response was rapid; within a few months, new car registrations fell by almost a quarter from the September figure. As families, earning on average just two thousand dollars a year, cut back on their spending, manufacturers, stuck with overstock and expensive overhead, began to lay off workers. As the unemployed struggled with bills and consumed even less, more companies cut back on workers or even closed up shop. The unemployment rate skyrocketed. In 1929 the nonagricultural sector was about 1.5 million, or 3.2 percent unemployed. By 1930 it was 8.7 percent, or about 4 million. By 1931, when Roth started writing down his thoughts on the events around him, the jobless had nearly doubled to 15.9 percent, or 8 million.

When Roth begins his "Notes" in 1931, he is conscious of a delineating crisis, one that obliterates the twenties-era intoxication forever (or so, I think, Roth would have believed). But he is not particularly scolding of the culture surrounding wealth or a bubble; rather, he seems dispassionately scientific in wanting to know how economic forces behave.

That he could summon such dispassion is itself remarkable, in an age that stoked passion into panic. More than in any economic downturn before or since, Americans during this era feared that the very pillars on which their society had always stood—democracy and free enterprise—could crumble and be replaced by something unrecognizable in the country's history. This was hardly an idle fear: Germany had elected a Nazi government in 1933, largely in response to years of an imploded economy. Japan and Italy were being run by Fascists, and Stalin was in the process of turning the Soviet Union into a ruthless dictatorship. Historian Arnold J. Toynbee, who would go on to write a twelve-volume history of how civilizations rise and fall, wrote at the time, "In 1931, men and women all over the world were seriously contemplating and frankly discussing the possibility that the Western system of Society might break down and cease to work."

And there was no shortage of advocates, on the Left or Right, who were eager to fill that void on American soil. The very first days of Franklin Roosevelt's presidency saw not only a reversal of the largely ineffective Hoover policies but an extension of federal control over the economy that Americans had never witnessed. Some on the Right attacked Roosevelt for dabbling in socialism, a position with which Roth seemed to sympathize in certain instances. Whether the various programs of the New Deal constituted socialism or partial socialism depends on one's definition of that elastic term, and many historians take the position that even if Roosevelt had to curtail aspects of the free market, it was in order to save capitalism. But certainly the National Industrial Recovery Act, Social Security, the Agricultural Administration Act, Securities and Exchange Act, and Federal Deposit Insurance Corporation constituted government intervention into the minutiae of business activity that had no peacetime precedent in the United States. Furthermore, jobs programs in the Civil Works Administration, Works Progress Administration (WPA), and Civilian Conservation Corps resembled the types of government-sponsored employment that was often a feature of Socialist or Fascist governments. The fact that key parts of Roosevelt's agenda were struck down as unconstitutional—which the legally trained Roth often pointed out—lends some credence to the idea that Roosevelt's view of government and executive power tipped over into antidemocratic extremes.

For many others, however, the New Deal was not extreme enough. Due in part to the surge in labor organizing made possible by the National Industrial Recovery Act, the Communist Party of the United States flourished in the 1930s. Its leaders advocated that the United States follow the Soviet model of revolution, eliminating capitalism and anointing the working class to run the society. It is doubtful that more than a few million Americans genuinely preferred this direction; actual CPUSA membership never topped one hundred thousand, and while party-affiliated organizations might have brought that number more comfortably into six figures, not all factions would have shared a Soviet-style society as a goal.

At the same time, there were many Americans who felt that if the fall of Democratic Capitalism was inevitable, Socialism in some form was preferable to other alternatives. And certainly Communists, Socialists, and their allies—particularly in trade unions—had a significant impact on social and cultural life during this period. Roth's writing does not dwell on the politics of the Left, especially not before the introduction of the New Deal. Still, it is worth noting that Roth begins his diary on June 5, 1931; just six days earlier, one of the most violent confrontations in Youngstown's history had taken place. A group of hundreds of Communists had been trucked into Youngstown from all across Ohio, Pennsylvania, and West Virginia to recruit members from its newly opened flophouses and soup kitchens and disrupt the city's Memorial Day celebration. A violent clash with police ensued, and more than two hundred people were arrested and dozens injured and hospitalized.

Other extremists and populists also tempted America. The chameleon-like Father Charles Coughlin mesmerized millions of Americans over the radio, railing against Jews, capitalism, communism, Roosevelt, and the Federal Reserve system. In Youngstown the Ku Klux Klan had a particular appeal. Steel-industry jobs attracted workers from all over the world;

according to the 1920 census, 60 percent of the city's population had been born outside the United States. Such a large, and mostly Catholic, immigrant population made the Klan's nativist message popular among Protestants, and in 1923 a majority of Youngstown's city council was affiliated with the Klan. It was not fantasy to believe at this time that Socialists, Communists, Fascists, or extreme populists might take power in parts of the United States, whether by force or sympathy.

Not that such political ferment was Roth's day-to-day concern. By dint of his professional standing and class, Roth was a natural-born Republican. He notes in the diary that he supports Hoover's reelection in 1932, Alf Landon in 1936, and Wendell Willkie in 1940. For that reason it's all the more remarkable that Roth became a public advocate for Roosevelt's National Recovery Act in 1933. At one point that year he notes that he is doing so much on behalf of the NRA—including five speeches on a single Sunday—that he has time for little else. Yet within weeks he is questioning whether the NRA (or indeed any of the early New Deal programs) is doing any good and fears that the tremendous government debt may be doing harm. Supporting the NRA was, he explains, a simple civic duty, although reading between the lines, it seems clear that Roth was an effective public speaker and that he may well have developed a taste for the public spotlight (he would go on to hold elective office in Youngstown).

In our shorthand history of the period, we tend to think of a 1920s stock market boom—which Roth documents vividly, if retrospectively—followed by abject dust-bowl poverty, in which no one had money even for sufficient food or decent shelter, the Roaring Twenties replaced by haunting images from Dorothea Lange. Roth's diary is a firsthand reminder that the reality was far more complex, that minibooms and minibusts existed during this period, in which post-1929 fortunes were being made as well as lost. Granted, the crash was one of the most devastating events in stock market history; the 1929 high in the Dow Jones Industrial Average of 381.17 would not be reached again for another quarter century. Yet in the period from 1929 to 1939, neither the stock market nor the economy as a whole went in one continuous direction.

Benjamin Roth's writing asks a central question, namely, how should an honest, prudent person create wealth, protect it, and build it over the course of a lifetime?

It is fascinating to follow the evolution of Roth's thinking about investment. As he watches the market mostly plunge in the 1931–1932 period, he seems mostly to feel that stocks are a sucker's game. At the same time, he is tantalized by the prospect of bargain hunting among stocks—notably railroads and steel—that had lost nearly all their value, even though their underlying businesses seemed sure to rebound eventually. He also began to see that even though real estate seemed like a reliable investment—it is finite, tangible, and can be self-financing by charging rent—in a prolonged downturn, it could be devastating. The costs of upkeep, taxes, mortgage payments, and insurance are usually inflexible, whereas rental income could easily dry up if renters don't have jobs. All around him buildings were being torn down because the owners would rather lose their investment than be forced into bankruptcy by their inability to pay property tax.

In the mid-thirties Roth begins to lay out an approach to investing based on controlling risk, maintaining liquidity, and protecting principle. Today, even casual investors are familiar with ways to describe the types of investment strategies toward which Roth gravitated: "value investing," "buy and hold," even "dollar-cost averaging." But for Roth, these were not strategies to be bought off the rack; he had to build them himself—studiously, patiently, and, at least during the period covered by this book, entirely theoretically. He later regretted not having had the available cash to buy stocks when they hit historic lows and then recovered. (Roth would eventually come to buy individual stocks although, according to his son, only in very large companies, and always part of an investment portfolio that also included bonds and real estate.)

Roth's preoccupation with personal finance makes this diary something of an anomaly in Depression-era literature. Visit the nicely appointed library or historical society in Youngstown (they are practically kitty-corner across Wick Avenue from one another) and you will find volumes about the struggles of Youngstown's working class: the fight to unionize, the need for relief and decent housing. Much of Depression-era scholarship understandably adopts that lens. On the other end of the spectrum, the very wealthy of every time and place always have their lives documented, immediately by local media and later by biographers. If anything, the modern wealth-and-celebrity industry had its origins in the Depression, spawned by people's need to be entertained out of their dreary realities. But if there is—to use a Depression-era phrase—a "forgotten man" of this period's history, it is the honest, striving professional. There is no question that millions of Americans had a harder time during the 1930s than Benjamin Roth and his immediate family. Presumably, those hardest hit left little by way of a permanent record of their experience, because they died of starvation or were silenced by abject poverty. A step up from that level provides us with the Depression images we carry in our collective back pocket: dust-bowl refugees, urban soup-kitchen lines, Tom Joad and *The Grapes of Wrath*.

The endurance of those images is testimony to their truth, but Roth's diary insists on an equal truth that is somewhat surprisingly absent from the nation's 1930s yearbooks. Here is history told from the point of view of the Depression's dramatically affected, but not its thoroughly trampled. At times—both when government aid is targeted directly at the poor and when a degree of prosperity returns in 1936—Roth seems a bit jealous that very little of the wealth being redistributed is ending up in the coffers of, say, lawyers such as himself. But he does not complain, and he does not propose a bailout for the professional class; instead, he redoubles his effort to understand the cycles of the economy and stock market and how best to invest. His mind is set on the potential for recovery, a particularly American predisposition.

That was not typical of his time; it seems fair to say that no one in the 1930s paid as much attention to the stock market as Benjamin Roth, unless they were actually invested in it. Strangely, though, it is far more typical of our own era, when (depending on how one measures it) about half of Americans have money invested in stocks and when a simple act like sitting in an airport lounge or getting on an elevator can mean being bombarded with opinions of buy, sell, or hold. We are, as a consumer spending–driven, service-oriented, market-led country, more like Benjamin Roth today than we were when he was writing, and certainly more than we are like the steelworkers who were his contemporaries. Benjamin is our CNBC Everyman, transported back in time.

Roth's work has surprising literary power. He was not a professional writer; he was not immediately expecting a wide audience for these entries, and thus did not load them with fancy words, dazzling metaphors, or aphoristic sentences. (He did, though, have an ear for a cliffhanger ending to the individual notebooks.) Neither was he a trained economist or financial professional; especially in the early years of this diary, Roth seemed to genuinely struggle with some basics of investment and economics. He admirably held no illusions about his acquired expertise. As if constructing a kind of economic palimpsest, Roth would occasionally go back and annotate his earlier entries and did not hesitate to pronounce himself wrong. (Here, this hindsight commentary is indented on the page and marked with all-numeric dates [e.g., 8/13/52] to distinguish it from the real-time entries, where the full name of the month is spelled out.) Perhaps most important, though, Roth did not have the novelist's or screenwriter's luxury of knowing where the story was ultimately going.

Yet it is the very limitations of Roth's expertise that make the diary so compelling to us today. The diary forces us to confront that buried, throbbing sensation that tells us that no matter how prosperous or lucky or cunning the American economy has been for the past century, we still don't have definitive, universal answers to some very fundamental economic questions, large and small, that almost obsessed Roth. How much debt is too much debt—for a household, a company, or a government? What is the most secure way to guarantee return on an investment without exposure to excessive risk (whatever excessive risk is)? How much can government prop up private enterprise without creating a moral hazard that hinders market dynamism? Why can't economies continue to expand at a steady, manageable pace without lapsing into destructive boom-and-bust cycles?

It is humbling and a little scary to realize that, since Benjamin Roth first began keeping his journal, millions and millions of man-hours have been spent framing, quantifying, and hypothesizing these questions without creating bulletproof answers or even much of a permanent consensus. Economics uses the statistics and ostensible precision one associates with, say, physics and astronomy. Yet to survey economic opinion on even seemingly simple questions gives the impression that economists as a group cannot consent to their equivalent of the hypothesis that the earth orbits the sun rather than the other way around.

It's easy (and instructive) to read this diary and reassure ourselves about how many lessons policy makers learned from the 1930s and how many more economic safety mechanisms are in place. Insurance for the unemployed and guaranteed Social Security income for the elderly and infirm are standard features of the American economy; without them, the impact of current recessions on individuals could easily be as bad as it was during the Depression. On the federal policy level, the government guarantee of bank deposits up to a certain monetary amount makes panicky bank runs less likely and less damaging (though by no means impossible, and of course there are those who argue that such guarantees are harmful; see the above observation about the earth and the sun). And when banks do close, the process is orderly and the impact on the overall financial system minimized. Moreover, decades of experience with monetary policy have given the Federal Reserve—a relatively new institution in Roth's time—much greater power in steering the economy away from extremes of inflation or unemployment. In the decade covered by this diary, Roth rarely takes the time and the perspective to assess the value of these lessons learned in the New Deal and beyond; he wasn't, after all, seeing many permanent signs of their efficacy. Still, there is much in Roth's descriptions to bolster the arguments of those who wish to argue that today's economic managers are much better off than their counterparts in the thirties.

And yet: It's nearly impossible for any reader in 2009 to examine this work without seeing stark, sometimes eerily prescient, parallels to our own age. Here, for example, is an entry from May 1933: "Investigations are the order of the day. The Senate is investigating private banking and in particular J. P. Morgan & Co. Mr. Morgan was on the witness stand all day yesterday and today. The evidence shows that his firm made loans to many men now prominent in public affairs." There is this on June 1, 1933: "In looking back over the 3 months since Roosevelt became President it seems that the U.S. has traveled a long way toward some form of socialism or managed economy." And this in 1932: "It looks as though the Democrats will win because everybody wants a 'change.'"

The point here is not whether bulls or bears are right or wrong within any snapshot of any decade, or whether critics of FDR in 1933 or Barack Obama in 2009 are off base or right on the money. Rather, Roth's diary is a reminder that our economic security, individually and collectively, always rests on a complex interaction of market forces, politics, consumer perception, and the impact of unforeseen (and sometimes unforeseeable) events. As in so many other areas, those offering predictions for the future or even detailed readings of the present are often wrong because of incomplete information, flawed statistical models, or hidden agendas.

And even when they are right within a particular time frame, history often has other plans in mind. The Youngstown that Benjamin Roth knew and hoped to see revived—the booming steel town, where soot-choked skies meant prosperity—did in fact survive the Depression, thanks in large part to the military buildup during World War II, a major theme of this book's final chapter. But Youngstown today has a fraction of the steel industry and population that it had in 1930; even by the late thirties, the steel industry's need for cheap water-based transportation had moved much of the area's production westward to the South Chicago–Gary, Indiana, area, so that shipments could go out via Lake Michigan. In a triumphant document issued in 1950 to celebrate its first half century of existence, Youngstown Sheet & Tube declared that it "looks forward to another fifty years, and then another, ad infinitum, of continued service to its buying public, its employees, its shareholders and its country." That infinite vision no doubt made sense to the company and even to Roth at the time—this was one of the largest firms in a region that in midcentury was alone producing more steel than, say, France. But in reality the company would not last another two decades on its own, nor Youngstown's industry as a whole much more than another thirty years.

As I write this in June 2009, General Motors, once the largest private company in the world, has been delisted from the New York Stock Exchange. Benjamin Roth, I think, would probably not have recognized a world in which General Motors was not a major engine of the U.S. economy. Based on his diary, however, I think he would have soon grasped how it could come about. Stock markets and individual sectors may go up or down, for months or decades at a time, but certain broader economic forces—in his time, the international movement of gold or the buildup to war; in ours, deindustrialization and globalization—will always assert themselves.

THE GREAT DEPRESSION: A DIARY

Foreword

For the first time in my personal business life I am witnessing a major financial crisis. I am anxious to learn the lessons of this depression. To the man past middle life it spells ~~it spells~~ tragedy and disaster but to those of us in the middle ~~thirties~~ it may be a great school of experience out of which some worth while lesson may be salvaged. With this thought in mind I am going to write down brief accounts of developments as they occur from time to time.

June 5- 1931

The actual diary page.

CHAPTER 1
JUNE 5, 1931–OCTOBER 17, 1931

FOREWORD

For the first time in my personal business life I am witnessing a major financial crisis. I am anxious to learn the lessons of this depression. To the man past middle life it spells tragedy and disaster but to those of us in the middle thirties it may be a great school of experience out of which some worthwhile lesson may be salvaged. With this thought in mind I am going to write down brief accounts of developments as they occur from time to time.

JUNE 5, 1931

Benjamin Roth
2032 Elm Street
Youngstown, Ohio

VOLUME I

PERSONAL NOTES ON THE PANIC OF 1929

BRIEF RESUME OF EVENTS PRECEDING THE PANIC
1931

JUNE 5, 1931

I was mustered out of military service on December 5, 1918 and returned to Youngstown to open a law office. I found business humming. The return of thousands of soldiers to civil life had brought a boom to real estate, clothing and other retail trades. When I purchased my first civilian suit I found I had to pay $70 for a suit that might have cost half that amount a few years before. Silk shirts with big candy stripes were in style for the men and the usual price was $10 to $12 for an ordinary shirt. In a similar way shoes and other items were expensive. I was amazed to find mill-workers in Youngstown wearing these silk shirts without a murmur. I also learned that during the war and still in 1919 these mill-workers had earned enormous wages—from $10 to $35 a day.

This feverish prosperity and easy money continued through 1919 and 1920. In 1921 came a steel strike in Youngstown and for awhile it looked as tho we were heading for a depression but in 1922 things picked up again and continued in a hectic spiral upward until the big stock market crash in October 1929.

As I look back now I can understand how America during the years 1919 to 1929 was called upon to supply the needs of both Europe and America—after five years of wartime destruction. In Europe the industries and railroads had been destroyed and America was called upon to rebuild Europe to supply her returned soldiers with food and clothing and other necessities. At the same time the enormous similar demands of our own country had to be satisfied. I know now—but I did not know it then—America also supplied Europe with the money and credits to purchase our merchandise and we have not been paid back to this day.

At any rate things began to hum again in 1922. Our steel industries and other factories turned from the making of war material to the making of automobiles, radios, etc. We had a real estate boom and later in 1925 there was a tremendous boom of real estate in Florida. Prohibition was in effect but actually the amount of boot-leg liquor consumed exceeded that before Prohibition.

As I look back now to the 1922–29 period it seems to me unreal and almost unbelievable. After the war pressure people wanted to have a good time and to spend money. The flapper appeared upon the scene. Women's dresses became shorter and shorter until they hardly reached the knee and in the latter stages of the delirium they wore their stockings rolled and their bare knees rouged. Morality and religion were pushed into the back-ground and in its place came Negro jazz bands and night clubs and all its attendant evils.

To an older man it must have seemed inevitable that we were heading for a crash but to most of us it seemed that we were in a "New Era" which would never end.

On the industrial side of the picture, mass production led to the formation of larger and larger mergers. We began to hear of stock market millionaires, huge extra dividends, stock split-ups, and 99 year leases in real estate, shoestring financing and all manner of speculation.

In my own law business I began to feel a change in 1924 but did not know what was happening until several years later. My practice dealt largely with independent merchants. In 1924 these independent merchants began to be replaced by chain stores. The A & P and Kroger grocery stores probably put over 1000 merchants out of business in Youngstown. Today almost every building on Federal St. is occupied by a chain store. For many of these independent merchants I performed one last rite—bankruptcy—and never saw them again. In this way I lost considerable legal business because these independent merchants had been a substantial group of citizens owning real estate, etc. As for the chain stores, their legal business and banking was done in New York or Chicago and the local lawyers and banks gained nothing by the change.

In a similar way beginning in 1924 real estate and building transactions became fewer and fewer. An experienced economist might have recognized all these signs but to most of us it meant nothing. We believed in the New Era and were not going to sell the U.S.A. short. Dictatorship, Communism and Socialism might rear its head in Europe but we were sure in those days that none of those things could come to America.

Businesses in downtown Youngstown, Ohio, still appeared to thrive in 1930 and would not feel the full effects of the Great Depression for another year. (The Mahoning Valley Historical Society)

The picture would not be complete without a word about the stock market. Before the war the average man knew nothing about stocks and bonds and the stock-market was something he had read about in connection with Wall St. propaganda. The average man who wanted to invest or speculate used real estate as a medium and it was still considered a truism that the most sure way to build a fortune was through the ownership of real estate. I believed this and my parents believed it but my faith has been considerably shaken by what happened to real estate and mortgage investments since the depression.

During the war people bought Liberty Bonds from the government under high pressure propaganda and after the war when they sold these bonds many of them for the first time entered a stockbroker's office. Many holders of Liberty Bonds did not even know how to sell them and after the war "Liberty Bond Scalpers" opened offices, advertised and purchased these bonds from ignorant investors at discounts ranging from 25% to 50%. The scalper then sold these bonds on the market at par and with the money scalped some more bonds.

Without being able to explain it the fact remains that after the war people became stock-market conscious. Much publicity had been given to war babies (stocks of companies that made war supplies and paid huge dividends) and from 1922–1929 it seemed as tho every man, woman and child had determined to make a fortune by "playing the market" on margin. In 1929 when the crash came all sorts of people were into the market on margins over their heads—doctors, lawyers, merchants, bootblacks, waitresses, etc. They bought stocks on tips, did not know what the company sold or made and did not know how to investigate a stock even if such a thought had occurred to them.

....

EDITOR'S NOTE

Entering the stock market had become a lot cheaper by the 1920s. In the mid-nineteenth century, industries that required massive amounts of capital, like the railroads, raised money by dividing up the ownership of a company into shares. But in the early twentieth century, and especially after World War I, all kinds of enterprises needing money to fund their operations began splitting their stock shares into smaller and smaller amounts so more Americans could afford the opportunity to "own" a part of a company. Furthermore, cheaper "common stocks," stocks with no guaranteed return if the company wasn't profitable, gained popularity in the 1920s. They carried higher risk, but they were also less costly than "preferred" stocks, which generally guaranteed investors a dividend paying 6 to 8 percent return a year. Many buyers of these common stocks were speculators who would snatch up "bargains" that were traded enough to drive up their price. When the sales of these common stocks rose too high (sometimes, twenty to forty times their earnings), the stock was split into smaller shares (within the $10 to $250 range), so as not to price out even more potential buyers. To today's investors, these are everyday occurrences, but in Roth's day they were innovations whose full impact was not yet widely understood; IBM, for example, first began paying a dividend in 1925, and had its first stock split (three to one) in 1926.

By summer of 1929 stocks were selling at twenty, thirty and forty times their earnings. Stocks were split and re-split until the most capable accountant would have found it difficult to make a reasonable calculation. All sense of caution was lost, stocks were bought blindly and good bonds earning 4% or 5% were sneered at. Even tho the air was full of warnings, very few people took heed and when the crash came in the fall of 1929 the casualties were terrific. Many of my friends with small earnings had run up stockholdings on margin as high as $50,000 or $75,000. The crash wiped them out and in many cases left them indebted to banks and brokerage houses. I visited a stock exchange on the day following the crash (my first visit to one) and the place was filled with perspiring and white-faced people. Suicide and bankruptcy became the order of the day.

Following is a list of some of the stock market quote shares just before the crash:

Am T & T. 310 1/4; Atcheson, Topeka & Santa Fe 298 5/8; Bethlehem St. 140 3/4; J. J. Case Co. 50; Central R.R. of N. J. 360; Coca Cola 344; Detroit Edison 385; Eastman Kodak 284; General Motors 91 (after many split ups); New York, Chi & St. L. RR 192 (later went down to 1 1/2); Peoples Gas 404; Radio 114 (after many split-ups—later down below 10); Truscon 51 1/2 (later below 10); Union Pacific RR 290; U.S. Steel 262 3/4; Western Union 272 1/4 (later lost about 90%); Youngstown Sheet & Tube 175.

At the present time (June 5, 1931) some of these stock quotations have dropped to the following:

Truscon 61 5/8 to 12; Republic 140 to 12; AT&T 310 to 170; U.S. Steel 261 to 84; Sheet & Tube 175 to 43.

Immediately after the 1929 crash the speculators rushed in to buy "bargains" but were badly mistaken because the market kept going down and down even tho industrial leaders kept on assuring the people that everything was fine and the worst was over. At the present time the newspapers are urging people to buy these "bargains" but opinion is much divided as to whether or not the bottom has been reached.

What has happened to date (6-5-1931) in real estate and mortgage investments

Investments in real estate and mortgages fared almost as badly as stocks. Since 1929 foreclosure by the banks has been the order of the day.

Day after day real estate can be bought for the price of the 1st mortgage and there are no bidders except the bank which holds the first mortgage. In this way the banks are becoming the holders of huge quantities of real estate.

Most property bought in the last few years was bought subject to a large first mortgage and in many cases subject also to a second or third mortgage. In case of foreclosure the owner not only loses his property but is also subject to a large deficiency judgment. In this way many people have lost all.

The worst feature about real estate in a depression is that it is illiquid and cannot be sold at any price. If it is free of mortgage the owner may hold on until normal times—but in most cases it is subject to mortgage—he cannot collect his rent from the tenants—and cannot pay on his mortgage or taxes and eventually loses his equity by the foreclosure route.

It is almost impossible to collect real estate rentals. Taxes and repairs are high, banks are calling their loans and are terrible if interest is not paid promptly—and the real estate owner has a difficult situation to face.

Second Mortgages

During the boom years it became popular to buy real estate at inflated prices on a shoestring. This was done by encumbering it with a 1st, 2nd and 3rd mtge. Second mortgage loan companies were formed to buy these 2nd mortgages at a discount of 10% to 25% per year. It has proven to be a bad investment because at each sheriff sale the 2nd mortgage is wiped out. Most of these companies have frozen assets and seem to be heading for bankruptcies.

Good, conservative first mortgages have proven to be good investments altho' in many cases the mortgagee has been forced to take over the property.

The sheriff has been selling recently at public sale many vacant lots on which accumulated taxes amount to $500 or more. At these sales the lots are selling as low as $25 apiece clear of taxes. One of my clients bought ten of them ranging from $10 to $50. Of course they are mostly located in undesirable neighborhoods. Another client had 10 buildings razed because he could not collect rents and the taxes are exorbitant. This is a popular way to reduce taxes.

Here as elsewhere there are lessons to be learned and I am very much confused. Where can a person safely invest—in real estate, stocks, bonds? The constant supervision required by real estate, the costly upkeep, its illiquidity, the danger of a deficiency judgment—all have cooled me considerably. I begin to realize that changing business conditions and the growth of the country make almost essential a knowledge of stocks and bonds—not for the purpose of speculation but to preserve principal and to get a fair return on the investment.

2/12/36

I am re-reading this. These early buyers were badly mistaken and many of them were wiped out. The market reached bottom in the summer of 1932 when Truscon sold at 2; Sheet & Tube 4; Republic 2; U.S. Steel 23; AT&T 73 etc. After the summer of 1932 a slow up-turn began. Prices today (2/12/36) are Truscon 9; Sheet & Tube 51; Republic 25; AT&T 165 etc.

In the last analysis however the rules of conservative investment apply whether you buy real estate or stocks or bonds. Thorough investigation is the first necessity—safety of the principal—and it usually follows that only a fair return on the investment can be expected. To seek a high or unusual return means greater risk and speculation. This was true of 2nd mortgages on real estate which brought a return as high as 20% but in the end proved worthless. A pretty safe rule to follow is to stick to the conservative investments. There are times, however, in a depression when cash money is king and many good investments can be purchased at a big discount.

JUNE 15, 1931

Stocks continue to go lower and lower and dividends are being slashed right and left. For over a year now people have been buying stocks at what they think are bargain prices. These prices are much below 1929 but there is no way to tell if they have reached bottom. Some present day prices are: Sheet & Tube 43; Truscon 13; US. Steel 83. Only the blue chip stocks are still high: AT&T 170; G.E. 42; Consol. Gas 95 etc. It seems there should be no rush to buy bargains in a panic. The opportunities are many and the period is often protracted. The best time to buy of course is when the panic is almost over. My guess is that we haven't seen the end yet.

JULY 30, 1931

Magazines and newspapers are full of articles telling people to buy stocks, real estate etc. at present bargain prices. They say that times are sure to get better and that many big fortunes have been built this way. The trouble is that nobody has any money. On account of numerous bank failures, the few people who have money are afraid to spend it and are buying government securities. From the extreme of speculation in 1929 people have now turned to the extreme of caution. In my own case I find it a problem to take in enough to pay expenses and there is nothing left for investment.

5/16/32

This advice was premature. Here a year later prices are 1/3 of what they were in 1931.

EDITOR'S NOTE

The collapse of so much commercial activity strained the banking system in the United States and abroad. Banks had overextended their loans, and the rate of nonpayment was putting pressure on the supply of gold. In December 1930 the Bank of the United States (a private bank with no actual government status) collapsed in what was the largest bank failure in U.S. history at the time, freezing some $200 million in depositors' funds. Similar collapses took place in Austria and Germany in mid-1931. Because the world banking system is always interconnected, and because world currencies at the time operated on a gold standard with only a finite amount of gold in the world, it was inevitable that these failures would hit very close to home for Roth and his neighbors, with devastating effects on businesses and the real estate market. By the time 1931 came to a close, several major countries had been forced to take their currencies off the gold standard, a development that Roth would come to view with increasing alarm. In addition, a worldwide cratering of prices on commodities—coffee, cotton, rubber, and wheat had all fallen more than 50 percent since the stock market crash—destroyed the farming sector, bringing food prices to absurd lows, but still not low enough for the jobless to afford.

AUGUST 5, 1931

The town is stunned by the news that the Home Savings & Loan Co. has suspended payments and would demand 60 day notice of withdrawals. This is followed quickly by similar announcements from The Federal Savings & Loan Co. and The Metropolitan Savings & Loan Co. All of these loan companies paid 5 1/2% on savings deposits and earned their money by lending on real estate. With the coming of the depression people stopped payments on their mortgages—mortgages became frozen and the banks had no way to get cash. Mortgages are a safe investment but cannot be liquidated quickly and are not a good investment for a bank which has agreed to pay out its deposits on demand. For the past three days, these institutions have been besieged by hysterical depositors demanding their money. I am only afraid the banks will become more stringent in their collections and that foreclosures will become the order of the day.

Wheat sells today at 45¢ and corn at 42¢. This is the lowest since 1855.

I went to the fruit market house this evening. It was almost deserted. The farmers cannot sell their produce because men are not working and it has become popular for each family to have its own vegetable garden.

AUGUST 6, 1931

At a public sale by the sheriff today on foreclosure by the bank, the Carosella home at 1915 Elm St. was offered for the third time but no buyer found. It could be bought for $4400—and is really worth conservatively $7500. In 1929 the owner thought it was worth $11,000.

8/14/52

The same house today at 1915 Elm is still in good condition and is worth about $12,000.

AUGUST 7, 1931

Business is at an absolute standstill and the big stores are deserted even tho they are all running sales and almost giving the merchandise away. Since the Home Savings & Loan Co. and other loan companies stopped paying out, nobody has any money and everybody seems scared and blue. We seem to have touched bottom in Youngstown and it hardly seems possible that things could get worse.

3/8/33

This was a poor guess. Conditions in 1932 were much worse.

AUGUST 8, 1931

My brother Morris has been out of work now for almost 2 years and can't find a thing to do. He is an engineer and draftsman. Jerome Burger was laid off by by the Truscon Steel Co. two months ago and is not very optimistic. Joe is still at Truscon but is afraid for his job. He says the air is tense and men are being discharged every day.

The Chicago Tribune announces that 100 theaters in Chicago and vicinity will close up. This is because of the tremendous overbuilding of theaters during the last 5 years of the boom. Each producer built his own chain of theaters and bought the real estate at fancy prices. Now they are going broke. In Youngstown movie admissions have dropped from 60¢ to 35¢.

AUGUST 9, 1931

Professional men have been hard hit by the depression. This is particularly true of doctors and dentists. Their overhead is high and collections are impossible. One doctor smoothed a dollar bill out on his desk the other day and said that was all the money he had taken in for a week. Lawyers are almost as badly off and most are not taking in enough to pay. We have been helped a little by bankruptcy and foreclosure work which followed in the wake of the depression but most of it does not pay because the assets are worthless. Most professional men for the past two years have been living on money borrowed on insurance policies, etc. The only work that comes in now are impossible collections on a contingent fee basis. Everybody is digging up old claims and trying to realize on them. Tempers are short and people are distrustful and suspicious. There is nothing to do but work harder for less money and cut expenses to the bone.

8/26/36

I am re-reading this when the depression is about over. Profes-sional men have not yet had a break. In normal times the average professional man makes just a living and lives up to the limit of his income because he must dress well, etc. In times of depression he not only fails to make a living but has no surplus capital to buy bargains in stocks and real estate. I see now how very important it is for the professional man to build up a surplus in normal times. A surplus capital of $2500 wisely invested during the depression might have meant financial security for the rest of his life. Without it he is at the mercy of the economic winds. His practice suffers and he has no chance of rising above the level of the ordinary practitioner who lives from day to day and from hand to mouth.

AUGUST 10, 1931

I note in today's Legal News that the Kirsch home on Coronada Ave. is being foreclosed by the bank on a $7500 mortgage. It can be bought for the price of the mortgage and is worth $10000. This and many other bargains are being offered today. The Legal News carries advertisements today of 78 sheriff sales to be held within the next 30 days. In almost every case, the properties will be bought back by the bank for the 1st mortgage plus taxes and court costs. There are no bona fide bidders. Among the properties offered for sale is the old Gallagher property—corner Ardale and Rayen—132 front running back to Erie RR. and appraised at $3000.

8/26/36

The Kirsch property was bought eventually by the U— family for about $7500 but instead of using cash they used Home Savings & Loan Co. pass books which were selling at 50¢ on the dollar. This family has bought much real estate this way and in the next few years will reap a harvest.

6/28/62

The U— family bought half of East Federal St. at sheriff sales in the 1930s. However down-town real estate has gone to pot because of the growth of suburban shopping centers. The U— family still owns half of E. Federal St. but the buildings are empty and they cannot sell.

7/10/70

Almost all of E. Federal has been purchased by Urban Renewal at modest prices. The stores are vacant or have been torn down. The cheap E. Federal stores have moved to W. Federal and the good stores have moved to the suburbs.

AUGUST 17, 1931

I just came back from a short stay at Geneva-on-the-Lake. Summer resorts seem to be particularly hard hit. Hotels are empty and everybody is bidding for business at cut-rate prices. This is a good time to buy summer resort homes or even large mansions of the rich people. Nobody wants them at any price because they are too expensive to carry. Many formerly rich families are living in the chauffeur quarters above the garage while the mansion stands closed.

AUGUST 17, 1931

Today's *Vindicator* carries the news that four of the largest commercial banks in Toledo, Ohio closed their doors (total deposits over $100 million). Also that eleven Savings & Loan companies in Toledo stopped paying out money. The conclusion seems clear that savings and loan companies are not good places to deposit money even tho they pay a high rate of interest.

I had lunch and a talk with Russell McKay of the Home Savings and Loan Co. He is not very optimistic about the near future. Says that the City of Toledo is completely tied up for lack of money. Money is either in hoarding or tied up in closed banks and business is crippled. He does not think bank money will be released for a long time. He also fears that people who owe money on mortgages will withhold their payments and thus make the situation worse. Foreclosure does not help much because there is no re-sale market. The bank simply becomes the owner of the real estate. Moratoriums of one year are being considered on mortgage payments in many states.

8/26/36

Looking back now it is clear that the Toledo bank failures were but a fore-runner of the closing of the Youngstown banks later and of the National Bank holiday in March 1933. Very few people foresaw. We could not believe that Youngstown banks like the Dollar Bank, the

Commercial and the City Banks would close their doors. We thought it could not happen here—and yet it did. It is cheering however to note that both Toledo and Youngstown survived the bank closings and are prosperous cities again with bright futures. In the Commercial and Dollar Banks the depositors lost nothing. In the City Bank they lost about 40% altho even for that they hold certificates against questionable assets.

AUGUST 18, 1931

This town is fast becoming panic-stricken. Everybody is talking about the depression and wondering where it will end. The failure of the four big Toledo banks and the stoppage of withdrawals by practically all of the Savings and Loan companies has tied up everything. There is no money in circulation and all business is at a standstill. Dr. W— our family dentist stopped me today and urged me to continue to send my family in for dental work even tho we could not pay promptly. This was a very unusual thing for him to do but people have simply stopped worrying about dental needs. If a tooth aches they have it extracted but neglect all other dental services that might be expensive.

Today's Legal News recites that vacant lots on Main St. in Wickliffe sold for taxes at $25 each. I did not bid on them because each carries future special tax assessments of $200. I suppose I will be sorry 10 years from now.

10/30/41

I am not sorry I did not buy the lots. Vacant residential lots in Youngstown have not been a good investment unless you build on them at once and get a return on your investment. If those Wickliffe lots had been purchased at $25 each in 1931 they would be worth less today than the original $25 investment plus accumulated taxes and interest for 10 years.

AUGUST 19, 1931

Another large bank in Toledo closes its doors today. This leaves only two open banks in this hard-hit city. The Federal Reserve Bank of Cleveland announces that it will back these two banks to the limit and rushes 11 million in gold down there to meet the steady withdrawals.

EDITOR'S NOTE

The strain on charitable organizations, in Roth's Youngstown as elsewhere, was tremendous. Without public assistance programs to help the poor and out of work feed their families in the 1920s, charities stood on the front lines. Until the Great Depression, joblessness was usually perceived as a temporary setback; if a man tried hard enough to get another job, his need for charity would end. Family members, ethnic communities, or neighbors came to his aid until he "got back on his feet." Neighbors or relatives would contribute a dollar apiece to feed a down-and-out family; churches or private charities provided meals.

But the sheer volume of the needy in the first few years of the Depression tapped the normal capabilities of these organizations. In Youngstown the Allied Council, the local charity, handed out relief to 100 people in August 1931. By September 4 they handled 1,150 desperate calls. Furthermore, initiatives that raised funds in the past had dried up: A fund in Detroit that needed $3.5 million in 1931, for example, could raise only $645,000. On this score, President Hoover was tragically out of touch. In the winter of 1930–1931 he felt the country's unified "'sense of voluntary organization and community service' could take care of the unemployed," according to Arthur Schlesinger Jr. About a year later, in late 1931, President Hoover did create the Organization for Unemployment Relief to help drive the wealthy to donate money to private charities, but he simply did not believe the government needed to directly assist the unemployed. For one, Hoover considered it the responsibility of local communities to handle and feed their own out-of-work citizens. But he was also afraid that any federal assistance would provide an excuse for the wealthy in America to stop providing charity and funds to the needy "have-nots" in their communities. Amazingly, many Americans sided with Hoover on this topic in the early days of the Depression.

AUGUST 20, 1931

The Allied Council—the charity organization of Youngstown—has been busy during the depression handing out grocery orders. When I came to work this morning I counted about 50 of them coming down the steps that lead to the office. The elevator man tells me this happens every day and that people start drifting in at about 7 A.M. Many of them look well fed and are probably taking advantage of the situation. The city is planning a bond issue to provide for relief needs this winter. Hold-ups and killings are becoming more frequent and it becomes dangerous to walk the streets after dark.

AUGUST 20, 1931

This morning a client 65 years of age came into the office and we had a long talk about his personal affairs. He had been in the liquor business and in 1921 when Prohibition put an end to his activity he had accumulated about $200,000 in liquid cash. He is now broke except for some worthless real estate. He became a prey to high pressure salesmen of worthless stocks, tried one business after the other, speculated in real estate and in many ways tried to make more money quickly. We discussed 7 or 8 other men to whom the same thing happened. Not one was able to hold his money. They were good saloonkeepers but had not learned how to keep their money or to make it work for them. They knew absolutely nothing about sound investments and were not satisfied with a moderate return of 4% or 5%. I asked him what he would do again in the same circumstances. With tears in his eyes he said he would preserve and protect the principal at all hazards. He would invest safely for a small but certain return. On $8,000 a year, he could have lived well in Youngstown and he and his family would have had the peace of mind that financial security can bring. He was particularly rabid against his investments in real estate.

AUGUST 21, 1931

The Union Savings Bank of Warren closes its doors today. It was one of the oldest in the community. People seem to have lost all confidence in banks and are quietly withdrawing their funds and putting it in safety vaults. It is impossible to say how far the movement will go. In Youngstown just now the Commercial Bank seems to be the strongest with 50% liquidity. The other banks are not so good with about 20% liquidity. Government and postal savings are popular today.

AUGUST 22, 1931

Things are happening fast and the people are getting more demoralized each day. Two more large commercial banks in Warren and one Savings &

Loan Co. closed their doors. Nate got back from his vacation yesterday and said his personal account was tied up and also a commercial account he uses in his business and consisting of money that belongs to clients. His personal account was not much but the other was more substantial.

This morning about 100 men were standing in line before the Allied Council Headquarters waiting to get grocery orders. The line grows longer each day.

Just heard that the bank at Cortland closed today. The closing of a bank in a city seems to drag down banks in the small communities nearby.

AUGUST 22, 1931

There is a quiet but steady stream of depositors at every bank in Youngstown this morning quietly withdrawing their funds. The closing of banks in Toledo and Warren received much publicity and distrust of all banks is growing like a cancer. It is a movement which feeds on itself and is hard to stop. At the Dollar and Union Banks there are about 4 or 5 depositors at each withdrawal window. There is no excitement but a quiet look of intensity on the faces of both depositors and bank officials. Even the strongest banks can't keep this up long. They do not have enough cash to pay everybody. Much of their funds are invested in railroad bonds and other securities which were once considered gilt-edged but are now selling below par so that the banks cannot afford to liquidate. Investments like mortgages are frozen tight. There is clearly something wrong with our banking system which permits such a situation to come about. It is hard to rent a safety box today because there has been such a demand by hoarders. Actually the liquid cash of the bank is being transferred from the bank vaults to the private safety vaults where it is taken out of circulation and becomes sterilized.

AUGUST 25, 1931

I talked today to Serena Shlesinger who works for the Allied Council. She tells me they had 750 applicants for charity on one day of last week and had 300 on another day.

Everybody is afraid of the banks. Both in Warren and Youngstown the depositors are withdrawing money—the thing simply cannot go on. I tried to warn W. W. Z. who is a large depositor but he laughed at me. Nate transferred his office account to the Commercial Bank at Youngstown so he can continue his business.

AUGUST 26, 1931

Good properties on almost every business street in the city are being offered for sale by the sheriff. Oh! If I only had some money. As little as $1000 or $1500 in cash would swing the deal if the buyer is willing to assume the mortgage. I am still hoping I can pick up some of these bargains before the depression is over but unless a lucky large fee comes in I do not see how it can be done.

International politics are boiling but I cannot quite understand everything that is going on. Germany is on the verge of financial bankruptcy and is asking for delay and cancellation of war debts. England is in the same position and yesterday Prime Minister MacDonald resigned. France seems to be richer than ever and is using every advantage to crush Germany.

AUGUST 29, 1931

The Legal News advertises a foreclosure against Dr. B— covering about 5 apartment buildings in poor neighborhoods. The mortgage is $12000 and the whole thing can be bought for this amount. Four years ago, the owner was willing to sacrifice the property for $45000 and thought it was worth $75000. In normal times the rental income was $1000 per month. This is another example why a professional man should not invest in low-grade real estate. It takes almost full time to collect the rent, make the repairs, etc. The overhead is high and he is fortunate if he makes 6% clear over a period of years with nothing for his labor. Properties of this kind seldom have a speculative value.

People who have savings accounts in the Home Savings & Loan Co. are willing to sell them at a discount. They are also being accepted as payments on real estate, autos, and merchandise but the buyer always suffers a loss. If necessary I will accept them in fees and apply them on my mortgage.

Now that fall is coming I feel a little more cheerful for the coming winter although there is no sign of betterment. The steel mills are operating at 30% capacity, the lowest of any depression and farm products are still selling at record lows. I still do not understand why the prices of "blue chip" stocks do not come down. Amer. Tel. & T. is still selling at $170 and should come down at least to $100. General Electric is at 40 instead of about 18. Railroad stocks are way down but people are afraid of them because motor competition has made the future doubtful. [Later undated entry: "In the summer of 1932 AT&T went to 70. Blue chips could be held all thru."]

8/26/36

Before long the pass books on Home Savings; Federal; Dollar and City Banks sold as low as 40¢ on the dollar. Prices were quoted every day in the papers and the sales were made mostly through regular brokerage houses. Speculators bought the books and used them for various purposes. Many bought real estate at foreclosure and from the banks—paid for it in passbooks they had purchased at a discount. In this way they bought valuable real estate at about 1/2 the amount of the first mortgage balance. Likewise when the Central Bank was liquidated speculators exchanged passbooks purchased at a big discount for 1st mortgages at face value. Money was king.

SEPTEMBER 1, 1931

Another big mob today waiting in line before the office of the Allied Council. They blocked the stairway and extended down through the Dollar Bank lobby.

Most people think another boom will start as soon as this depression ends. I cannot agree with them. I think the next five years will be a period of gradual recovery and that bargains in stocks and real estate will be available through the entire recovery period. The boom may then come in about 10 years after this period of recovery. Hard work, low wages and a period of accumulation are ahead of us.

Signs of the times: Prices are falling rapidly. The 1929 dollar buys $1.40 in merchandise. Men are beginning to "roll-their-own" cigarettes and pipe smoking has been increased because it is cheaper than cigars. A good cigar can again be bought for a nickel and the 3 for 10 and 2 for 5 stogies are back in popular favor. Office men and women take their lunch to work or go home during the noon hour instead of eating in town. It has become popular to wear old clothes—to brag about poverty and how much you lost in the 1929 crash. It is almost bad taste to give a big party or to drive a new car.

A good plan for the next 5 years would be to save and invest cautiously and plan to have funds in liquid form when the next crash comes.

Our wash-woman said yesterday was the first day's work she has had in 3 months—her price is $2 instead of $3 and she is willing to work for almost anything she can get.

8/26/36

Looking back now this was a fair guess. Recovery has been moving gradually forward since the bottom was reached in summer of 1932. A spurt came in March 1935 and has continued to date. Bargains are still available in stocks altho they do not compare with what could have been done in 1932. The real estate taken back by the banks during past 5 years is still being liquidated at bargain prices but the choice is now limited. Rents are going up and it is probable that in another year the banks will have liquidated all their foreclosed real estate and then a more normal market will be established. As to the future—it is hard to say if we are heading for a boom or for a few years of normal business. The possibility of inflation makes a guess difficult.

SEPTEMBER 2, 1931

As nearly as I can make out from a study of past panics, the cycle of business is always moving down toward a panic or up toward a boom. It rarely for long travels in a straight line. At the present time we are clearly moving down and the turn has not yet come. In the making of investments it would also seem wise to wait for some sign of the upturn before jumping in. It is impossible to hit the exact turn but as long as things are still definitely on the downgrade there would seem to be no hurry. When the final upturn does come it seems to me it will continue up for 8 or 10 years and culminate in a boom and a crash. The wise investor will disregard the day-by-day fluctuations of the stock market or real estate market and base his buying and selling on these long periods of rise and fall. Above all, and I repeat it again and again—he must have liquid capital in time of depression to buy the bargains and then he must sell before the next crash. It is difficult if not impossible to do this but the conservative longtime investor who follows the general rule of buying stocks when they are selling far below their intrinsic value and nobody wants them, and of selling his stocks when people are bidding frantically for them at prices far above their intrinsic value—such an investor will pretty nearly hit the bull's-eye. Among such investors are the Morgans, the Mellons and the Bakers. Their secret to a large extent lies in having liquid capital available and the courage to invest when things look the blackest. They say of Mr. Baker that he always bought good stocks when they sold below their intrinsic value—and then held on until the cows came home. It seems to me he took very little risk.

8/26/36

This advice was pretty sound. The turn in the depression came in the summer of 1932 and since then it has worked up—with numerous breaks—but always up. Here is what would have happened to a buyer of stocks in summer of 1932 as contrasted today:

Amer T &T 70 to 170; Yo Sheet & Tube 6 to 80; Warner Bros. 1/2 to 14; Western Union 17 to 80; U.S. Steel 20 to 68; Gen. Motors 8 to 100; Gen. Elec. 8 to 46.

SEPTEMBER 4, 1931

The Allied Council broke all records the other day by handling 1150 calls for relief in one day. There is no accurate record of how many people are on relief in Youngstown today but it is estimated at about 30,000—almost 20% of the population. Several efforts are being made to care for the needy this winter which is expected to be severe:

1. The Community Chest will have an extra drive for funds.
2. The city will issue bonds.
3. All churches are acting as collectors of food, clothing, etc.

Farm prices are steadily going down. Peaches, apples and plums are selling at 50¢ a bushel.

Banks are absolutely terrible in their insistence on payments on notes and mortgages. It is the old story of lending you an umbrella when the sun is shining and then demanding it back when it rains. If a depositor asks for his money he is regarded with suspicion—sometimes he is sent to one of the officials who wants to know why he wants the money—if they think he is hoarding it they try to shame him out of a withdrawal and only if he becomes unpleasant and insistent does he get his money. It is a good time *not* to owe money to a bank and many businesses are being ruined because the banks insist on liquidating their loans. Some businesses owe the banks so much money that the banks are afraid to press them too far for fear they will go into bankruptcy and thus avoid the whole loan.

SEPTEMBER 8, 1931

The 2nd National Bank of Youngstown is today absorbed by the Mahoning Bank. Popular gossip says this was done to avoid another bank failure.

Reform and dissatisfaction are in the air everywhere. People who are ordinarily moderate predict freely that if things do not get better very soon we will have a revolution in the U.S.A. and some form of Communism or dictatorship. Judge David Jenkins predicted this definitely last week in a talk before the Kiwanis Club.

The *N.Y. Times* reported yesterday that numerous small real estate bond companies have been formed in the past year to buy up defaulted real estate bonds. There is no open or active bond market and the owner has no way of knowing what they are worth. An unscrupulous buyer can get them at 20 or 30¢ on the dollar even tho they may be worth par. Most of the large real estate bond houses which sold these bonds have gone broke. Lawyers in large cities like New York and Chicago are reaping a harvest in foreclosures and receivership involving large office buildings and apartments which were erected in the years of frenzied finance.

SEPTEMBER 9, 1931

The Youngstown Sheet & Tube Co. at a directors meeting decides to omit the quarterly dividend. The stock is now selling at $35 per share. This is lower than in the 1921 depression when it sold at 45. U.S. Steel is at 80 as compared to 70 in 1921. Railroads are all down to the 1921 levels—Penn at 34, NYC 64. It still seems to me that blue chip stocks such as AT&T at 165, Consolidated Gas at 90 and G.E. at 40 must come way down before it can be said that the market has been fully deflated.

I am getting weary of depression talk and patent remedies. You hear it on all sides. The favorite remedy is repeal of Prohibition and the bringing back of liquor in the hope that a new industry will give employment and that real estate values will be stimulated. Then there is a great deal of talk about socialism and Communism and revolution. It all seems silly to me. Everything will work itself out without these radical changes. The depression has loosed all the radical thinkers who call themselves "liberals." The true liberal and conservative has been silenced and is in disgrace.

8/29/36

This guess was pretty accurate. In summer of 1932 these stocks were selling as follows: Sheet & Tube at 6; U.S. Steel at 17; Penn R.R. 5; N.Y.C. 8; AT&T 70; Consol Gas 15; GE 10.

> *Liquor became legal in 1933 but failed to help recovery. It stimu-*
> *lated the imbibers but not general businesses. Today we have 2 or 3*
> *beer parlor lunchrooms in every block.*

SEPTEMBER 10, 1931

An item in the financial column today states that the Payne Whitney estate increased $59 million in value during the 1929 boom. It consisted entirely of high grade stocks. Even tho the high grade stocks suffered in the depression very few of them were wiped out and will probably come back.

AT&T is still paying its $9 dividend and has proven to be an outstanding stock.

Many Youngstown millionaires have been hard hit by the failure of Youngstown Sheet & Tube to pay its dividend. In a great many cases these families have over a million tied up in Sheet & Tube and Republic Steel and depended entirely on these stocks for their income.

I feel more and more convinced that the time to buy stocks has not yet arrived because the blue chip stocks have not yet come down even tho the depression is already two years old.

8/29/36

> *AT&T paid its usual dividend thru the depression. Other high*
> *grade stocks did not but practically all of them have come back again*
> *and the holder who did not sell will lose nothing except the unpaid*
> *dividends.*

SEPTEMBER 13, 1931

We bought peaches yesterday at 75¢ a bushel. The trees are still loaded to the ground and will go to waste because the fruit cannot be sold. In the meanwhile thousands are starving. It is hard to understand. There is no sign of a pick-up this fall. If anything things are worse. There is simply no money in circulation. This scarcity of money is what makes people think if more money were printed business would be better. This is a false and vicious theory.

SEPTEMBER 15, 1931

I talked to a very prominent real estate man today who developed one of the best residential plots in Youngstown but went broke with the coming of the depression because everything he had was heavily mortgaged and people stopped paying on the property they had bought. He tells me his wife is working in a millinery store and he is in Detroit selling Whiffle Boards (a 5¢ marble gambling game sold to drug stores, beer parlors, etc.). He owns many fine pieces of real estate, mostly vacant lots but cannot give them away. He says he waited too long—hoping the depression would be short—in the meanwhile spending all his liquid cash on taxes, etc.—and now it is too late to unload. Many investors would have been better to unload their real estate and stock investments during the first year of the depression rather than to have waited. They would at least have salvaged something rather than to have lost everything.

8/31/36

An interesting side light of the depression was that unemployed people became interested in small gambling games and the inventors of these games made considerable money. Some of the more popular games were the Whiffle board—a marble game charging 1¢ or 5¢; the "Bug" racket in which people bet from 1 cent up on what numbers would represent stock sales or bank clearings for the day—this is still going strong and is a million dollar racket; the dime chain letter game which offered a return of $200 or $300 for a dime plus a chain letter sent to 10 friends—the crossword puzzle game—Monopoly—finance—politics, etc.

People lost all confidence in the old virtues of saving. They were willing to bet small amounts in the hope of getting large returns. They wanted something to occupy their minds and they wanted some gamble to buoy their hopes.

SEPTEMBER 28, 1931

A great deal of bad news came out in the past week. England, Denmark and Norway go off the gold standard and their currency values drop. The pound goes to $3.50. On top of this, Japan starts a war in China and hopes to grab off some land—knowing the other nations are too much involved in their own troubles to interfere.

There is no fall pickup in business and conditions are worse. During the past week 10 banks in Pittsburgh closed—and one in Alliance.

Following England's abandonment of the gold standard the U.S. market had a bad break and for the first time since 1929 the blue chip stocks are sliding down. AT&T is now 136—G.E. 30 and Consol Gas 70. The second-rate stocks are certainly low enough—Sheet & Tube 25 1/2; Republic 7; Truscon 8. I wish I had some money to invest but law business is bad and we are all operating on a day to day basis. Stock exchanges in England and Germany are closed.

SEPTEMBER 29, 1931

The Niles Savings & Trust Co. closed its doors yesterday. The effect was immediately felt in Youngstown by a steady stream of withdrawals at all banks. It is all being done so quietly that I cannot believe anything can happen here and yet I know that this cannot go on much longer. I also marvel at the quiet way in which people take bad news of bank closings. A quiet crowd of white-faced people gather in front of the banks for a day or two—read the notice of closing signed by the Ohio State Bank examiner and then quietly slip away. In France I can imagine a similar crowd breaking windows and stirring up revolution.

I am really afraid for at least two of our big banks here. It would be a calamity. My emotions tell me it just can't happen and yet—my logic says it *must* happen unless some drastic solution is found at once. Last night's paper listed further bank failures in Philadelphia, Detroit and Pittsburgh. This means additional failures in the small surrounding towns. In a great many instances fraud is shown on the part of bank officials who used bank funds to play the stock market. The whole banking fraternity is in public disfavor and many of them face prison.

I am a little puzzled by the complications of international finance but I am learning fast and a good deal of what I was taught in college as theory is now being put to the test of actual practice. What is meant by a country going off the gold standard? As far as I can see it is like a bank refusing to pay out deposits because of lack of funds. I can see I will have to read up on the subject and I shall get started at once. Politics, economics, and international finance—the depression has been a postgraduate college course for me and from that standpoint at least has been a worth-while experience.

OCTOBER 2, 1931

Things get gloomier and the stock market continues on its downward path. Sheet & Tube sells at 22 1/2. Small banks close their doors all over the country as newspapers try to minimize it as much as possible so that the panic will not spread. Yesterday the largest and oldest bank in Steubenville (1854) closed its doors. The Canadian dollar is worth 70¢ in U.S. because England went off gold standard. In the U.S. the silver mining states are urging a return to bi-metalism in order to bring prosperity back to their states.

OCTOBER 6, 1931

The big new zeppelin made in Akron just flew over Youngstown in a trial flight. It is the biggest thing I ever saw. It makes one wonder what will be the future of travel by air.

Stocks have been going down, down, down for over a month now. The latest explanation is that *English* investors are selling their U.S. investments in order to get U.S. dollars which are worth about 25% more in depreciated English currency.

U.S. Steel 62; Sheet & Tube 20; Truscon 7; Republic Steel 5 1/2.

Only public utilities are still high such as AT&T, Consol Gas, etc.

One financial writer says stocks are not too low—in fact too high—because future profits of industry will be lower on account of lower prices etc.—and that profits in the last 10 years of prosperity are not a good gauge.

OCTOBER 7, 1931

A large bank in Philadelphia and 5 smaller ones closed up yesterday. The bank closing movement started in the mid-west and now seems to be penetrating the east.

OCTOBER 8, 1931

Everybody is excited about Pres. Hoover's plan to end the depression and stocks go up as high as 10 and 15 points. Under this plan a huge national banking corporation is to be formed backed by government money which will discount frozen mortgages and other illiquid assets of the banks in order to give them cash to pay depositors. It will be something like the Federal Reserve Bank except that it can discount mortgages and other paper not now eligible. The plan also contemplates making the

Federal Reserve more flexible so that in time of depression it can widen its discount basis.

9/1/36

This organization was formed and known as the RFC (Reconstruction Finance Corp.). It came too late to prevent a bank collapse but in 1933–36 under Pres. Roosevelt it loaned huge amounts to banks and corporations and did a great deal of good.

OCTOBER 10, 1931

Ruth Bryan Owen makes claim that the prophecies of her father William Jennings Bryan who urged free silver 30 years ago are now coming true. I am faithfully reading books on economics so I can fully understand all this talk of free silver and bi-metalism. It is a complicated subject and I have almost come to the conclusion that nobody knows very much about it. Many of these theories sound fine but do not work out so well in actual practice.

OCTOBER 10, 1931

When I visited my safety box in the vault of the Dollar Bank today, Mr. Owen told me that "the last two days—since President Hoover announced his plan to help the banks—has been the quietest we have had for several months. Before that we had a number of new applicants for safety boxes every day but since then we have had none." He felt that Hoover's announcement had strengthened faith in the banks and had put a stop to hoarding.

Again and again I am forced to the conclusion that in prosperous times a man must be cautious and preserve his capital and be careful not to over-expand his business or to go too deeply in debt relying on a continuation of good business to pay the debt. In time of depression a man can be brave and if the depression is nearing an end he can invest his money or expand his business or open a new business with confidence that he is facing 5 or 10 years of prosperity. He can feel sure that the road ahead will be up—not down. Many great prosperous businesses were founded on the ruins of depression. This may be why so many Federal St. merchants are now beginning to put in a new store front, etc.

A great many losses and failures in business and in investment are due to the reversal of this policy. At the height of prosperity they rush in to buy stocks or real estate or businesses at boom prices and assume enormous indebtedness which can be liquidated only if the boom spiral mounts higher and higher. Then comes an abrupt end to prosperity—a crash—and down go these businesses and investments purchased at top prices. If the purchase was made mostly with borrowed capital as so often happens— then you can write finis to the chapter.

3/8/33

The difficulty of course is to know when the depression is over. People who bought "bargains" in stocks in 1931 now find they were too quick and these same stocks are now selling at 1/3 of 1931 prices. If they can hold on long enough they will come out alright but it is a soul-trying period of waiting. It might be best to wait until the upturn actually begins. It may come suddenly and the opportunity may be lost.

8/31/36

The bottom was reached in summer 1932 and the upturn gradually started. There had been so many false starts however that it was not until 1934–5 that people really realized that the turn had been passed. Then a glance at a business or stock market chart showed what had happened. The upward advance was irregular—it went up and down just like a half dozen earlier false starts but finally in March 1935 it started up and has continued up until the present day. All of these charts followed the pattern of 1873 and 1893 closely and it will probably happen again.

OCTOBER 12, 1931

Bank failures continue in spite of President Hoover's plan. Yesterday saw the closing of the National Bank of Uniontown—one of the largest in western Pennsylvania.

The Strouss-Hirshberg Company employees some time ago received a 25% cut in wages. Yesterday the employees on the second floor were informed they could work only on alternate days. At the Truscon Steel employees also received a 25% cut some time ago and now they can work only 5 days a week. The stock market has been going up for several days now since the Hoover announcement.

OCTOBER 13, 1931

The good effect of President Hoover's plan is wearing off rapidly. Last night's paper publishes the quarterly reports of the local banks. All were in pretty frozen shape (about 20% liquid) except the Commercial Bank which is about 65% liquid. Long lines of people can be seen this morning quietly withdrawing deposits and bank officials seem more worried than ever. More people are renting safety deposit boxes or taking their money to the post office to open a U.S. Postal savings account.

In the meanwhile, the Japanese-Chino war grows more imminent.

OCTOBER 14, 1931

Last night's paper reports the closing of eight banks in West Virginia and Philadelphia. Also that the 14 banks in Atlantic City have been combined into 4 banks. Also that the government bank aid plan is not going so good because the stronger banks do not want to guarantee the weaker. The proposed capital has been cut from $500 million to $100 million.

Stocks are on the way down again.

OCTOBER 15, 1931

Great excitement in Youngstown. It finally happened here. The Dollar Savings & Trust Co., The City Trust and the 1st National Banks all fail to open for business this morning. This leaves only the Mahoning Bank and The Commercial open for business. Both of them are besieged by depositors seeking to withdraw their deposits. I do not see how it can last. The town is panic-stricken and the streets are crowded with people excitedly discussing the situation. I was aroused this morning at 4 A.M. by newsboys shouting Xtras. It still seems like a bad dream. [Later undated entry: "This was before the days of television and radio."]

OCTOBER 15, 1931, 2 P.M.

Banks in the small towns around Youngstown are either closing their doors or refusing to permit withdrawals except for emergency use.

Several of the wealthiest families in Youngstown had all their funds invested in local bank stocks or in the local steel mills. With these investments almost worthless and with double liability attached to the bank stocks they are wiped out. This seems to show the wisdom of a partial investment in sound bonds or government securities.

Announcement is made that the proposed Bethlehem–Sheet & Tube merger has been called off.

OCTOBER 15, 1931, 3 P.M.

The run continues on the Mahoning and Commercial banks. Both banks are still open but trying to talk depositors out of making withdrawals or giving them part of their money. A large street car bus filled with armed guards just unloaded money for the Mahoning Bank brought from the Federal Reserve Bank at Cleveland.

I have some money and checks to deposit but do not know where to go to open a checking account. I was a depositor at the Dollar Bank which is now closed.

8/31/36

Many bitter enmities were made during these days. Friends of bankers who were loyal to the bank and left their money in later became embittered against the officials who persuaded them to do so. One large law firm was later dissolved because one partner insisted in withdrawing his funds from a bank in which the other partners were deeply interested. Many a feud destined to last many years had its beginnings here.

OCTOBER 16, 1931

The Commercial and Mahoning Banks are still open and jammed with depositors but only partial withdrawals are being permitted.

Business is being operated this morning in crazy-quilt fashion. No one will accept checks—and nobody has cash. The wholesalers, most of whom have their offices in other cities, refuse to deliver merchandise to the stores except C.O.D. cash. A good many professional men are also likely broke and admit it without hesitation. When I came downtown yesterday morning my total assets consisted of a $15 check on a Hubbard Bank and $6 in cash. I rushed to Hubbard—was the 1st one to enter the bank at 9 A.M. and succeeded in getting the check cashed. So far so good—but what of tomorrow! The following thoughts occur to me:

1. It pays to do business only with the strongest bank in the community.
2. The depositor should learn how to read a bank statement and then

follow the progress of the bank. Such a depositor could have long foreseen the bank crash in Youngstown.

3. In the same way money should be invested in the *best* bonds, stocks, real estate even tho the return is less.

4. Life insurance proved to be a cushion for me in the depression. Money borrowed on life insurance policies should be paid back as quickly as possible. It has so far proven to be the next best investment after government bonds.

5. Money should be invested not locally but on a national scale if possible, including stocks and bonds in companies located in other communities and operating nationally. Many wealthy families in Youngstown grew rich on only local industries and banks but they are pretty well cleaned out now.

OCTOBER 17, 1931

The financial situation would be ridiculous if it were not tragic. Everybody demands cash—no checks are accepted. The Truscon Steel Co. paid its employees with checks drawn on a large New York Bank and the local banks refused to cash them. The check may be good today and bad tomorrow. Even certified checks are regarded suspiciously. One large department store had no cash to pay its employees. The streets are full of rumors that the City Bank will re-open with a subscription of a million in new capital but nothing can be verified.

As I bring to a close the first volume of my personal observations on the depression I must breathe deeply and pinch myself to be sure I am awake and not dreaming. I still cannot believe that the Dollar Bank—the Gibraltar of Youngstown—has closed its doors—or that the old First National Bank is no more. It is all unreal to me. Each day I move about in a dream. I feel as tho I am experiencing an historic thing which will be long remembered. So far I have not been badly hurt personally—we are all well—I still have faith in Youngstown and in the United States in spite of the dire prophecies that are heard on every side! Somehow it all reminds me of the war days of 1917–18 when with bated breath we asked "What next?"

CHAPTER 2
OCTOBER 20, 1931–NOVEMBER 11, 1932

"There is much suffering."

VOLUME II

EDITOR'S NOTE

By 1931, the economic downturn had gone from bad to worse. Joblessness continued to rise, reaching eleven million by October 1932; by some estimates one in every four eligible Americans was out of work. Many who kept jobs saw their hours or wages reduced. And banks were collapsing at an ever-increasing rate, taking their depositors' money with them; during Hoover's presidency more than 20 percent of America's banks shuttered their doors.

Roth chronicled the bank closures in neighboring Warren and in Toledo when he started his diary. Yet bank closures were not unique to the Depression. Even during the booming 1920s, almost five thousand small, independent state-chartered banks and savings and loans had shut their doors, primarily in the South and Midwest. With little extra capital to handle a series of bad loans, defaulted mortgages, failed speculative investments, or even just a run of large withdrawals from depositors, bank failures were a relatively common occurrence. To an important degree this was a deliberate policy. Many economists and the bankers who made up the Federal Reserve (which, founded in 1914, was still a relatively young institution) believed that bank closures were a desirable effect of an economic depression, because they weeded out banks that had weakened themselves through excessive lending. Of course, for local communities the effects could be destabilizing. When a bank was struggling, it would often freeze its assets and limit withdrawals. If it collapsed, it could even lose all of its depositors' money. As a result, bank customers would try to protect themselves by rushing to withdraw their funds at the slightest indication that their local bank had cash problems. These mass withdrawals would only exacerbate a troubled bank's financial straits.

Opening a postal savings account became one popular alternative to banks. President William Taft established the postal savings system in 1910 as a means to regain the trust of Americans who felt it was unsafe to store their money in uninsured banks after the panic of

1907. In contrast to banks, a postal savings account was a government-protected alternative that took deposits as little as $1 and up to $2,500. It also offered people the opportunity to convert their deposits into certificates or bonds that accrued interest. By 1933 these federally secured accounts grew to more than $1 billion. The number of postal savings depositors would drop after banks received federal insurance protection.

But in 1931, as 2,294 banks with $1.7 billion in depositors' money failed, the massive loss meant a huge disruption to everyday money transactions. People didn't have the money to pay bills or buy food, businesses couldn't pay employees, and shops wouldn't accept checks that they couldn't cash. In Youngstown people created alternative ways to get funds. Promissory notes called "scrips" were distributed as a substitute for cash. Some companies even used scrips as paychecks to workers. But scrips could be redeemed only once the banks with frozen assets allowed people to take their money out again. A market for buying bank "passbooks" also cropped up in places like Youngstown. If you were desperate enough in 1931 for money to buy the basic necessities, you could get 60 to 70 cents on the dollar for your passbooks' value. Local newspapers even printed the weekly rates for buying and selling these passbooks as they became a commodity; Roth pasted one such rate chart into his diary.

In Washington President Hoover resisted involving the federal government in rescuing the banks. It conflicted with his political philosophy of "self-reliance" in personal as well as business life. Nevertheless, by 1931 he did see a need to save the smaller banks and boost their dismal reserves. He organized a "secret meeting" of major bank leaders to convince them to put their money together and provide a reserve for the weaker banks. At first the bankers resisted. They believed it was the role of the federal government to bail out the smaller institutions. Furthermore, they had their own problems with cash, partly due to foreign investors who were dumping American securities and withdrawing gold in record numbers. They did eventually agree to Hoover's request and created the National Credit Association, but briefly. Within a few weeks this organization failed, simply because the bankers refused to save their colleagues—including the Bank of Pittsburgh—with their cash. Under pressure from Congress, which had been taken over by Democrats in the 1930 election, President Hoover eventually succumbed to the notion that federal help was necessary. The Reconstruction Finance Corporation was created. By the time the RFC had the power to provide about $2 billion in loans to banks, railroads, and insurance companies in February 1932, even the reserves of the big banks pegged to the Federal Reserve had dropped within $50 million of the lowest amount allowed by law. In August of that year $336,000 would arrive in Youngstown to help the local banks.

As he watched banks fail all around him, one of Roth's particular concerns—and a subject still examined by economists today—concerned the "double liability" of bank shareholders. Beginning in the nineteenth century, many state governments mandated that a shareholder in a bank would be liable not only for the amount of money that he originally invested but also for the value of the shares that he owned; in short, if the institution failed, he could easily lose more money than he had put in. The goal of double liability was to prevent banks from pursuing high-risk activities; if shareholders knew that their own fortunes were at stake, they were presumed to be more cautious. By 1931 federal banking law and all but ten states had some type of multiple-liability provision on their books. But the massive bank failures of the Depression indicated that this was not an effective technique; after federal deposit insurance was introduced, most states did away with multiple-liability rules.

OCTOBER 20, 1931

This is a continuation of personal impressions and observations in connection with the first depression or panic that I have gone thru during my business life.

The big stock crash which marked the real beginning of the depression came exactly two years ago. Stocks and prices and wages are still on the down-grade; unemployment has increased and the outlook for the winter is very bleak.

Locally the three large banks which closed last week (The Dollar—The City—The 1st Nat'l) are being liquidated by the state. This morning about 2000 people watched armed guards load all the City Bank money into armored trucks to be carted away for safe-keeping. Mass meetings are being held every day to consider plans to re-open the banks but so far nothing accomplished. The City Bank depositors are making the hardest fight. It has been interesting to note the large number of real estate transfers by stockholders of the banks who fear double liability. Actual money in Youngstown can't be gotten and business is at a standstill.

OCTOBER 21, 1931

It is interesting to note that none of the plans started by Pres. Hoover and other leaders has produced results. Even the National Credit Bank which Hoover started a few weeks ago seems to have been forgotten.

In the meanwhile this morning's paper carries the news that Japan launches a military attack on Manchuria in defiance of the League of Nations and the Kellogg Treaty. Japan probably thinks the other nations are too busy with their own troubles to interfere.

10 banks failed yesterday in Pittsburgh and vicinity. In New Castle and in Akron the banks combined to prevent failures.

7/10/70

Under present law shareholders of banks are no longer subject to double personal liability if the bank fails. Likewise personal liability is limited on real estate foreclosure deficiency judgment.

OCTOBER 22, 1931

I never thought I would live to see things like this happening in Youngstown. The farther I get away from the closing of our 3 oldest banks the more horrible are the consequences and the more unbelievable it becomes. Something is wrong with our banking system yet in spite of the Federal Reserve. I am reminded of the early war days where the military draft started to operate and people held their breath and asked "what next."

Banks in Canton, Massillon, Alliance and Pittsburgh closed yesterday. Included were two old banks—The Harter National of Canton and the Monongahela of Pittsburgh.

At a mass meeting last night at South High an attempt was made to re-open the city banks by urging depositors to buy new stock with 25% of their deposits and to agree to let the balance remain for an agreed period of 1 to 3 years.

OCTOBER 24, 1931

Pessimism grows deeper locally and little hope is held out for re-opening the banks altho new plans spring up every day. It is interesting to watch the list of daily real estate and mortgage transfers. Most of our established families were stock-holders in the banks and every day sees a half dozen transfers to wife or child or a large mortgage.

I am told that 200 young priests have been sent here from Cleveland to make a house-to-house canvas to help re-open the City Bank. The bank was favored by a large number of Jewish and Catholic depositors.

Sermons are being delivered in all the churches urging courage. A large bill-board is being erected on the public square with the caption "forward Youngstown." I attended services at Rodef Sholom Temple last night and it was crowded. It seems true that religion and the church grow stronger in adversity.

OCTOBER 25, 1931

It is unbelievable that in one year so many old established fortunes in Youngstown could be swept away. I can find very little to criticize in their list of investments. They relied on local bank stocks, Sheet & Tube, Republic and Bank deposits. They might possibly be criticized for not selling all their Sheet & Tube Common and Republic Common at boom prices in 1929 and switching to good bonds. Also they might be criticized for holding too much bank stock entirely or in one community. If Youngstown went bad, all their investments went bad. On the other hand they had held all these investments for over 25 years and had grown rich on them. The only conclusion I can come to is that at least half of the investor's money should be in good bonds. Also the double liability attached to bank stocks is a dangerous feature.

OCTOBER 27, 1931

The situation remains the same and the banks remain closed. The latest howl comes from school teachers who have not been paid since school started. They must wait until the bonding company pays bank losses. The same situation exists in Chicago and other cities.

OCTOBER 28, 1931

Small banks in Kinsman and several other little nearby towns closed yesterday. Akron and Dayton get organized to bring in outside capital to prevent a situation such as exists now in Toledo and Youngstown.

NOVEMBER 3, 1931

The Union Trust of Dayton—one of its largest banks—closed yesterday. Also one of the largest labor union banks in New York has closed. The National Credit Bank proposed by Pres. Hoover has failed to function so far. More talk of "bi-metalism" as a remedy for the depression and also of Russian-Japanese-Chinese War. About 500 unemployed held a meeting on the front steps of the courthouse today and demanded a "dole" of $1 per week. No signs of business improvement in sight.

NOVEMBER 5, 1931

Banks continue to close all over the state. Yesterday the Farmers Bank of Mansfield closed its doors. This is where Jake banked. All discussion in Youngstown about re-opening the banks has died down. "Hunger Meetings" are being held daily in front of courthouse, City Hall and our Square.

NOVEMBER 7, 1931

During past week wheat went up from 40¢ to 80¢ per bushel. Stocks also push up and claim is made that in 1873 and in 1893 the turn for better came with the rise in wheat and the removal of fear that U.S. would go off gold standard. There seems to be little danger of this.

Japan is practically at war with China and Russia and ignores League of Nations warning. In past month Japan sent 75 million gold to U.S. presumably in preparation for purchase of war munitions.

NOVEMBER 8, 1931

It is really funny to see professional men "pull in their horns." Those who became "specialists" during the boom by taking a 3 months trip to Europe are now back in general practice. A good many doctors and dentists have given up their down-town office and are using their home. Same with lawyers. It is the old story of expanding too far and living too high.

Practically every country club including the Youngstown Country Club has closed for the winter.

NOVEMBER 12, 1931

Things remain at a standstill. There is no money in circulation, the stores and business places are deserted and everybody seems to have given up their initiative. The banks are still closed, school teachers are unpaid and there is no money to pay salaries of county and city officials. There is some talk about issuing scrip against bank deposits. Vacant store-rooms on W Federal St. are on the increase and half-price sales are numerous.

Russia-China-Japan seem to be actually at war with over 1000 killed to date and the League of Nations seems helpless. Because of this war scare the price of wheat and of silver has trebled in the past week. All of these countries are on a silver basis.

There will be a meeting tonight of the Congregation Rodef Sholom to consider ways and means. Both the temple funds and the members funds are tied up in the banks. The choir has been fired and other economies affected but this does not seem enough. The same is true of other churches and institutions.

NOVEMBER 14, 1931

The congregational meeting at Rodef Sholom Temple last night was very "blue." Money tied up in banks, members dropping out, reducing dues or not paying at all, etc. Entire budget is cut down and various resolutions passed promising co-operation. Rabbi Philo's salary cut from $10,000 to $8,500.

Hoover launches another national bank system to rediscount small mtges. It is like the National Credit Corporation which will rediscount commercial loans not eligible for Federal Reserve Banks. One mortgage discount bank will be established in each Federal Reserve District—capital to be supplied by the member banks.

Another bank in Toledo voluntarily quit business and tells the depositors to come and get their money.

The bi-metalism argument rages hot. Bryan advocated a ratio of 16 to 1 but at present the ratio of 22 to 1 is being advocated. At present prices silver is about 70 times cheaper than gold but its price is rising due to buying of Japan and China.

Strong rumor that the Mellons of Pittsburgh will come to Youngstown—place a three million mortgage on the Dollar-First buildings and re-open the banks. This would be a bargain for them for they would have good security for the money they advanced and get control of the banks for nothing.

NOVEMBER 18, 1931

Everything is still at a stand-still. The banks remain closed and business is worse if anything. We bought apples Sunday for 30¢ per bushel. Drove thru Niles and Warren and were impressed by the number of vacant stores on the main street. The same is true of Youngstown with many chain stores leaving. Movie prices are down to 25¢ and the State Theater is closed "temporarily."

NOVEMBER 24, 1931

Business as usual—and that is rotten. Large delegation of Youngstown goes to St. Louis to urge the canal matter. The weather remains unbelievably warm and we have had no winter. A large crowd of 400 or 500 men still assembles each morning in front of City Hall hoping for a day's work.

Stocks are going down again to lowest point in 15 yrs. And in some cases (rails) all time record lows: West. Union 52; U.S. Steel 58; Sheet & Tube 22; Beth St. 25, etc. There is more talk of script and bi-metalism.

EDITOR'S NOTE

Even traditionally secure industries witnessed a quick, sharp decline in business between 1929 and 1932. Construction of residential properties, for example, saw an 82 percent drop in those years. U.S. Steel Corporation, headquartered near Youngstown in Pittsburgh and founded by Andrew Carnegie, J. P. Morgan, and Charles Schwab, had cut 75 percent of its workforce to part-time hours in 1931. By September of that year it had adopted a 10 percent wage reduction. Other industries quickly followed the example of U.S. Steel. Another 1.7 million workers experienced similar cuts in their wages within ten days.

The beleaguered agricultural sector fared even worse. Farmers had experienced a downturn as early as 1920. From 1910 to about 1920, and especially during World War I, there seemed to be a nearly endless need for the food that American farmers provided. Farms grew bigger and output increased, as the demand in hungry, war-torn Europe seemed insatiable. But after the war, though the postwar consumer culture created profits in the business sector, Americans simply couldn't consume all the surplus of wheat, corn, dairy, or beef that the farmers were accustomed to producing and selling. Farmers saw their gross agricultural income fall to $10.5 billion in 1921 from $17.7 billion in 1919. Wheat prices, for example, had gone from $2.19 a bushel in 1919 to $1.05 in 1929. Farmers, however, didn't reduce their production even as prices plummeted. So President Hoover, in contrast to his slow response to the banking and unemployment situation, enacted the Agricultural Marketing Act of 1929 to handle the glut of production and try to raise the price of agricultural commodities. This policy created the Federal Farm Board, armed with $500 million to develop agricultural cooperatives and stabilization corporations to keep prices steady and store surplus produce as a means to heighten demand and raise prices.

Only the effort did not save the farmers. As the new era gave way to the Great Depression, farmers' plight had moved beyond the price of milk. Their debt had ballooned from $3.2 billion in 1910 to $8.4 billion in 1920. Farmers financed much of the expansion during the good times by remortgaging their properties with easy loans from banks. They also snatched up modern plows, cultivators, tractors, and other equipment aimed at boosting productivity when demand was high on credit from farming companies. By 1932 many farmers could barely afford the seed to plant on their land to feed even their own families.

DECEMBER 2, 1931

The Wabash Railroad goes into receivership. Also the other R.R.s are all in bad shape. Local banks are still closed and very little hope of opening. Stocks continue to go down to new low records. U.S. Steel and Western Union are both selling at 50 and Atcheson (Topeka & Santa Fe Railroad) pays $10 div. on a price below 87.

DECEMBER 7, 1931

The weather has turned bitter cold for the first time this winter and there is much suffering. About 1000 unemployed were lined up at 6 A.M. today in front of City Hall hoping to get a day's work. Business is at a standstill although a little Xmas shopping appeared last Saturday.

DECEMBER 8, 1931

A party from Detroit tells me that conditions are far worse there than in

Youngstown. Real estate bonds and large family hotels etc. have become worthless and at foreclosure sale these large hotels etc. sell for less than land value. In some cases the large buildings have been destroyed rather than pay taxes. Likewise Detroit had its bank failures.

DECEMBER 10, 1931

Four large railroad companies fail to pay dividends yesterday—including New York Central—for first time since 1870. Stocks go to new lows. Some samples are NYCRR 24; Penn R. R. 20; U.S. Steel 46; Western Union 43; Yo. Sh. & Tube 20; Republic St. 5 5/8.

Many old businesses are going to the wall and many of them lived thru 5 previous panics but never saw anything like this.

DECEMBER 11, 1931

A very conservative young married man with a large family to support tells me that during the past 10 years he succeeded in paying off the mortgage on his house. A few weeks ago, he placed a new mortgage on it for $5000 and invested the proceeds in good stocks for long-term investment. I think in two or three years he will show a handsome profit. It is generally believed that good stocks and bonds can now be bought at very attractive prices. The difficulty is that nobody has the cash to buy.

DECEMBER 14, 1931

According to this morning's paper the new Japanese government abandons the gold standard. This makes a total of 15 countries that have gone off the gold standard. France and U.S. are the only 2 large countries remaining on the gold standard. China has always had silver money—the Scandinavian countries and India followed England and report has it that Canada will do the same thing. There is very little danger that U.S. will follow suit.

I received over the mail instructions to collect against a local man a balance of $50 due as subscription price to an "investment service." The record shows that in 1930—over a year after the big stock crash—this man invested over $100,000 in common stocks at what then seemed to be bargain prices. The total value today at market prices is $30,000. At least half of his funds should have been invested in high grade bonds.

DECEMBER 18, 1931

It seems that if a bank once closes its doors, it remains closed forever. For awhile a fuss is made, efforts to reopen, etc. but nothing happens. That is the situation in Youngstown now with the City, Dollar & 1st Nat'l still closed. In Chicago 59 banks were closed this year and only 2 re-opened. In Toledo—out of 4 large banks—only 1 re-opened. The stock holders now are getting double-liability notices.

Down-Down-Down goes the stock market.

Many interesting stock market stories now float about. In 1929 one Youngstown man owned 4000 shares Sheet & Tube on which he received an income of $20,000. He sold at boom price of $150 per share and received $600,000. Then bought 6000 shares Republic pfd which gave him an income of about $30,000 net. Now the Republic pfd pays no dividend and is selling at $10.

The only moral I can see is to limit investments to the highest grade issues and to diversify. If he had invested in a diversified list of blue chip stocks and bonds he would still be a loser but not nearly so much and he would still be getting a comfortable income. A portion of good old government bonds is the backbone of many an investment list today.

DECEMBER 23, 1931

Almost Christmas and we haven't had a snow-fall this year. The weather is like spring and it has been the warmest winter I can recall. Nothing new in business. Predictions for the new year have all been very conservative so far. A number of enterprising auto merchants and real estate dealers have been offering a bonus of 10 or more shares of common stocks in Republic Steel, Continental and other low stocks with each sale made. Others are giving cheap stocks as Xmas gifts to elevator boys, etc.

DECEMBER 30, 1931

Good news for Youngstown. The Commercial Bank and the (now closed) First National Bank will combine and reopen on Jan 4th as a new bank under the name of Union National Bank. It is said that the old stockholders of the First National Bank get nothing for their stock. Stock-holders of the old Second National have already been assessed double.

Stocks and bonds are still going down. Even U.S. gov'ts are selling as low as 82.

[Quarry owner Jacob] Coxey of Massillon, Ohio plans to issue his own city money backed the same as city bonds. He says this will help unemployment.

The papers are now full of the usual predictions for the new year but they are very conservative.

1932

JANUARY 2, 1932

The *N.Y. Times* yesterday had the usual new year predictions by business leaders. It was comical how each and every one refused to be definite. Last year they almost gave a date for the expected revival. The slump is now looked upon as of indefinite duration.

It was "interesting" to watch the workmen this morning eradicating the "First" and substituting "Union" on the old First National Bank Bldg.

The bank failure movement having swept thru the West and Middle-west is now devastating the East and South. Several large bank "consolidations" are announced in New York. Today's paper announces the failure of a South Carolina bank with 44 branches. I think the old-style "country banker" is out of the picture forever. Local business men are more hopeless than ever and a good many bankruptcies are looked for in the near future.

JANUARY 4, 1932

The new Union National Bank (merger of 1st and Commercial) opens this morning and starts with a bad run. The entire room is packed like sardines and everybody is withdrawing. I don't know how they can stand the pace long. Seems to me that they should put a limit on withdrawals.

JANUARY 5, 1932

The new Union National Bank is again crowded this morning. A few minutes after the doors opened there was a lineup of about fifty people in front of each paying window. Fortunately most of them seem to be working people who would have very small accounts.

JANUARY 7, 1932

The run on the Union National still continues. Yesterday was the 3rd day and crowds seem as big as ever. Progress is slow—about 10 minutes for each person. If a large withdrawal is demanded they are told to take it up with one of the officers.

Other signs of the times:

1. Sheet & Tube, preferred, sells at 40.
2. In almost every state an "army of unemployed" marches toward the capital for relief.
3. In Massillon, Coxey issues $100 city bonds to be used as money.
4. Frequently some girl or man advertises that they will marry or "sell themself" to any person for a certain sum of money which they need very badly.
5. No sign of betterment and dark predictions of large business failures this year.

JANUARY 9, 1932

The run continues on the Union National but it is much smaller. A statement published yesterday shows that even during the run the deposits exceeded the withdrawals and the bank is about 40% liquid.

JANUARY 11, 1932

The run on the Union National has practically subsided and the new bank has settled down to business.

The stock market continues downward and there seems no end to it. The contrast between 1929 prices and today is unbelievable. A few samples of some of the drops are Truscon 63 to 5; Sheet & Tube 175 to 12; U.S. Steel 250 to 35; Republic Steel 140 to 4; Treasury Bonds at 83; Sheet & Tube bonds at 65; good railroad bonds at 75 etc. etc. Even now there is no way of telling if the bottom has been reached.

In looking back now it seems that the only safe rule to follow is to sell everything when prices are high, stocks, bonds, real estate. If this had been done and the money converted into liquid form such as treasuries or municipal bonds, then today the change could be made to good, high-grade stocks and bonds. The real tragedy is that people who never speculated but invested only in banks, railroad bonds, etc. are suffering with the rest.

Even those who invested in 1930—after the crash—at what they considered bargain prices, now find their "bargains" selling at half price or lower.

The war between Japan and China drags along. Threats made by the U.S. are disregarded. Germany announces she cannot and will not pay further reparations and France threatens to collect by force what is coming to her.

JANUARY 27, 1932

Just returned from Warren. Both Youngstown and Warren look "lean and hungry." The streets are crowded with shabby, unemployed—vacant store rooms everywhere—signs on closed banks—bankruptcy sales and half-price sales in the stores that are open—soup kitchens. It will take long to forget these things.

Business shows no sign of pick-up. People are already looking toward the next presidential election when a Democrat will probably replace Hoover. In the meanwhile Hoover adds to his long list of artificial stimulants his "reconstruction finance company" which will loan government money to frozen banks and industries. By the last election the Republicans lost the control of Congress to the Democrats. This seems to reflect the desire of the people for a change—altho I personally feel that Hoover or the Republican Party should not be held responsible.

FEBRUARY 22, 1932

Conditions get worse instead of better and unemployment increases. In our own family the following lost their jobs since Jan. 1st: Joe Roth; M. I. Benjamin; Roy Elliot; Morris (out 2 years).

The war in China continues to rage and there is grave danger that U.S. will be dragged in.

Youngstown is now operating several soup kitchens. The people come with buckets to take home soup and a loaf of stale bread. I visited the one being operated in the old St. Columba's church. About 500 people were in line.

Pres. Hoover starts an "anti-hoarding" campaign in which people with hidden money are asked to buy government bonds.

MARCH 8, 1932

3000 unemployed riot at Ford plant in Detroit and 4 are killed by police.

About a month ago Ford announced he would re-employ 100,000 men but so far has failed to live up to his promise.

No definite change for the better although people are more cheerful and feel they are on the up-grade. It looks as tho the Dollar Bank and City Bank will re-open soon. Depositors have signed agreements as to limit withdrawals.

We have had mild summer weather all winter so far but yesterday the first real blizzard of the year visited us.

MARCH 28, 1932

The first quarter of 1932 comes to a close with industry stagnant and no sign of betterment. Unemployment increases—various efforts are being made to help things but so far they have all failed. Congress is trying to pass bills to raise taxes to balance the budget and everywhere there is unrest.

The City and Dollar Banks are still closed. Steel industry is operating at 20%. Stocks are again going down and are now at the all-time low for this bear market.

It now seems that the only person who could have evaded this panic would be a person who sold everything he had at the top of the boom and then invested everything in government bonds. Even then he would lose at least 10% but he could now reinvest. Good railroad and other bonds are selling for 40 to 50%.

APRIL 5, 1932

Stocks still going down and breaking low records for the depression. The price of stock exchange seats has fallen from a high of $650,000 in 1929 to a present price of $85,000.

APRIL 6, 1932

It is common street talk now that we have not yet seen the worst of the depression. Rumors of all kind. One is that the Yo. Steel & Tube will shut down entirely and is building a fence around its property for protection. At the same time there is talk that the Sheet & Tube–Bethlehem-Inland merger will be revived. There is nothing else to add. Insanity and suicide among prominent business men is on the increase.

APRIL 13, 1932

For the 12th consecutive day stocks have been drifting lower. Congress starts an investigation of short selling. Business indexes reach new low. Steel mills operate at 20%. Sharon Steel Hoop and Ohio Works (of U.S. Steel) Plants shut down completely. B&O 8 1/2; N.Y. Central 20; Continental shares—comm. 3/8—pffd 7.8—Gen Fireproofing 5; Sheet & Tube pfd @ 35 and common @ 10. Some of these low priced stocks are bargains. Local predictors say Truscon (now 4 7/8) will go to 2.

Organized demand by soldiers for two billion cash bonus leads to revival of talks of U.S. going off gold standard. France again leads attack against value of U.S. dollar.

Locally the big stores are still deserted except when they run a sale and almost give away merchandise. I don't see how they keep going.

APRIL 14, 1932

Talked to W. W. Zimmerman today. He said, "This is the most puzzling period of my life. I can't understand things. Everything that I thought was right is now proving to be wrong." And the same thought is in the minds of other thinking people. All sense of value, optimism and initiative seems to have disappeared. That is why the depression period presents so many opportunities to the man who has the nerve to buy stocks and real estate and businesses when the outlook is the blackest.

Signs of the times: The demand for gold metal by foreign countries on account of money scarcity has made it worthwhile to melt old gold ornaments, etc. The jewelers on E. Federal St. are running large ads saying they will pay high prices for old gold in any form. As a result many old watches, heavy rings, etc. are going back to the melting pot. Several out-of-town concerns have solicitors going from house to house.

Recently advertising and house-to-house canvassing has increased—buying up pass books on closed banks at 50¢ to 60¢ on the dollar. It is possible the committee trying to open the banks has something to do with this.

APRIL 20, 1932

Chile goes off gold standard, Brazil may follow and still the stock market continues its unbroken decline.

APRIL 30, 1932

No change for better. First quarter reports show that Sheet & Tube lost 3 million. Republic lost 2 million and U.S. Steel lost about 12 million. U.S. Steel drops common dividend and sells at 27. Western Union sells at 24. Receiver asked for Continental Shares. With most people it has come to a daily effort to get food. It is almost funny today to see how quickly people are willing to plead poverty and brag about how much they lost.

EDITOR'S NOTE

In 1924 war veterans of World War I were rewarded a pension, or "bonus," of about a thousand dollars for their service to be delivered in 1945. But beginning in the late '20s, war veterans—who had become a major national political force—began demanding that the government pay the bonus immediately. In May 1932 a few veterans in Portland, Oregon, led by a sergeant named Walter W. Waters who'd endured joblessness for eighteen months, decided to march on Washington and demand an early distribution of their bonuses. They dubbed themselves the Bonus Expeditionary Force, a reference to the American Expeditionary Force that was dispatched to Europe during World War I. The small Portland group jumped onto boxcars and began their trek to Washington. Their voyage was mostly peaceful and orderly. But in East St. Louis, after they were booted from a freight train and the Illinois National Guard came to break them up, the "bonus army" didn't just become front-page news but a national movement. More and more out-of-work vets from around the country joined the march; Roth would see a group of veterans in Youngstown in June. By the time Waters and his crew reached Washington, one thousand vets, dressed in their old, tattered army attire, had descended on the capital. In the coming months, their number would swell to more than twenty thousand. As Roth notes, the incident ended in violence.

MAY 6, 1932

In connection with the two billion dollar bonus for soldiers of the world war there is considerable agitation for the issue of "fast" money and again there is considerable talk in Congress and on the street on the subject of sound currency, controlled inflation, silver and gold standard, bringing back

Awaiting the Congressional vote on a "bonus bill" that would release the pensions promised to World War I veterans in 1932—rather than 1945 as originally planned—thousands of men camped in front of the Capitol on June 13, 1932, to the agitation of President Hoover. (Library of Congress)

prices to 1926 level, etc. So far Congress has failed to balance the budget. The veterans of the world war appear to have unlimited power over Congress and it is possible their demand for bonus money will have to be satisfied.

Food prices are way down—eggs fresh from the farm sell in the city at 15¢ per doz. Butter @ 25, etc.

Stocks are almost back to 1900 levels and receiverships for railroads are often mentioned. Railroads are fighting back by cutting fares, improving service, etc.

It seems certain now that the Dollar Bank will re-open shortly with the help of a large loan from the government reconstruction corporation. No news about the City Bank.

MAY 9, 1932

Tomorrow is primary election day and there is literally a swarm of candidates for each office—17 for sheriff; 7 for prosecutor, etc. Hard times has a great deal to do with it.

Signs of the times:

French premier shot and killed by a fanatic.

Five people killed in Chicago communistic rioting.

Community chest drive opens tomorrow with much greater needs and little chance of getting it.

Dr. Philo [a Youngstown rabbi] chooses as his topic last night "If I Were Dictator of the U.S." He makes numerous radical statements.

Again I question if any man could have foreseen the severity of this depression. Both stocks and commodity prices are back to 1899 level. Those men who were wise enough to sell during the boom and then keep their funds liquid in the form of government bonds, etc. were not far-sighted or patient enough to wait almost three years to re-invest. Most of them re-invested a year or more ago and now find stock prices have sagged to 1/3 of what they were when they thought they were buying bargains. Of course they will come out ahead if they can hold on long enough and—most important of all just now—if a receivership does not intervene. Patience, rather than boldness, seems to be required just now. A receivership is possible today for any corporation except possibly the very largest such as U.S. Steel, AT&T etc.

I question whether it is not a wiser plan today for the purchase (of either stocks, bonds or a business) to actually wait until the turn has come before he does any buying. Of course he will have to pay more but at least he avoids further depression with the possibility of a receivership if the interim of waiting for business to turn is too long extended.

Rodef Sholom Temple holds its annual meeting tonight and the congregation faces grave problems in planning a budget for next year.

MAY 11, 1932

All "wet" candidates win in today's poll. Looks as tho present unrest will bring with it prohibition repeal.

The Keith-Albee Theater announces policy of exhibiting only moving pictures hereafter without vaudeville b/c of the economic conditions. This leaves Youngstown without a vaudeville theater.

Beginning next week employees in McKelvey store will be paid by commission on sales—instead of a regular salary.

MAY 12, 1932

Good news at last. The court today authorized the re-opening of the Dollar Bank. Checking accounts can be withdrawn in full but savings accounts only to the extent of 10%. There remains among the larger banks only the City Bank to be re-opened. Even in the banks that re-opened, the stockholders are heavy losers.

MAY 16, 1932

An armored truck from Cleveland Federal Reserve Bank just delivered three million dollars in cash to the Dollar Savings & Trust Co. which reopens tomorrow morning. This represents a loan from the government Reconstruction Finance. As collateral, the Dollar Bank turned over to the Federal Reserve Banks its "frozen assets" consisting of mortgages, notes, etc. Without this loan the Dollar Bank could not have re-opened. It is likely that the City Bank will be re-opened in the same way.

I talked to Miss K— this morning. She says that at time of Bethlehem Sheet & Tube merger fight, she was owner of 1200 Sheet & Tube common. Sold most of it to the highest bidder at $165 per share and almost immediately re-invested in Republic Steel at 70. She did not realize that she would have to pay a huge income tax and later was hard put to raise cash to pay this tax because in the meanwhile the banks had closed and Republic Steel was selling at about $3 per share. Here again an ideal situation would have been created if she had placed all the cash in government securities and then reinvested during the panic when Republic and other stocks were way down. Such foresight was apparently given to a few people.

Signs of the time:

Japanese Premier is assassinated. This is the second Japanese premier to die this way in the past year.

Peru and Brazil are now both off the gold standard. France continues to withdraw gold from the U.S.

The stock market continues its steady decline without a halt. This has been going on for several weeks.

MAY 18, 1932

The Dollar Savings and Trust Co. re-opens this morning with a great deal of ceremony including blowing of whistles, flags on the stores, etc. The bank is now filled with people withdrawing money in an orderly fashion. The line of people outside is 4 abreast and extends from the main entrance back to the Wick Ave. entrance. Approximately five million dollars will be put into circulation by these withdrawals.

MAY 19, 1932

Withdrawal depositors of Dollar Bank again stand all day in line four abreast extending back to Wick Ave. entrance. Everything is quiet and orderly. The interior of the bank is full of flowers. I just congratulated Carl Ullman who was named executive vice-president.

Each day brings new and interesting stories of great fortunes wiped out in the past year. Here are a few that appear to be well-founded:

1. W. G. Mather of Cleveland held steel stocks (most Sheet & Tube) worth forty million in 1929. When he died in 1931 his estate had dwindled to six million and his will gave to charity bequests amounting to $3 million. At the present date the estate has further dwindled so as to leave nothing to the heirs. His estate contained no bonds or government bonds.

2. Mr. F. F. of Youngstown invested his all in Dollar Bank stock and for years had lived comfortably on a monthly income of about $1000. With closing of bank last October his income stopped and he faced the possibility of double liability. The re-opening of the Dollar Bank may eventually pull him through but he faces a long period of uncertainty. Here again there was no diversity.

3. Mr. M. T.'s story is about the same. In 1929 he sold at top price his holdings in Sheet & Tube. Immediately reinvested in City Bank stock and the other 1/2 in Republic Steel Common @ 70. City Bank now closed with possible double liability to stockholders and Republic @ 3. Again no back-log of governments or other high grade bonds.

4. Miss K—who is of German extraction invested considerable money in German bonds during the post-war currency inflation period. These bonds are now about worthless. To make the investors feel better she tells me the German government now runs a lottery by "drawing" a few bond numbers each month. The lucky holders get 5 times the original cost of the bond—the others get nothing.

And so the stories run without end. It all comes to the same point. Every investor should at all times have a reasonable portion of his holdings in liquid securities that can't shrink much. In boom times everything should be sold and converted into government securities. When prices of more speculative stocks and bonds and businesses have reached bottom—then is the time to buy again.

MAY 20, 1932

The line of depositors withdrawing money from the Dollar Bank becomes shorter every day.

It occurs to me that preferred stocks are better to gamble with today than common. If prices keep going down, then corporate earnings (and price of common stocks) will be low.

When conditions pick up the common stocks will still sell at about 7 or 8 times earnings but the preferred (if the company survives) will then be worth $100 par plus three or four years accumulated dividends at 6 or 7 %. For instance Republic pffd @ 8 serves a better gamble than the common @ 3 and likewise Sheet & Tube pffd @ 25 looks better than common @ 8. Both stocks now have more than 2 years of cumulative dividends due. For real investment purposes many good bonds can be bought today at a yield of 8 to 10%.

3/5/68

This proved to be correct. Almost all of these preferred stocks eventually paid off in full plus accumulated dividends.

MAY 25, 1932

The line of withdrawing depositors has disappeared from in front of the Dollar Bank and the bank is settling down to normal business.

All classes of professional men (including lawyers) are very hard hit by the depression. Fees have been drastically reduced and most of the men are unable to pay the office rent.

Two good building lots on Selma near Gypsy Lane have (65 ft front each) can be bought for $1000 each. This is about the cost of the improvements. They cost the owner $3250 each and he has since paid for most of the improvements.

It is interesting to note the stringent rules covering withdrawals as set forth in the new passbooks being issued by the Dollar Bank. These rules in brief require notice of withdrawals and in time of stringency gives Board of Directors the right to stop all withdrawals. All withdrawals are payable "in money bank notes at the time current in the City of Youngstown."

MAY 26, 1932

Yo. Sheet & Tube common sells yesterday on the stock exchange at $4 per share. It seems unbelievable. As far as I am personally concerned I think the company will survive the depression and that the opportunity is now on hand to buy stock cheap. The pessimist on the street talks already of receivership. It is hard to believe that this stock comprises the backbone of most of the large fortunes in Youngstown. Without dividends for two years people are selling the stock for actual bread and butter needs.

MAY 31, 1932

And still conditions get worse. After a steady decline of over two months the stock market yesterday again plunges down. Railroad averages are down to 1904 levels.

Hoover personally appears before Senate today to demand that the National Budget be balanced with the sales tax and they defy him.

300 war veterans are camped in Washington after "bumming" their way from Oregon—and insist that they will stay until the bonus is passed.

Things are quiet at Dollar Bank but not much new money seems to be coming in on account of restrictions on deposits.

JUNE 2, 1932

Mahoning County Real Estate Tax Collection comes to a close with only 1 1/2 millions collected out of six million. With the old arrears this makes a total tax delinquency of about 10 million.

Yesterday Congress passes a revenue to "balance the budget" and for awhile stocks spurt up but after a day they are back to old level.

It is reported on pretty good authority today that Yo. Sheet & Tube Co. is losing money at the rate of a million a month.

A tremendous number of casualty and liability insurance companies are going broke in this storm. The life and fire companies are standing firm so far. A prominent insurance man told me that this was because the life & fire companies were limited by law to investments in good bonds, etc. Also the Casualty Cos. expanded *rapidly* in past 10 yrs. with the growth of the automobile.

JUNE 5, 1932

Thousands of world war veterans are marching toward Washington to demand that Congress pay them their bonus. They are coming from all parts of the United States. In Cleveland they took possession of the Penn R.R. system until driven away by police. About 100 passed thru Youngstown yesterday. They were orderly and were fed at the bread lines. The bonus if issued would mean the printing of two billion dollars of paper currency and it is feared would result in inflation. With a national election coming next fall, it is possible Congress will listen to their demand.

A good many people are leaving Youngstown to live elsewhere—most of them going to the West Coast. They say Youngstown will never come back. I think they are mistaken and they will find the same situation wherever they go.

JUNE 9, 1932

For the first time in 30 yrs. the Sheet & Tube fails to pay its preferred dividend. It is selling now: Comm. 5 1/2; pffd—Bid 15 asked 20.

8000 war veterans camped in Washington and refuse to leave until Congress grants their bonus.

JUNE 10, 1932

For the past two months there has been a complete lull in business activity of all kind. Far worse than any period during the past two years. There is very little bankruptcy even because creditors have found it is useless to push their debtors. I personally think the upturn will come soon—possibly by next fall after the election. Everybody seems to be holding on and expectantly waiting for something to happen.

The stock market continues lower but with very little activity. It seems to me an ideal time to invest money but I may be mistaken again. Railroad stocks and bonds are selling at ridiculous prices but the conservative investor fears a repetition of the receivership period of 1893.

I still think that right now the preferred stocks of good companies is a better investment than the common because the next few years may show small earnings on the common but if the company survives at all, the preferred will go back to par with cumulative dividends. For instance I feel sure that Radio Corporation will survive the storm. Its common sold recently at 2 3/4 and its pffd B at 3 7/8. This pffd B pays $5 ann. dividends. Assuming that the company survives, this preferred should go back to 75 plus the accumulated dividends. The common seems to me more uncertain. I am curious to see how this theory works out but unfortunately (?) have no money to test it.

3/28/38

This theory was right. In 1935 Radio B sold at 92 and comm. at 13 3/8. Pfd B is now 40.

JUNE 11, 1932

I just saw the Youngstown contingent (about 150) of the "Bonus Army Expeditionary Force" start out for Washington to demand payment of the bonus. It was thrilling as well as pathetic. Most of the men wore remnants of their old uniforms such as overseas caps, mess equipment etc. One truck will go all the way to Washington carrying contributed food supplies. Several other trucks carried the men to New Castle. From there they will walk or hitch-hike to Washington. From all parts of U.S. about 50,000 ex-soldiers are concentrating on Washington and there is possibility of trouble. For the most part the men are of the better type and well behaved.

JUNE 13, 1932

I attended a joint meeting of all Bar Association Committees today with the Judges of Common Pleas Court to devise means to keep the courts open in view of failure of tax collections. A motion was carried that all cases (with a few exceptions) be tried hereafter without a jury—or with a jury of only 8; also that jury pay be reduced to $2 per day. Other suggestions including an effort by the Bar Association to collect the taxes without charge.

The situation in the County has almost reached a breakdown. The whole county government has already been reduced to a skeleton and even this will collapse when present fund is used up next November. Former City Solicitor Carl Armstrong said in a very effective speech: "By next December the city of Youngstown will be feeding a bread line of 30,000 people. There is no money for juries or courts and these must wait while the people are fed. If this is not done we will witness a collapse of law and order this coming winter." He also predicted that the real depression would start this coming winter and would last another two years. Other talks along the same line pictured a similar situation in other cities with no money to operate the schools, courts, etc.

I cannot agree with this dismal picture. I think the turn for the better will come within the next six months and that there will be no such break-down as is predicted. If I am wrong there will be h— to pay because things cannot go along this way much longer.

JUNE 17, 1932

It is very disagreeable as well as unprofitable to practice laws these days. The work is of a destructive nature such as foreclosure, receivership and bankruptcies. Estates are dragged out interminably because they can't be liquidated, particularly as to the real estate. Nothing can be brought to a conclusion and even jury verdicts have been affected. As to fees—well they have shrunken beyond recognition and in some cases we are offered pass books on closed banks etc.

JUNE 21, 1932

It is now clear to me that in normal times the average person does business with about 25% his own capital and the other 75% of borrowed credit. This is particularly true of big corporations who got their capital thru bond issues or bank loans. When the crash came the bank called their loans—people stopped buying bonds—and many bond issues defaulted because they were not even earning interest charges. U.S. Steel at the height of the boom pd off its entire bond issue and now is an outstanding example of good financing.

O.P.M. (Other People's Money—or credit) are the three most powerful letters in business but must be wisely and moderately used. Most of the banks are now almost liquid and these vast resources will soon again be loaned out for business expansion. To use these funds for business expansion and yet with moderation is the height of good business management. To operate today without access to such credits is almost impossible in this day of big business.

JUNE 22, 1932

The Dome Theater closed its doors. This makes three dark theaters lying idle on West Federal St.

JUNE 23, 1932

These are stirring days and in spite of our troubles it is good to be alive. I am reminded often of the days of the world war when families and businesses were mercilessly uprooted and broken. It is the same today. Fundamentals are being changed and new foundations are being placed for what we all hope will be a new era of prosperity. Amongst many of our friends—formerly safe from want—it has become a daily problem to supply their family with food and shelter. A little money today and a lot of courage will go a long way to guarantee the future.

JULY 1, 1932

I listened over the radio last night to the Democratic National Convention which is dead-locked over the selection of a presidential candidate. The speakers blame the depression entirely on the mis-rule of the Republican Party. Both parties adopt a plank advocating repeal of 18th Amendment but the Democratic plank is more drastic including a demand for "beer and light wine" at once.

I just returned from visit to Struthers by bus. It is heart-sickening to see the deserted houses and stores and buildings falling to pieces for lack of repairs. Almost all stores are boarded up and more than half of the houses are vacant. Both Campbell and Struthers seem harder hit than Youngstown.

JULY 6, 1932

It is just announced that the last of our closed banks—The City Trust & Savings Bank—will open its doors on July 14. This is made possible by a loan of $2,300,000 from the U.S. Reconstruction Finance Corp. and by permitting depositors to withdraw only 10% balance when available. Several depositors contested the opening.

Except for the re-opening of all of our closed banks there has not been the slightest sign of revival. In fact for past 6 months things have been moving downward. Almost everybody is down to a point where it is a problem to get money for bread and butter bills.

H. R. Hopper—who led the fight to get City Bank Depositors to sign proxies—has been named president. He was formerly an automobile dealer. Carl Ullman headed Dollar Bank reorganization committee and was named executive vice president.

JULY 12, 1932

We drove up to Geneva-on-the-Lake Sunday. The place is deserted and yet prices for cottages have not been reduced by much.

A small store opens on E. Federal St. called "Men's 15 cent Shop." Here can be bought neckties, socks etc. for 15¢.

One of the tragedies of this depression is the fact that young college and professional school graduates are unable to get placed. Some have been looking for work for two years and others are driving bakery wagons, clerking in stores, etc. They are getting cynical. The number of lawyers in Youngstown has almost tripled in past 10 years and of doctors has doubled.

JULY 13, 1932

As far as I am personally concerned this depression has been a "postgraduate" course for me in economics and public finance. It has caused me to read widely of economic subjects and for the first time I am following, intelligently and with intense interest, the doings of Congress and the coming national election. This interest in books and economic subjects has been followed by history and biography. I am now completing the reading of Beveridge's *Life of John Marshall* and have gotten quite a kick out of it because it fits right into the present political picture with the Democratic Party appealing to the half-starved "forgotten man" and pleading "state rights" on the prohibition question. If it weren't for the suffering that it has caused I would say that the depression has brought with it a good many worthwhile results. Among other things library circulation has trebled and people are once again turning to home pleasures etc. and to simple living.

Congress expects to adjourn this week and the B.E.F. (Bonus Expeditionary Force) in Washington is making a final effort to get the bonus. Soldiers formed a protesting circle completely around the Capitol building and remained there all night.

JULY 19, 1932

The City Trust & Savings Bank re-opens for business today but allows only $50 withdrawals. Very few people appear to make withdrawals. A great deal of skepticism is expressed on the street about its ultimate success. This is the 3rd bank in Youngstown to re-open with the assistance of Hoover's Reconstruction Finance Corporation.

For the first time in American history the tide of immigration is away from the U.S.

I have recently talked to people from Florida and also from California. In both cases they insist the conditions are worse there than here.

Florida in particular is absolutely flat since the land boom of 1925. Literally whole communities can be bought up with little cash.

It is almost funny to talk to professional men on the street today. They are all flat broke and in most cases are in arrears for office rent and household necessities.

Last week dad went down to the West Rayen Avenue–St. Clair district to look over our property. He says most of the buildings have been torn down by the owners rather than to pay the taxes and small gardens have taken the place of former store buildings. He says the district is reverting to farm land and is beginning to look as it did 40 years ago when we first settled there.

JULY 21, 1932

There seems to have developed a new feeling of optimism among the people lately and it is hard to explain because there are very few tangible signs of improvement. I have a feeling that the Republican administration will be able to produce at least a temporary upswing during September and October preceding election but I am not so sure it will be permanent.

In the meanwhile a new banking crisis has appeared in Chicago and elsewhere. The big Continental-Illinois Bank of Chicago was saved by an eighty million reconstruction gov't loan. I do not believe our re-opened banks here can be affected because no further withdrawals can be made by depositors under the terms of their new pass books.

JULY 25, 1932

The Keith-Albee Theater is the latest theater to close "temporarily" and it is said that the Warner Theater will also close at the end of this week. If this happens Youngstown will be left with only one first-class picture show—the "Paramount."

A considerable traffic has grown up in Youngstown in purchase and sale at a discount of Pass-Books on the Dollar Bank, City Trust and Home Savings Banks. Prices vary from 60% to 70% cash. All of these banks are now open but are not paying out funds.

Steel operations are at 17% capacity. The newspapers this evening give a big head-line to the fact that U.S. Steel today decides to pay its preferred dividend. Almost everybody thought it would be omitted. This is done in spite of the fact that U.S. Steel only earned 1/2 its pffd div. in 1931 and lost 13 million in first quarter of 1932.

EDITOR'S NOTE

The Bonus March standoff became tense and confrontational after the Senate rejected an early release of the veterans' bonuses. The veterans had established camps throughout Washington, D.C., including a settlement right near the White House on Pennsylvania Avenue. Negotiations between protesters and city police for an orderly withdrawal broke down. While police removed the Pennsylvania Avenue veterans, fighting and rock throwing broke out, and police shot and killed one veteran and wounded three others. This in turn triggered the involvement of the federal army, who took to the streets of Washington with cavalry forces and tanks against World War I veterans with whom some of them had served. The army forces, under the command of Army Chief of Staff Douglas MacArthur, pushed the marchers out of the city using bayonets and tear gas, then proceeded over the Potomac to Anacostia and burned down the shantytown where some 15,000 veterans had camped. The result was a public relations debacle for Hoover and MacArthur. Intriguingly, leading the cavalry was Maj. George Patton and acting as MacArthur's liaison to the police was Maj. Dwight D. Eisenhower; all three men would become household names during World War II.

JULY 28, 1932

The stock-market has been making up for past two weeks and newspaper headlines hail it as a sign of permanent betterment. I wonder how much of this sentiment between now and election day will be manufactured by the Republican Party.

War veterans riot in Washington because bonus is refused and one veteran is killed by police in an attempt to picket the White House.

Beggars going from house to house are getting more numerous and more bold. I dread what the coming winter will bring forth.

AUGUST 1, 1932

It is almost unbelievable the ways prices have fallen in past two years. Haircuts are now 25¢; shoe shine 5¢; a fairly good suit for men can be purchased for $25 (Strauss-Hirshberg has a window display at $9.90). The only lunch counters doing any business are those selling sandwiches for 10¢; pie for a nickel and a bowl of soup for a nickel.

Business this summer has been at a complete standstill—legal fees almost non-existent. Conversation between professional men is always the same—about the depression. Many have sent their stenographers away— others haven't paid office rent for several months and still others have given up their office. It is one of the most difficult summers I've witnessed.

Both Youngstown Sheet & Tube Co. and Republic show tremendous losses for the second quarter. Their average loss is over a million dollars per month for past year.

AUGUST 5, 1932

The U.S. Engineers, after months of survey, just report unfavorably as to the canal from Youngstown to Lake Erie and Ohio River. They say there is insufficient natural water supply, too great an encroachment on the river bed by railroads and mills and too great an expense involved to raise present bridges. This is a sad blow to Youngstown because the large steel mills say they cannot exist here against competition with cheap water transportation. This becomes still harder since ocean travel may be soon opened to lake and river cities by the agreement recently made between U.S. and Canada to push completion of the St. Lawrence Canal to the Great Lakes. A good many thoughtful citizens are wondering if the next 25 years in Youngstown will show progress.

The stock market continues upward for two weeks now in the face of unfavorable semi-annual reports and predictions are again made freely that we have turned the corner.

6/6/33

It now seems that this prediction was true and that the summer of 1932 marked the bottom of the depression.

Once again the U.S. Government thru the Reconstruction Finance Corporation comes to the help of Youngstown. This time it lends $336,000 to Mahoning County for relief work. It may save considerable suffering this coming winter.

AUGUST 8, 1932

In the last 30 days the stock market has given one of the most strenuous rallies in its history. Even the *N.Y. Times* yesterday devoted considerable front page space to it. There is no tangible explanation for this by way of industrial revival and yet there is plenty of optimism and feeling that this fall will see a turn for the period. In this 30 day period most of the popular common stocks have doubled and tripled in value. The entire list shows a 70% increase in value. A few samples are: U.S. Steel from 22 to 42; Western Union from 13 to 34; G.E. 8 to 19; IT&T 3 to 8; Anaconda 5 to 14; Sheet & Tube 4 to 12; Republic 2 to 5 etc. We will probably see a number of these movements before permanent betterment sets in.

AUGUST 8, 1932

It is interesting to note that the real estate situation is worse now than ever. The banks are loaded down with foreclosed properties and won't fully dispose of them for the amount of their mortgage. Tenants don't pay rent, people don't pay taxes or their mortgages, the property goes without much needed repairs. It is a vicious circle. As far as Youngstown is concerned real estate has been on the down grade and hard to dispose of ever since the war boom collapsed in 1921. Since bank books can now be bought at large discounts some people are buying them up and then trading them in on foreclosed properties held by the bank. As usual it takes some cash to benefit by the situation.

AUGUST 12, 1932

President Hoover delivers a splendid political speech over the radio last night. He points out that this depression has consisted of two phases. The first phase was an ordinary depression and we in U.S. were recovering from it 18 months ago. But then 18 months ago European countries began to collapse, went off gold standard, withdrew gold from U.S. and had revolutions. 75% of European countries went thru this—they had no (real) money with which to buy U.S. mdse. and as a result we had in U.S. bank closings and almost complete paralysis.

It was to fight this that Hoover 18 months ago used government funds to loan to banks and private business and for public works. This is still going on and will continue as long as possible. It is remarkable that so far in U.S. we have had no labor strikes, no bloodshed or other violent exhibitions.

AUGUST 14, 1932

The movement back to the farm has grown stronger during the past two years until today it is almost an exodus from the city to the farm. Farmers and children of farmers who were attracted to the city by high industrial wages during the past 10 years are now moving back. This is made easier due to the large number of foreclosed farms now on the market at low prices. Many good farms near Youngstown improved with fairly good buildings can be bought at $15 to $20 per acre—which is less than the cost of the improvements. In most cases the people moving to the farm feel they will at least be sure of plenty of food for their families.

AUGUST 20, 1932

The stock market continues to move upward. This has continued for over 30 days except for a short pause of a few days last week. A great many stocks have tripled and quadrupled in value in that time. The speculative interest of the public seems as strong as ever in spite of their experience of 1929. Most of them seem determined to recover part of their losses. Both commodity prices and the bond market are also moving up. In the meanwhile there is no visible sign of improvement in businesses or industry and on the contrary it seems to be getting worse. The situation is hard to explain. Most observers believe that between now and election day the Republican Party will try to boost the market, raise commodities, urge corporations to maintain dividends and in other ways create sentiment to the effect that the depression is over. I won't believe this until industry itself shows signs of pickup.

AUGUST 24, 1932

The stock market has quieted down a little but the trend of both stocks and bonds is still upward. This market spurt differs from the others only in that bonds have advanced as rapidly as the stocks. It seems to me that a good many stocks are too high now in view of prevailing conditions. For instance General Motors sells at 18 and General Electric at 20 while at present rate of earnings neither one is worth more than 10. In the meanwhile business is at a complete standstill and my earnings this month perhaps the worst of the depression. People are absolutely flat and except for the stock market they would be pretty hopeless. Also nobody seems to be able to figure out just why the market should go up except perhaps that it is being maneuvered for political purposes.

AUGUST 27, 1932

A "farmers strike" is in progress in Iowa and other Western states. The farmers claim they don't get enough for produce to pay for the labor. In this strike they are dumping and destroying milk and food products and blockading all roads leading into the city so that no farmer can sell his products until the price is raised.

The national labor unions yesterday go on record as being opposed to all wage cuts. Everything else has been reduced and I don't see how there can be permanent recovery until wages are reduced accordingly. On the Federal

Post Office job in Youngstown, a strike was declared last month and the men walked out because the contractor refused to pay a $10 rate. In view of the present low cost of living this seems ridiculous to me. It still bears the stamp of inflation.

AUGUST 29, 1932

In a speech delivered the other day Pres. Hoover summarized the present depression so far as follows:

1. In 1929 and 1930 it seemed to be an ordinary depression and in early 1931 the U.S. seemed on way to recovery.
2. In 1931 European countries became demoralized and suffered break-down and revolution. England went off gold standard and was rapidly followed by Sweden, Denmark, Norway, Finland, Australia, India and Egypt. All Europe withdrew her gold from U.S.—European investors were scared and dumped their American stocks and bonds on the market and withdrew more gold. Then the people of U.S. followed suit and withdrew their savings for the purpose of hoarding and this caused our banks to fail. This was followed by Japanese war and a breakdown in Germany. This went on for 18 months.
3. We have now survived this financial panic. We paid Europe every dollar we owed them and we are still strong and will remain on gold standard. With the help of Reconstruction Corp. and other government agencies we are now lending credit to railroads and other private industry. The recovery will be slow because Europe also must recover but it is certain we will succeed.

AUGUST 30, 1932

It is interesting to note that during the first three years of depression a wave of bankruptcy swept out of existence most of the small independent merchants. Recently the movement has included large national chain stores. Yesterday the United Cigar Stores Corporation with over 800 stores went into bankruptcy. This also happened recently to several drug stores, ladies dress and shoe shop chains. In almost every case a reorganization is affected. In each case also the main trouble has been long-term leases taken at exorbitant prices during the boom period. One chain organization took three 99 year leases in 1929 in the best locations in Youngstown. They

*Angry dairy farmers who were unable to feed their families—
or pay their real estate taxes or mortgage on the 1¢ a quart
that they received for their milk—went on strike in 1933 to
seek higher prices. They poured milk on the road and block-
aded trucks from transporting their products to cities like
Detroit, Michigan, and Toledo, Ohio. (Library of Congress)*

remodeled and subdivided each building so that for awhile it showed a profit. Indirectly they made more money out of their real estate speculations than they did out of their business. Today their rents are entirely out of line and they are being forced to liquidate. In most cases the landlord is the winner.

SEPTEMBER 1, 1932

The month of August just ended has been the lowest point so far in the depression for all kinds of business and professional men. The heat has been severe and all kinds of activity are at a complete standstill. The stock market on the contrary tripled its value during August in one of the quickest climbs ever witnessed. I believe this also established a record. Nobody seems to know even yet why the stock market went up because business has gotten worse instead of better.

Here is another bona fide depression story. An individual in Detroit was worth five million in 1929. His holdings consisted of 8000 shares of stock in a Detroit Bank selling at $300 per share; balance in good real estate and miscellaneous securities. The bank stock is now selling at $3 per share; the real estate is vacant and the other securities have also shrunken and are paying no dividends. Here again his only salvation lay in having at least half of his funds in hi-grade bonds. Here again real estate and bank stocks proved to be highly speculative.

As far as bonds are concerned most all first and second grade issues have continued to pay interest all thru the depression. High grade bonds like AT&T suffered very little. Second grade bonds like Yo. Sheet & Tube and most of the railroad bonds went below 50 but continued to pay interest. Most of the real estate bonds defaulted in their interest or resulted in receivership. The conclusion seems to be that when bonds are purchased only the highest grade—preferably municipal or governments—should be purchased.

The farmers' strike in Iowa grows intense and 12 farmers are killed. The state militia is called out to preserve order. The movement is spreading to farmers in other states. They are dumping and destroying their produce. In Youngstown corn sells at retail 2 dz. for 15¢. Tomatoes, potatoes, peaches and apples at 20¢ a half-bushel basket out of which the farmer must pay a nickel for the basket. Other produce at corresponding prices.

SEPTEMBER 7, 1932

The stock market still continues upward with hardly a pause since the middle of July. In the meanwhile industry is still stagnant and shows very little sign of pick-up. Most financial writers refer to the stock market as an election market and believe it will break badly after the November elections unless there is an unexpected pick-up in business. Some comparison between stock prices between July and September follows: Aluminum Co. of Am. 25–85; Sheet & Tube 4 to 27; Bethlehem Steel 7 to 30; AT&T 70 to 120; U.S. Steel 22 to 50; Western Union 13 to 50; United Aircraft 7 to 30. Most of railroads are 400% higher now than in July although railroad business continues to get worse.

I believe it can be truly said that the man who has money during this depression to invest in the highest grade investment stocks and can hold on for 2 or 3 years will be the rich man of 1935.

SEPTEMBER 8, 1932

Judge Griffith said to me today: "I was a young man when the panic of 1873 occurred and I can remember how my father after that always insisted that government bonds were the only real safe investment and were a necessary part of every investment list. In my law practice in later years I found that other successful men who lived thru the panic of 1873 felt the same way. One particular client—a successful steel executive—always held $100,000 in government bonds out of a total estate of $250,000. His theory was that he could always live on the interest from the bonds no matter what happened to the rest. Now that I am experiencing the 1929 panic I can see how those men felt and I now agree with them. Banks and large corporations will continue to fail in great crises but our ultimate faith must be in the government."

SEPTEMBER 10, 1932

The lawyer who is engaged in general practice in this city is having a hard time making ends meet. On the other hand the "bankruptcy lawyer" is reaping a harvest from bankruptcies and from forced reorganizations. This work is monopolized in Youngstown by 2 or 3 law firms by solicitation of claims and by control of credit organizations. Because the work is so very destructive these lawyers are also reaping a harvest of hatred and distrust from the merchants forced into liquidation.

Directly after the war period it became popular for small local concerns to expand by selling stocks to the public. In almost every single instance these investments have proven to be worthless. This is also true of a number of small state banks that were organized in this period. An investment in a new enterprise seems to have proven far more hazardous than in established companies with a proven record of earnings.

SEPTEMBER 19, 1932

In spite of the activity in the stock market, business conditions get worse. Steel mills operate at 15% capacity. There is a slight increase in fall business but it is probably only seasonal. The national elections begin to warm up.

After a rising stock market of six weeks which increased values 150%—the market broke badly last week. Stock prices are still 100% higher than last July and seem to me too high in view of present tremendous losses to all business. It is impossible to tell if the improvement is permanent or only an "election market." So far in last 2 years the stock market has made 8 fake starts upward and then eventually came back to record lows. Commodities have also steadily declined and show no definite sign of upward turn.

Moving picture operators go on strike in Youngstown last week. The theaters are being operated by strike-breakers under guard—while the entrance to each theater is being patrolled by union men. The union rate is $85 per week and they won't take a cut. Public sympathy is not with the union in their attempt to maintain wartime wages. I am afraid we will witness many strikes in the next two years before wages are finally adjusted and I am also afraid the depression can't end until wages come down. The disparity between cost of raw material and finished product is entirely too high.

The issues involved in the coming National Election are mainly economic and I am intensely interested. I feel that the Republican Party should be continued in power. I never delivered a political speech in my life but I am tempted to try it in the coming campaign. It looks as tho the Democrats will win because everybody wants a "change."

OCTOBER 4, 1932

Business remains at a complete stand-still and it looks like a tough winter. The national election campaign grows intense and people are very partisan.

The stock market still retains most of the gains it made in September and it will probably stay there until after election. There has been some improvement in business but mostly seasonal. And steel mills are operating at about 18% capacity. Most of the lawyers are discharging their stenographers and fees are simply non-existent.

OCTOBER 12, 1932

Nothing startling has happened in past few weeks. The stock market is sagging again and business at a complete standstill. Everybody seems to be waiting for the election to be over.

The national election grows heated. I made my first political speech last night on behalf of Republican Party—spoke on national issues in the Mt. Zion Baptist Church on Himrod Ave.

The 14th of this month will mark a year since the big banks in Youngstown closed. They have all been re-opened with government loans but are not doing any business.

OCTOBER 19, 1932

This is becoming the battle-ground for the National Political Campaign. Both President Hoover and Franklin D. Roosevelt were here in person last week. It is a repetition of the campaign of 1896. All indicators point to a Democratic victory but I personally think that Hoover will get stronger in the next two weeks and win.

I have already remarked how the real estate owner can collect no rents and must pay taxes. The situation is almost ridiculous. Tenants occupy a house for 6 months without rent and then move on to a new location. It is useless to sue.

Recently the down-town real estate situation has come to light. One owner told me that his taxes are $250 per month and his rental income is $75 per month—when he gets it. Formerly the same property brought in $800 per month. Another property was formerly leased at $10,000 per year plus taxes—now rents for $125 per month. Another downtown property owner owes $60,000 in delinquent taxes. There are at least 20 good storerooms between the public square and Spring-common. Others are occupied by temporary tenants selling fruits or 15¢ neckties, etc.

Not very much down-town property has been foreclosed or has changed hands so far. This is due to the fact that these properties are in strong hands. Most of these properties are subject only to moderate mortgages. The wisdom of this is now apparent.

The city is borrowing $300,000 from the government to feed 30,000 people in bread lines here this winter. It looks like a winter of hardship and suffering and possibly of violence. Many people in good homes have no food or coal and are too proud to make known their situation. The beggars have become obstinate and sullen.

OCTOBER 22, 1932

The Savings & Loan companies of the city seem to have started a regular drive to foreclose real estate. This may be because there has been so much public talk about a moratorium on mortgages. Every day sees about 30 new cases started and many of our friends in fine homes on the north side are included in the list of casualties.

NOVEMBER 1, 1932

The month just closed has been the poorest in my entire law practice. Everybody is waiting for the November election. Betting of 2 1/2 to 1 favors the Democrats but Hoover is getting stronger every day and I think he has a chance to win. The main issues are "tariff" and "sound currency." Just now the United States has become a dumping ground for cheap European merchandise which is made possible by depreciated European currency. I made my first political speech on this subject a few days ago.

The stock market is at a standstill. Commodities are again going down. Wheat is selling at 44 1/8¢ per bushel. This is an all time low record for U.S. and is a record low for almost 300 years in Europe.

U.S. Steel lost 27 million in last 3 months. Sheet & Tube still loses at a rate of more than a million per month.

NOVEMBER 7, 1932

The political campaign is over and tomorrow is election day. It has been a bitter campaign and will be long remembered. The "forgotten" man who is out of a job will probably decide the election. On Wall St. the betting is 6 to 1 in favor of Franklin D. Roosevelt, the Democratic candidate. In spite of this I still hold some hope for Hoover. I delivered seven political speeches for Hoover—mostly on the tariff question and other national issues—and I thoroughly enjoyed the experience. Because of the depression and the national election I have developed a keen interest in economic and governmental questions. This is also true of a great many people.

NOVEMBER 9, 1932

The election is over and Franklin D. Roosevelt, the Democratic candidate, becomes President in one of the greatest landslides in all history. He captured the electoral votes in 42 states and his opponent Hoover got only 6. In 1928 Hoover got the electoral vote of 40 states. By a plurality of over 15 million votes the people decided they wanted the "new deal" promised by Roosevelt. It is interesting to note that Mahoning County elected all of its Republican candidates in spite of this national landslide. I will follow with interest the question of "lower tariff" promised by the Democratic Party. I don't see how it can be done in the face of depreciated European currencies.

NOVEMBER 11, 1932

It seems that earlier newspaper reports of election results were exaggerated. The Democratic candidate for President (Roosevelt) won by a popular plurality of about six million instead of fifteen million as first reported.

"Business is at an absolute standstill."

President Franklin Roosevelt made a number of visits to Youngstown. Here, he is accompanied by Frank Purnell (far left), president of Youngstown Sheet & Tube, and two uniden-tified men. (The Mahoning Valley Historical Society)

EDITOR'S NOTE

By the end of 1932 one out of every four families in Youngstown needed the support of charity. In January 1933 Benjamin Roth wrote in his diary that people seemed to be "marking time" until the new Democratic president took office. But in the short time between Franklin D. Roosevelt's November landslide victory as the thirty-second president of the United States and his inauguration on March 4, 1933, the economic crisis actually deepened. Throughout the nation events taking place in the banking system, farming, the Hoover administration, and overseas created a more turbulent social and economic environment. As Richard H. Pells puts it, "Economically, the winter of 1932–1933 was the worst in American History."

In 1933 more than 40 percent of home mortgages were in default. Foreclosures, notes Roth, "are no longer a disgrace." In the nonexistent real estate market of the Great Depression, banks often deferred foreclosure proceedings. Banks realized there would be no recoup on a seized property that they couldn't sell, rent, or even afford to maintain adequately.

Farmers were the most vulnerable to foreclosure in the Depression. "In Iowa, the most heavily mortgaged state, nearly one-third of the value of farms was in thrall, mainly to banks and insurance," describes Arthur M. Schlesinger Jr. With bread selling for three cents a loaf and milk at eight cents a quart, farmers organized an influential movement called the Farmers' Holiday Association to protest, sometimes violently, price devaluation. In May 1932 hundreds of farmers disrupted the nation's food supply by destroying their crops and blockading highways and rails to prevent trucks or trains from distributing their milk or chickens. They overpowered and disarmed local sheriffs who tried to bring order. Though Americans were starving throughout the country because they didn't have the means to eat anymore, farmers poured milk onto the side of the road. "Seems to me there was a Tea-party in Boston that was illegal too," rationalized one farmer, according to historian T. H. Watkins.

Militant farmers also intimidated, even injured, sheriffs, bank officials, or lawyers who attempted to foreclose farms or seize properties
due to unpaid taxes. By 1932 the typical farmer's income had fallen
by 64 percent, yet his indebtedness had only been adjusted to drop 7
percent. As Schlesinger explains, "A cotton farmer who borrowed
$800 when cotton was 16 cents a pound borrowed the equivalent of
5,000 pounds of cotton; now with cotton toward 5 cents, he must pay
back the debt with over 15,000 pounds of cotton." Considering no
one had the purchasing power in 1932 to buy 15,000 pounds of cotton from each and every cotton farmer who needed to pay back
loans, farmers took the notion of loan forgiveness into their own cal-
lused hands. Mobs of angry farmers gathered at bankruptcy proceedings and farm auctions, carrying clubs and swinging a noose around
a nearby tree to deter outside bidding. One Iowa debtor was able to
pay back the $800 mortgage on his property for just $1.90. Sometimes, the practices turned to violence. A New York Life Insurance officer was attacked by a mob when he offered a price for a farm that was
less than the value of the mortgage. In January and February 1933
farmers sabotaged at least seventy-six auctions. The outcry worked.
The Iowa state legislature passed a moratorium on foreclosures on
February 17, 1933. Minnesota and other farm states soon passed similar laws that winter.

NOVEMBER 19, 1932

It seems unbelievable but conditions seem to be even worse. The month
of October was the worst ever experienced in my law practice but November is on the way to beat even that low record. So far this month I have
taken in $19 in cash. I believe that is better than most lawyers have done.

Congress will convene in 2 weeks and a great many serious problems are
coming up for consideration. One of them is a possible cancellation of the
war debts of foreign countries. In the meanwhile the steel industry operates
at 15%—bank failures start again with 4 last week closing in Pittsburgh and
5 in Oklahoma. The newspapers are suppressing reports of these failures in
order not to alarm the people.

DECEMBER 1, 1932

Nothing new to report. Several hundred "hunger" marchers passed thru

Youngstown on their way to Washington where they will demand "food instead of bullets" from Congress when it convenes on Monday. I passed about 200 of them on West Rayen Ave. and they were singing "Battle Hymn of the Republic" as they marched.

Everybody on the street is talking about Europe's request that U.S. cancel the war debts. In the meanwhile the pound sterling goes to a new low of $3.12. Also wheat, oats, and corn reach new low levels. At Chicago wheat sells at 42¢ bu; oats at 19¢ and corn at 14¢. After a farmer in Montana pays transportation to Chicago he gets a net of about 12¢ a bushel for his wheat. As a result they are burning corn for coal and using wheat and oats for cattle. It is hard to explain this situation while so many people go hungry. There is also considerable discussion about the new science of "technography" which holds that new machinery and electricity have replaced many men in industry who will never find a job again. I am confident that new inventions and scientific discoveries will remedy this situation.

DECEMBER 5, 1932

A salesman just tried to sell me a small pass-book on the Dollar Bank at 72¢ on the dollar. He states the tenants of the Dollar Bank are using this means to pay their office rent, notes, mortgages, etc. Books on Home Savings and on City Bank are selling at 62¢ on dollar. It is a fine opportunity to pay off notes and other obligations at a discount.

DECEMBER 10, 1932

Congress is now in session and promptly ejected the "hunger marchers." Also it refused to cancel the foreign war debts but agreed to reconsider them later.

Five lawyers are up for disbarment in Warren on a charge of misappropriating money belonging to clients. It seems that all misdeeds and grievances are coming to the surface during this time of depression.

In the meanwhile business is at an absolute standstill. Merchants are fighting hard for Christmas business but report there is none in sight. Last night's paper states that in Youngstown one out of every four families is being supported by charity.

DECEMBER 24, 1932

The year draws to a close with business stagnant and no sign of improvement. Money is non-existent and "scrip" is being used in increasing proportion all over the country. Wheat and other commodities are reaching new lows and the stock market is again on the way down.

Both 1931 and 1932 will take their place as the poorest years of my law practice. In both years my earnings fell below the very first year of my practice.

It is becoming increasingly evident that we will not see normal business for another year or two.

DECEMBER 28, 1932

Predictions are freely made that a great many railroads will go into receivership in the coming year. Traffic on railroads is steadily declining and interest charges on bonds have not been earned for some time. During the past two years defaults have been prevented by loans from the government. Many junior railroad bonds are now selling to yield 20% to 70%—if the interest is paid. B&O bonds sell at 10 and yield 4 1/2%. The claim is made by railroads that they were unable to build up a surplus during good times because of severe government regulations and now they are up against it.

Again and again it is being proven that the only man who can survive this storm is the fellow who put his earnings into government bonds before the crash came or second to that—built up a large life insurance reserve on which he could borrow. So far life insurance has come thru with flying colors.

DECEMBER 30, 1932

I interviewed five clients this morning and in not a single instance was a fee even remotely possible. Following are samples of why law practice is unprofitable today:

1. Mrs. A's boy received a broken leg and other injuries while coasting on a street by collision with an automobile. The facts present a fair case of liability. Investigation shows that the driver of the automobile carries no insurance; has no property except the automobile which is mortgaged for more than its real value; is out of a job and has 3 children to support and will soon have to look to the city for support. To file suit would be a waste of time and money. In normal times this

man would have been collectible, would have carried liability insurance and the case might have been worth $500. Today almost all personal injury cases are worthless because no insurance is carried and defendants are judgment proof.

2. Mr. A, a merchant, came in with a 2nd mortgage of $1,200 on a property he wants foreclosed. Investigation shows that taxes, first mortgage, and delinquent interest will consume the property and leave nothing for the second mortgage. The mortgagors are personally judgment proof. Client therefore decides not to foreclose and a fee is lost.

Instances of this kind can be multiplied. Litigation of all kind is at a standstill because people are judgment proof or because their assets cannot be liquidated. Constructive legal work such as drawing leases, incorporating companies etc. is entirely lacking. Even divorce work and criminal cases are lacking because of want of funds.

DECEMBER 31, 1932

Today brings to a close the most difficult and dismal year in my business experience. The outlook for 1933 is not much better. Thirty thousand people in Youngstown are being supported by charity—steel mills operate 13%—begging and holdups and murder are frequent—bankruptcy and receiverships and foreclosures are no longer a disgrace. In 146 cities of the United States "scrip" money is being used or "barter exchanges" have been set up to exchange services for merchandise. Commodity prices are at lowest point in history and stocks are just above their all-time lows. Standard average is 49.

In looking back it is interesting to note that expansion of business during a boom is a mistake. The time to expand is at the end of a panic when the economic cycle is headed up again. In 1928 professional men rented larger offices and bought bigger homes—business men established chain stores, etc.—mergers took place—Warner Picture Co. built a million dollar theater in Youngstown etc. In almost every instance this expansion proved to be a mistake. On the other side of the picture it is interesting to note that the Strouss-Hirshberg Co. was started in 1875 after the panic of 1873 and prospered. Herman Ritter tells me he started the Ritter-Meyer Co. just after the panic of 1893 and prospered. He was also far-sighted enough to give up his business just when the present panic started. It is my judgment that in another year or so the time will be ripe to found new enterprises on a conservative basis and then expand slowly as the economic cycle again moves upward.

I believe that a fortune in wisely selected stocks could be bought very cheaply just now. The opportunity is here—but no money.

1933

We bid farewell to 1932 without regret and we welcome 1933 with a fervent prayer for better days.

JANUARY 6, 1933

Prices of all merchandise continue to plunge downward at a dizzy pace. The dollar today buys two and three times as much as it did two years ago.

The question of inflation of currency is coming forward as a dominant issue this year. It is being supported by many respectable and well-known economists. Personally I am opposed to it. During the boom everybody piled up debts to a dizzy height. Now it is hard to pay up because of increased value of the dollar. These economists claim that either the debt will have to be cut down or money inflated. The temper of the public is shown by the fact that last week about 500 enraged farmers mobbed a lawyer on the steps of a court house in Kansas when he attempted to bid on a foreclosed farm for the New York Life Insurance Co. at a price that would leave a deficiency judgment. They forced him to get permission to raise his bid to the full price of the mortgage.

JANUARY 12, 1933

Gasoline is selling at 14¢ per gallon. Out of this 5¢ goes to Ohio tax; 3¢ to the retail gasoline station owner; 2¢ to wholesaler and 4¢ to cost of distribution and transportation and production. Business in almost every line is being run at a loss. It looks as tho 1933 will be given over to the liquidation and reorganization of many businesses.

The use of scrip or "white rabbit" money is increasing in many cities. Real money continues to be almost non-existent.

After the closing of several large banks in Pittsburgh a few weeks ago, there followed the closing of banks in small surrounding towns. Last week the National Bank in Butler closed its doors. It is remarkable how these things take place with terrific loss to small depositors and yet so far there has been no violence.

JANUARY 17, 1933

Seven banks closed in St. Louis yesterday and a couple more in Kansas. The newspapers are suppressing news of this kind. Bankruptcy among merchants is on the increase and is now reaching the large corporations. Last week McCrory's went into bankruptcy (large 5¢ and 10¢ chain). I think exorbitant lease rentals is the cause. Other large national bankruptcies are United Cigars; Shulte; Whelan Drugs. Each of these chains had stores in almost every city in the U.S.

Protest against real estate foreclosures continues to grow. Youngstown Chamber of Commerce appoints a committee to advise with owner and banks.

Three lawyers are disbarred today in Warren: one is suspended and one is reprimanded. In each case they used money belonging to clients. The depression is bringing out many cases of misuse of funds by lawyers, banks, etc.

Congress is flooded with all kinds of plans to remedy the currency system. Everything is being advocated from printing money with no banking at all to silver currency.

The usual spring rise in the stock market has so far failed to materialize.

JANUARY 18, 1933

I am reading a book written by Claude Bowers entitled *The Tragic Era*. In it, he describes the panic of 1873 and I am amazed at the similarity to conditions today. He mentions the following high-lights all of which are true of this 1930 panic:

1. The 1873 panic was preceded by Civil War—then 8 or 9 years of hectic prosperity, speculation, rising prices, corruption in government— and then sudden panic, bank closings, etc.
2. In 1873 the farmers revolted for higher prices.
3. Organized movements to stop foreclosures.
4. Wild schemes to inflate currency, greenbacks, etc.
5. Talk against tariff.
6. Untold unemployment and suffering and considerable radical talk about capitalistic system, socialism, etc.—a change of political parties.

The panic of 1873 lasted 5 or 6 years and if this is any guide then we have 2 or 3 years more of hard times ahead of us.

Good news for Youngstown. The U.S. Army Engineers are ordered to re-survey the Ohio River canal project with the possibility of recommending the building of a canal as far as Struthers.

JANUARY 23, 1933

Bank closings are again coming to the front. The Warren State Bank of Warren closes last week and again Nate is the loser. This makes the third time he has lost money in bank closings in Warren in the past 18 months. These banks are not closed by runs but by steady withdrawals of depositors caused by necessity and by inability to collect on frozen mortgage loans.

All over the country farmers are mobilizing to prevent farm foreclosures. They appear at sheriff sales in mobs and intimidate the lawyers and court officials.

JANUARY 28, 1933

Conditions get steadily worse and no relief in sight. The Federal Store (a department store on W. Federal St.) closes its doors. For the third time in 2 years the employees of the Strouss-Hirshberg co. get a pay cut. This time 20%. Within the past 6 months about 6 tenants have given up their office rooms on the 6th floor of the Dollar Bank bldg. Office rentals are still too high. Money continues to be scarce and almost non-existent.

JANUARY 30, 1933

By an overwhelming vote Congress rejects a silver standard currency on a 16 to 1 basis. It seems that other inflationary schemes will be treated the same way.

I saw the following prices advertised along W. Federal St. store windows this noon: Bread 3¢ per loaf; hamburg 4 lbs. for 25¢; all steaks @ 15¢ per lb; fresh eggs @ 20¢ doz. Other high-grade stores were advertising men's over-coats @ $9; ladies shoes at $1.94; ladies dresses @ $1.98; hosiery @ 49¢. All of these prices are about 1/3 of their prices of a year ago.

The farmers are the best organized and most militant group in the coun-try today. By intimidation and by suppressing bidding, they have practically created a moratorium on debts. With a Democratic President, they will probably get most of their demands.

Since the election of a Democratic President last November the country has been marking time. Likewise the December session of the old out-going lame-duck Congress has accomplished nothing—except to reject silver currency and other patent remedies to bring back prosperity. The new President will have to call a new special session of Congress and business men are waiting to see what it will do.

I am reading a book called *War Debts and World Prosperity*. If its reasoning is correct we will probably have to cancel about twelve billion in war loans that Europe owes us. The main argument seems to be that we cannot be a creditor nation and at the same time refuse to accept European merchandise by erecting high tariff walls. The American Public seems to feel we have again been the goat and by cancelling these debts are paying the whole cost of the European war.

JANUARY 31, 1933

Two large banks close in Atlantic City. These are the first bank closings in the history of that city.

JANUARY 31, 1933

For the first time since its organization (32 yrs) the U.S. Steel corporation fails to pay the regular dividend on its preferred stock. Dividend on the common was suspended about a year ago.

Almost the entire Youngstown police force is gathered on the public square to control a protest parade by unemployed scheduled for this afternoon.

FEBRUARY 7, 1933

The process of involuntary and voluntary liquidation continues steadily. Bankruptcy receiverships and foreclosures are rapidly cutting down the mountain of debt created during the boom. Real estate and other property is going back to the real owner—the mortgagee and the speculative purchaser on a small margin loses his equity. In the case of the individual this liquidation is usually involuntary. In the case of the large corporation it is often voluntary for the purpose of breaking leases and getting rid of large bond issues, cutting down heavy capitalization etc. I do not see how real recovery can come until this liquidation movement is completed, old debts wiped out and business showing a profit on the basis of present capacity. I also do not believe that any legislation or artificial governmental stimulant can hasten the process. In this process of reorganization a great many holders of stocks and bonds are seeing their investments wiped out. Only the holders of government bonds etc. can feel any degree of safety.

In numerous talks with business men I find a higher valuation than ever placed on "financial security" and freedom from want. During the boom in 1928 business men scorned to leave their money in safe investments yielding only 4 or 5%. They sold such securities and bought speculative common stocks. Today the situation is just the reverse. The average man today would place enough money in government bonds so that in any emergency the income from this source alone would provide bread and butter.

Likewise the psychology of 1928 is different from that of today. In 1928 people were excited about big profits on the stock market: they read literature about investments, lived high and talked about the "new era." Today their outlook is gloomy, they think the depression will never end, the stock market is an abomination, real estate is no good, everybody is cynical, etc. Just as the public was mistaken in its excessive optimism of 1928 I believe it is mistaken in its excessive gloom. This situation, however, has created many opportunities for investment today for the man of faith, courage and a little capital. This last item is most important and it simply does not exist in any quantity.

FEBRUARY 13, 1933

I have done considerable reading about the depressions of 1837 and 1873 and I am struck by the similarity to the present crisis. If history repeats itself then we still have 2 or 3 years of bad times ahead of us. One article I read describes how John Jacob Astor accumulated most of his real estate in New York during the 14 year period from 1835 to 1849. It is entirely possible that the period for accumulation in the present crisis will last another 10 years. If so, I may yet be able to take advantage of it.

It is said that just before Astor died he was asked if he did not have too much real estate and he answered: "Could I begin life knowing what I know now I would buy every foot of land in Manhattan." Of course in his day, the country was agricultural and land was the most popular means of investment. The modern corporation and big business did not then exist. As it is, my own mind is not yet clear as to whether real estate or stocks or bonds or a combination of both is best.

EDITOR'S NOTE

When the crash hit in 1929, President Hoover had taken the position that the unregulated, unabashed speculation in the stock market was to blame for the brutal economic downturn. But he never perceived any systemic problems with the nation's production, distribution, and mass consumption. At first, Hoover attempted to resolve the nation's financial crisis with policies to foster credit, convince businesses to maintain wages, and boost production. But joblessness, debt, and frozen bank savings meant that tens of millions of Americans had no money even for the basic necessities. Over time Hoover began to fixate on two alternative tactics to solve the nation's financial troubles: balancing the domestic budget and boosting international trade with the United States. In the waning months of his presidency's befuddled attempts to pull the nation out of the Great Depression, Hoover urged Congress, the public, and even President-elect Roosevelt to carry on with his fiscal agenda: balance the budget and forgive Europe's war debt. Hoover thought the latter would get Europe back on the gold standard and in turn enable it to buy more American goods.

In fact, Hoover's fear of an unbalanced budget could almost be considered an obsession. Between 1929 and fiscal year 1932, federal revenue had dropped in half, while federal spending (on institutions like the Reconstruction Finance Corporation) ballooned by half. The fiscal budget of 1932 was about $2.735 billion. Between December 1931 and May 1932 President Hoover released more than twenty statements about "the absolute necessity of a balanced budget," according to Schlesinger. Businesses, from the American Bankers Association to the head of General Motors, publicly supported this agenda. And Hoover, in turn, believed that satisfying this fiscal responsibility would provide the confidence that private industry needed to lend and borrow and consequently get people back to work.

For Hoover, economic recovery also hinged on salvaging international trade relations. By June 1931 President Hoover was convinced that it was an overproduction of cheaper goods abroad that led to the drop in purchases of American goods by foreigners and increased the purchasing of lower-cost foreign goods in the United States. While Schlesinger points out that the "actual decline in foreign trade balance in 1930 was less than $60 million," it was Hoover's own tariff policy that had largely caused this imbalance of trade. The Smoot-Hawley tariff act of June 1930 prevented countries like Britain, Italy, Spain, and France from trading freely in the United States. These countries in turn actually raised barriers against American goods as a means to protect themselves.

By the time Congress went into session on December 5, 1932, the lame-duck president was asking Congress to forgive Europe's war debt. Since Europeans couldn't sell enough goods on the American market to repay their loans when the United States was the creditor nation of World War I, Hoover believed that a debt settlement would be the way to strengthen the international gold standard and therefore resolve America's economic problems. Instead, Congress decided to postpone any decision. On February 13, 1933, President Hoover would reiterate his agenda in his farewell address, mostly to polite silence.

In the meantime Michigan undertook dramatic action in an attempt to stem its banking panic. On February 14 Michigan governor William A. Comstock ordered an eight-day bank "holiday" to close the banks to help stabilize their thinning reserves and work on a reorganization. Nevada and Louisiana had initiated such "holidays" in 1932. But the situation in Michigan, with much of its mass of defaulted loans due to the faltering car industry, was much more dire. It involved fifty-five banks, $1.5 billion, and nine hundred thousand depositors' money. Car magnate Henry Ford was the primary depositor in the Union Guardian Trust Company, which teetered on the edge of closure. Two Hoover officials promised to provide government funds if Ford contributed $4 million to the Guardian and promised to keep his money in the bank. Ford defied them, and even threatened to pull his $25 million out of another struggling bank. As a result Michigan declared its bank holiday. Other states like Indiana, Arkansas, and Oklahoma followed. In the two and a half weeks between the beginning of Michigan's bank holiday and President Roosevelt's inauguration, more than thirty states would follow suit in what would be "the most exasperating two and a half weeks in financial history," according to historian Elmus Wicker. But as Roth would come to learn too well, the bank-closure crisis did not end then.

FEBRUARY 14, 1933

President Hoover delivered his "farewell address" yesterday. He pointed out that the world is now engaged in economic warfare which may spell ruin. 44 Nations are off gold standard and only U.S. and France are left among the leaders. These 44 nations have depreciated our almost worthless currency and are flooding U.S. with low priced merchandise paid for in worthless or depreciated currency. Even with our tariff walls we can't compete. If Europe wants us to cut down war debts she will have to go back on gold standard and stabilize her currency. Otherwise we will also have to go off the gold standard and depreciate our currency in order to compete in this destructive trade war.

FEBRUARY 14, 1933

The country is shocked by an order of the governor of Michigan closing every bank in the state for 8 days. The situation was created by the imminent closing of one of the largest banks in Detroit and the fear that other banks would follow. Detroit as an automobile center has been hit harder than the average city by the depression. It is feared that the action in Michigan will bring reactions in other states.

A similar situation existed in Louisiana last week but the situation was relieved after 24 hours by the help of government money.

FEBRUARY 21, 1933

So far there has been no serious reaction in other states of the Michigan Bank Holiday. Not only are the banks closed in that state but business is at a standstill because of lack of cash.

Other news items of the day:

Japan withdraws from League of Nation and continues her war against China.

Farmer strikes in the West continue. Milk is being dumped rather than sold at a penny a quart. Youngstown retail price of milk is 8¢ per quart.

President-elect Roosevelt is shot at five times by an Italian radical but escapes injury. Several other persons are seriously hurt.

The distrust in banks all over the country makes it difficult as well as risky to transact business.

FEBRUARY 24, 1933

The Michigan "Bank Holiday" ends and the banks re-open but restrict withdrawals to 5% of the amount on deposit. This will probably continue for some time.

Two banks in Indiana follow the Michigan example and severely restrict withdrawals. In actual practice this is almost as bad as closing the bank.

Japan is now invading China and a real war threatens.

There has been no "spring rise" this year in the stock market and the trend is downward. The average is 45 and some prices at random are: Truscon 3; Sheet & Tube 9—pffd 19; AT&T 97; U.S. Steel 26; Gen. Motr. 11; Gen. Elec. 11; Radio 3.

I am reading Beveridge's *Life of Abraham Lincoln*. It contains some description of the panic of 1837. I am again struck by the similarity between conditions in 1837–1873–1893 and now. Sound currency at all times has been one of the main issues.

FEBRUARY 25, 1933

Every bank in the State of Maryland closes today in an enforced "holiday" brought on by excessive withdrawals. The governor asks the State Legislature of Maryland to pass a law permitting the banks to reopen under very restricted withdrawals as in Michigan. At the same time the governor of Indiana gives to the State Banking Dept. full power to limit withdrawals to any extent that may become necessary. I hope the movement does not spread further because it paralyzes business.

The purchase and sale of pass books on restricted withdrawal banks has become a regular business in Youngstown. By state order it can be handled only by the regular brokerage houses. The daily newspapers list quotations the same as stocks and bonds. The following was taken from last night's *Vindicator*:

PASS BOOK PRICES

(Quoted by Licensed Brokers)

	Last Sales
Central Savings & Loan	25
City Trust & Savings Bank	52
Mutual Holding	36
Dollar Savings & Trust Co.	70
Federal Savings & Loan	63

Home Savings & Loan 50
Metropolitan Savings. 45

These books are purchased by debtors to pay off obligations owed to banks. Prices quoted are per $100.

Again and again dishonesty and speculation by bankers with bank funds becomes the subject of newspaper notoriety. The latest investigation discloses such practices on part of National City Bank of New York. By manipulation the officers boosted and unloaded on the public their own stock in National City Bank to the public as high as $650 per share when its book value was only $60. Likewise when the crash came this same bank sold out collateral of its customers but loaned money to its officers to save them from loss. Other similar practices enriched the bank officials at the expense of the depositors and the public. In spite of this the vast majority of banks and bankers were honest.

Thoughtful men everywhere express the thought that something is wrong with our banking system and Europe looks on in amazement. Over there the banks are part of the government and close only when the government itself goes bad. We may come to such a form of banking ourselves. As it is now the careful and thoughtful people who followed the maxim of saving for the "rainy day" are just as badly off as the most profligate spendthrift. In fact debtors who can lay their hands on a little money can pay their bills at 50% on the dollar by buying bank pass books. Very few however can avail themselves of the opportunity.

FEBRUARY 27, 1933

Again I witnessed happenings today that will be long remembered in the history of Youngstown and the State of Ohio. Without any warning this morning 69 banks in Ohio including three in Youngstown restricted withdrawals to approximately 5% of deposits. All day in the Union National Bank bedlam reigned with hundreds in line clamoring for money. There was no violence but I saw one woman faint. The same thing was happening in every other city of Ohio. The governor immediately called the State Legislature together to pass a restrictive banking law.

FEBRUARY 28, 1933

Practically every bank in State of Ohio is this morning restricting withdrawals to 5%. At 11:30 P.M. last night the governor of Ohio signed a law giving the banking dept. unlimited power to restrict withdrawals in any bank in any way he sees fit. As a result everything is at a standstill in Ohio, Michigan, Maryland and Indiana. I do not see how they can stop the movement from spreading to every state. If it does we will now have a "money panic" as we did in 1907.

I just returned from a tour of the banks. The Union National Bank seems hardest hit. About 300 people are lined up at the withdrawal windows. About 100 others are standing by waiting. At the other banks withdrawals are being made but very quietly.

Noon papers announce that the State of Pennsylvania has followed Ohio on a banking holiday. The streets outside are crowded with people all talking about banks.

MARCH 1, 1933

The run on local banks—particularly on the Union National Bank—continues into its 3rd day but is abating rapidly. I was fortunate this morning in having the Union National Bank pay me $530 in *cash* for an out-of-state check I had given them several days ago "for collection only." If I had originally deposited the check in my account in the usual way, it would have been indefinitely restricted. On the other hand I learned that the bank would not honor an insurance premium check I had issued prior to Feb. 28th.

The "bank holiday" movement has now spread into 8 states. If it ever reaches the large New York banks I don't know what will happen. There is considerable agitation for government control and guarantee of deposits. Also considerable blame is attached to the governor of Michigan who declared the original "holiday." In the meanwhile Henry Ford in Detroit becomes practically the sole owner of the two largest banks in Detroit by paying eight million in cash. The old stock holders and officials step out and he becomes virtually the financial dictator of the city.

MARCH 2, 1933

The "bank holiday" movement spreads to eight more states. It seems contagious. Also yesterday seven banks in Washington D.C. stopped withdrawals above 5%. So far New York has withstood the strain of withdrawals.

In the meanwhile, Congress has only two days to go before the inauguration of President-elect Roosevelt.

MARCH 3, 1933

Times are certainly exciting. Everybody is talking of banks and money. Twenty-two states have now declared "bank holidays." The latest to join the ranks are California and Texas. In most of the states the banks are not closed but withdrawals above 5% are refused. Only New England and New York still remain open. There is considerable talk of "scrip money" and of U.S. guarantee of deposits. In the meanwhile a new President will be inaugurated tomorrow. Backed by a united Democratic Congress and by Democratic administrations in nearly every state he has an unparalleled opportunity for service. The people are now waiting for the "new deal" he promised. It is my own guess that natural forces of recovery will go far toward making his administration a success.

Numerous lawsuits have been filed against banks in Cleveland to test the withdrawal restrictions. It is my guess the banks will be sustained by the courts on the grounds of "public policy."

There is talk about closing the stock exchange during the period of the emergency.

EDITOR'S NOTE

On March 4, 1933, as one hundred thousand Americans gathered at the Capitol to witness his swearing in, Franklin Roosevelt proclaimed a national bank holiday from March 6 to March 9, under the somewhat dubious auspices of the Trading with the Enemy Act of 1917. The closing would allow the treasury secretary to reorganize the sound banks, set up loans from the Reconstruction Finance Corporation, and close the banks that wouldn't make it. Roosevelt also chose not to issue scrip but to allow the Federal Reserve Board to print more currency to meet the demand so that, in under eight hours on March 9, Congress passed the Emergency Banking Act of 1933.

MARCH 4, 1933

Today is inauguration day at Washington. Banks in thirty states are closed or withdrawals restricted. The situation becomes hourly more serious. The governor of New York holds an all-night conference with leading New York Bankers. This may be a fore-runner of trouble in that state. If so there may be a complete collapse of the stock market. So far it has held fairly well. The inaugural message of the incoming President is awaited eagerly. Scrip issued by banks has appeared in several Ohio towns. In Jefferson, Ohio it cannot be cashed until it has 20 endorsements.

MARCH 4, 1933, 10:30 A.M.

Big news. An "extra" just announced that New York State and New York City Banks have joined "the bank holiday" and also that the New York Stock Exchange was closed at 9:15 to prevent trouble. It is also expected Chicago and other stock exchanges will be closed. Practically all banks of U.S. are under moratorium on payments. This last announcement comes at almost the exact moment that Franklin D. Roosevelt is being sworn in as President. It seems that every bank depositor in the country wants to withdraw his money and this of course is impossible. The closing of New York Banks and Stock Exchange was preceded by an all night session.

MARCH 4, 1933, NOON

During my lunch I listened in on the radio and heard Roosevelt take the oath of office and heard his inaugural. I was a little disappointed. He promised immediate action but gave no definite plan. A special session of Congress will meet shortly and he will ask broad war-time authority to deal with the situation. The whole situation is dramatic however because it comes at the most acute point in the depression thus far.

MARCH 6, 1933

We are greeted by a very dramatic announcement this morning. At 1:30 A.M. this morning as his first official act, President Roosevelt issues a proclamation ordering every bank in the United States to close for four days—including the U.S. Treasury and Federal Reserve Banks. It now appears that during the past two weeks foreign countries and domestic depositors have withdrawn gold from U.S. Treasury at an alarming rate. The proclamation also forbids exportation of gold. As a result of this announcement the U.S. will be technically off the gold standard for four days. I don't see how the government can resume gold payments at the end of that time because all

Europe will be waiting at the Treasury doors to withdraw gold. In Youngstown every bank and loan company is closed to all business and large placards in the windows bear notice of the President's proclamation. Everybody is fearful of the immediate future. In the meanwhile all over U.S. plans re going forward to issue scrip against bank deposits.

Likewise every stock exchange in the country is closed.

MARCH 7, 1933

We will close Volume II of this personal description of the economic situation at this time with the inauguration of Franklin D. Roosevelt. I will continue in Volume III to set down the developments from time to time under the "new deal" promised by the new administration. It has been a hectic period which has grown steadily worse for more than 3 1/2 years. The future just now seems more uncertain than ever. Every bank and stock exchange in the U.S.A. is closed—gold cannot be exported—scrip instead of money will be used nationally in a few days—everybody is alarmed. This morning Japan closes all its stock exchanges because of the U.S. situation.

VOLUME III

MARCH 8, 1933

When I started in 1930 to jot down the happenings during this depression I had no idea it would last so long and I did not think I would require more than one small notebook. Now after 3 1/2 years of the worst depression this country has ever seen, the end is not in sight. A very short summary of past events might be of assistance at this time. While the world war raged in Europe from 1914 to 1917 we had unparalleled prosperity in U.S. because of sale of war supplies to the belligerents. Stocks and bonds of "war industries" soared to $400 and $500 per share. Millionaires were made overnight. These securities were called "war babies." In 1917–1918 the U.S. participated in the war—became the greatest creditor nation in the world by loaning money to finance the war. Today these war debts are still unpaid in the sum of about twenty billion and Europe wants us to cancel them. From 1919 to 1921 we had the greatest real estate boom of all time because 2 million soldiers were released from the army, got married and established homes of their own. In 1921 we had a small scare because strikes came when war-time production of war supplies and war time wages stopped.

For awhile it looked as tho we had too much machinery and had built factories for war supplies that could not be used in peace time. Then suddenly Europe began to buy from U.S. on an unprecedented scale. The war torn countries had been almost completely devastated and had no factories to supply their needs. So from 1922 to 1929 America rebuilt Europe and because of this we had here the longest and wildest period of expansion and speculation ever seen. Everybody became stock-market conscious. Shares were split and re-split, new issues were introduced and gobbled up by the public at fabulous prices, foreign bonds (now worthless) absorbed billions of dollar. The collapse started with the stock market crash in 1929 (Oct.). Thru 1930 and 1931 and 1932 business leaders kept on preaching that nothing was wrong—do business as usual—spend money—and almost daily people expected a return to "normal." Then in 1932 all Europe seemed to collapse and for the first time people realized that the depression had just started and it would be many years before the "normal" period of 1929 would return. Forty-four European countries went off the gold standard, worthless currency was issued, government obligations went unpaid and even governments were overthrown. Russia tried Communism—Italy and Germany a dictatorship and even in the U.S. the red flag of Communism appeared on the streets. Prices of merchandise continued downward, wage reductions and unemployment followed. Then in November 1932 the people of U.S. showed their unrest by changing from a Republican to a Democratic government in the hope that the "new deal" promised would bring relief. In the meanwhile the banking situation of the U.S. utterly failed of its purpose. In 1931 thousands of banks (including 3 in Youngstown) closed their doors. "Frozen assets" was the reason given. The bank money could not be paid out because it was tied up in long-time mortgages. Liquid assets like bonds were sold by banks at losses of 25% or more. This bank situation was relieved for awhile by government loans but culminated on Feb. 14, 1933 when the governor of Michigan closed every bank in the state on a "bank holiday." This spread like fever to other states. First came Indiana, then Maryland and finally on March 4, 1933 (date of Roosevelt's inauguration) the New York State Banks closed and completed a list of 48 states under "bank holiday." On that same morning the New York and Chicago Stock Exchanges closed. Saturday, March 4, 1933 will be long remembered because almost at the moment of the inauguration of Roosevelt every bank and stock exchange in the U.S. closed its doors. Within 24 hours after his inauguration the new President issued a dramatic proclamation closing every bank and stock exchange in the U.S., forbidding the export of gold and technically removing the U.S. from the gold standard. As I write this every bank in Youngstown and all over the U.S. is closed and newsboys are selling "extras" stating that scrip will be issued soon by the banks. Times are exciting and personally I would not take a great deal for the privilege of participating in these events.

MARCH 8, 1933

At noon today, the Dollar Bank and City Bank, with permission of the government, opened its doors to make small change and transact routine business. No withdrawals of any kind permitted. New money deposited may be withdrawn on demand. Depositors are wary and distrustful because plans have been changed so often.

MARCH 9, 1933

The second day of the National Bank Holiday passes quietly. All Youngstown banks are open to make small change and to transact routine business but no withdrawals are permitted. Plans are being made to issue scrip against bank collateral such as notes, bonds and other liquid assets. It is not known yet whether this scrip will be issued by the government or by local bank clearing houses. I hope it will be issued by the government because then it will be received everywhere in payment of obligations.

It is pretty generally agreed that the U.S. is now off the gold standard and will not be able to go back on next Friday when the holiday ends. Banks have already been ordered to turn in all gold in exchange for paper currency. It is also pretty generally agreed that we are in for a period of currency inflation.

In the long run I am not sure that Roosevelt did the right thing in going off the gold standard. The American dollar has long been recognized as the standard of the world. For three years Pres. Hoover kept us on the gold standard and fought bitterly against inflation. This work is now undone. We may find ourselves competing with Europe on the basis of depreciated currency. One thing is certain—if bank depositors are permitted to draw out a portion of their deposits in the form of scrip—then we are in for a brief spending spree and rising prices. People need almost everything and also they will not consider the scrip seriously as money. If I get any surplus scrip I will use it to reduce fixed obligations such as loans on insurance policies, mortgage loan, etc.

MARCH 9, 1933

Scrip was issued yesterday by Truscon Steel Co. and General Fireproofing Co. in payment for wages. I saw today some of the General Fireproofing scrip. Legally it is a promissory note to bearer payable on or before 6 months. It is issued in $1 and $5 denominations. The Truscon is also a promissory note payable against frozen bank assets. This scrip is being refused in many cases because circulation is limited. Plans to issue scrip on a national scale are awaiting the President's message to Congress this noon. In the meanwhile the U.S. takes action against gold hoarders by demanding from each Federal Reserve Bank the names of persons who withdrew gold after Feb. 1, 1933. These persons will be shamed by publicity into returning the gold or will be taxed or punished.

MARCH 10, 1933

Yesterday saw legislation passed to reform the U.S. banking system. At noon the President delivered a short message to Congress asking full power to deal with the banking situation. At 7:30 last night both houses of Congress in record time passed legislation:

1. Giving President war-time powers.
2. Providing for opening of solvent banks and reorganization or closing of insolvent banks.
3. Permitting issue of U.S. currency based on notes, bank drafts, etc. Wide powers to pass this currency to members of Federal Reserve.
4. At 10:30 P.M. the President issued a new proclamation extending indefinitely the bank holiday and embargo on export of gold.

It is hoped that by tomorrow the sound banks will be selected and permitted to open.

In the meanwhile, gold hoarders have been alarmed by threats of publicity and punishment and are exchanging gold for paper currency.

Are we now going to have inflation and if so to what extent? Will prices rise? Will people rush to convert their money into real estate or other property? Fear of depreciation of money and rising prices may have many results. Locally the banks are still observing the legal holiday and the stock exchange is still closed.

MARCH 11, 1933

The national bank holiday continues and all banks and stock exchanges are still closed. Promise is made that "sound" banks will open next week. It must prove its soundness to the Secretary of U.S. Treasury and get a permit to open.

Hoarded gold flows back into banks on threat of exposure and arrest. Over $100,000,000 has returned this way in past two days. Mostly in large cities. One man in New York City is reported to have returned two million in gold.

Ohio and other states now pass a law to restrict withdrawals from life insurance companies. Loans cannot be made now on policies except to pay premiums. In case of necessity loans are limited to $100. Nothing is said about payment of death claims or trust funds.

Los Angeles district in California experiences 13 quakes yesterday. Almost as bad as San Francisco affair! Early reports indicate 150 dead; 2500 hurt; tremendous property loss.

In connection with inflated currency I heard an interesting story told today by Mr. Vasu, a real estate dealer. When the world war broke out his father owned real estate in Europe subject to mortgages of $50,000. After the war he paid off this indebtedness with inflated money actually worth about $18.

MARCH 13, 1933

President Roosevelt again breaks precedent by talking on radio last night and explaining the bank situation to the people in detail.

Banks will be re-opened all over nation in following order: Today (Monday) all "sound" banks in the 12 Federal Reserve cities; Tuesday all sound banks in cities with clearing houses; Wednesday all other sound banks in smaller communities.

Question: What is a sound bank? In Cleveland this morning only 3 banks were permitted to open. Two of the largest—Union Trust and Guardian Trust—are closed and will be reorganized. What will happen in Youngstown tomorrow?

I am again confused by "gold standard." Are we off because currency can no longer be redeemed? Are we having inflation when government issues two billion in new money, not backed by or redeemable in gold but backed by bank assets such as notes, drafts, etc.? The better economists say no— but I can't follow their argument. My own opinion would be otherwise.

The problem is simple—total gold supply of U.S. is now about $4 billion—total currency of all kind (including gold) is about $8 billion—total bank deposits $46 billion. Problem: how can all depositors be given the currency they demand? Also will only $2 billion of new money be enough? If more is issued, is it inflation?

MARCH 14, 1933

All of Youngstown banks open this morning with government permission for "normal business." City Bank and Dollar Bank do not permit withdrawals made prior to closing in October 1931. Same applies to Union National Bank. Also only withdrawals for "normal" requirements are permitted. No hoarding is permitted—an affidavit can be required to this effect. The largest bank in Akron must be re-organized. Same in other cities. Youngstown is fortunate in having had the house-cleaning experience in 1931.

People seem more optimistic now and talk of inflation dies down.

Sheet & Tube lost 13 million in 1932 and Truscon lost 1,600,000. Truscon does not seem to be in very strong shape.

MARCH 17, 1933

The stock market opened on March 16th after being closed for 10 days. Stocks boomed for 2 days and are now settling down. Since the banks re-opened people have gained considerable confidence and have become more optimistic. Retail sales in Youngstown have increased 300%. Banks permit check withdrawals but will not permit currency withdrawals. In this way currency is being slowly drawn out of hiding.

Roosevelt and Congress have made a record since March 4th by passing bills to (1.) Reorganize banking system (2.) To balance the budget (3.) To legalize beer and light wines. These are the 3 most important promises made in the Democrat platform. Quick passage was made possible by the emergency closing of the banks.

In 1907 most of our troubles came *after* the currency stringency. It is possible we still face a year or two of liquidation. U.S. Steel announces for 1932 the enormous loss of 39 million.

War clouds are again gathering over Europe and the situation begins to look serious.

MARCH 20, 1933

The stock market settles down and prices are back to where they were before the bank holiday. Also business settles down to "natural." More fear of inflation. Out of $2 billion new currency that was printed only 6 million has been put into circulation thus far. I haven't seen any of it. Scrip issued by local industries is being redeemed and no more will be issued. The time limit for returning hoarded gold has expired but it seems that threat of punishment or publicity was mostly a bluff.

MARCH 25, 1933

Reorganization and consolidation of closed banks take place all over country. It is interesting to note that lawyers were named to head large reorganized banks in Cleveland and Detroit.

Business continues at a standstill and the stock market drifts lower. Conditions in Europe are chaotic with continual threat. Hitler is named dictator of Germany and threatens to expel all Jews.

President Roosevelt signs bill permitting sale of beer and light wines—3.2% alcohol.

MARCH 27, 1933

The scarcity of gold and high prices of commodities has created a new interest in gold mining. In the west and in other parts of the country thousands of people are reworking old mines and streams. Most of them average about $2 per day. Likewise the sale of gold ornaments etc. has been spurred by the appeal of the government not to hoard gold.

The return of beer and light wines has caused considerable activity in this line. Already shares of stock are being offered for sale to the public in newly organized companies. Personally I think the whole thing is over-rated and that the excitement will die down in a few months.

MARCH 28, 1933

I have finally concluded that the issue of two billion new currency by Roosevelt will not mean inflation at this time. This is because the usual supply of currency has been cut down by hoarding, freezing of bank assets, etc. The one counterbalances the other and there has been no actual increase in the amount of money in actual circulation. If the government in the near future fails to balance the budget and issues new currency to pay its deficit—then inflation will follow.

We are now feeling the after-effect of the permanent closing of thousands of banks which were not permitted to re-open after the bank holiday. About six billion in assets have become "frozen" in this way. As a result, currency is more restricted than ever. The industrial reports for the 1st quarter of 1933 will be the worst of the depression. This will result in many more business reorganizations.

APRIL 1, 1933

The month just closed established an all-time low record in my law practice. My total cash receipts for the month amounted to $18. The same thing is happening to every professional man in town.

Unemployment, business stagnation and bankruptcy get steadily worse. Yesterday the Missouri-Pacific Railroad went into bankruptcy. This is the 8th railroad liquidation so far. The plan of re-organization contemplates exchange of bonds for preferred, preferred for common and practically the wiping out of the old common. Also the Liggett Drug Chain goes into bankruptcy with 450 stores in 340 cities. Blame is placed on high-priced leases.

Banking troubles are not over. Banks which were not permitted to re-open after the bank holiday are found to be in very bad shape. Indictment of bankers and investigations are the order of the day. Because the Union and Guardian Banks of Cleveland are still closed—84 small banks in Ohio cities cannot reopen. They used these Cleveland banks as depositories. Lawyer Burton will head the new Guardian Bank of Cleveland and lawyer Cannon will head the new Union. Likewise a lawyer heads the large new Detroit bank. None of them have previous banking experience.

In Germany the new dictator Hitler declares a boycott against Jewish merchants and professional men and arouses world protest.

Talk of inflation again appears. The powerful farm organization demands a "new dollar" with less gold content. They would raise the price of an ounce of gold from $20.67 to $30. They claim this would raise agricultural prices so they could pay their debts. If this is not done they claim they are ruined. This seems to be inflation pure and simple and I am afraid the long-run result will be disastrous. The same arguments are being used now as appeared in 1866, 1873, and 1893. I wonder if this will be a political issue in the next political campaign.

APRIL 5, 1933

The "gold" question comes to the front again. President Roosevelt issues an order forbidding any person to hold more than $100 in gold or gold certificates. Any amount above this must be taken to Federal Reserve Banks.

APRIL 11, 1933

Business drifts along with a little optimism on account of a late Spring and Easter spurt. Talk of "controlled inflation" continues. In 31 states now loans on insurance policies have been restricted to $100. Death benefits and annuities are still paid in full. Since the bank closed, the hoarding movement turned against the insurance companies.

The return of "legal beer" caused activity in certain lines. I don't believe it will continue after the first novelty wears off.

The Receiver in Bankruptcy of the Paramount Picture Corporation cancelled the leases on 3 local theaters (Paramount, State and Cameo) and returned them to the property owners. This is happening every day with large chain organizations.

The embargo on foreign exportation of gold from U.S. is still in force and so is the rule permitting paper money to be converted into gold on demand. Hence we are still technically off the gold standard. No change in commodity prices has resulted as yet. The value of U.S. dollar on foreign markets remains at par because of restrictions on foreign exchange and because of "pegging" by U.S. I don't quite understand this foreign exchange situation.

APRIL 18, 1933

Business still in the dumps altho optimism comes back with the nice spring weather. Steel production jumps from 13% to 20%. Inflation talk grows stronger. Yesterday a 16 to 1 silver currency bill was defeated in the Senate by a narrow margin of 46 to 33. There is a great deal of radical legislation being proposed in Washington.

It now appears that Great Britain and other countries have been taking advantage of U.S. by manipulating their depreciated currency and foreign exchange. With use of appreciated currency, they have been dumping their mdse produced by cheap labor into the U.S. At the coming economic conference this question and also "war debts" will be taken up. Instead of raising tariff barriers against this depreciated currency the present administration is pledged to lower them. By technically going off the gold standard and forbidding gold exports the U.S. serves notice on Europe that if necessary we will manipulate our own currency in order to prevent an unfair advantage in foreign trade. It is hoped that the coming Economic Conference will iron this out and make further steps unnecessary.

In spite of much reading on the subject I am still confused by the inflation theories. Briefly the following inflation theories are now being pressed in Congress:

1. Devalue the dollar by reducing gold content and thus issuing more currency.
2. Use silver as a base—bi-metalism.
3. Simply print more money—fiat money.
4. Increase credit instead of money because a normal $40 billion credit has been reduced to $20 billion by frozen bank deposits etc.
    a. One plan is the new farm plan to refinance mortgages with government bonds.
    b. Loans to industry by the government.
    c. Federal Reserve Banks to buy bonds and thus put money into banks. This was tried but the money stayed in banks and was not loaned out.
    d. Put the money directly into hands of consumers by huge public works plans. Bonds are first issued to pay for these improvements and then under the emergency law new currency can be issued against these bonds.

All of these plans are directly or indirectly inflationary. In my own judgment none of them will help. I think deflation and reorganization will continue for another year or two until consumption equals production and we start at rock bottom again. This process is extremely painful but possibly the only way out. I can't believe that legislation on tampering with the currency will provide work for the unemployed. In the end somebody will have to pay for all these improvements, etc.

In the meanwhile the stock market jerks up and down with each new threat of inflation. Most people believe that if inflation comes they should sell bonds and buy common stocks.

APRIL 19, 1933

In order to fight European depreciation in money President Roosevelt places a formal embargo on gold and indirectly promises to raise domestic prices by some form of inflation. The stock market rushes up on the news and has a hectic day. Many stocks jump 11 points. The dollar falls in value on European exchanges.

APRIL 20, 1933

The papers are full of details today of how and why U.S. went off gold standard. Stocks soar upward on theory that commodity prices will go up. I don't see how or why prices should advance simply because we are off the gold standard unless real currency inflation follows by deflating value of the dollar. Everywhere the subject is being discussed and everybody seems to think they know all about the subject. A great deal depends now on further steps of the government toward inflation.

APRIL 21, 1933

Times are again exciting. Everybody is talking inflation and the stock market is booming. Hectic crowds fill brokers' offices. U.S. is definitely off the gold standard both internationally and at home. The President asks wartime powers to inflate the currency:

1. By issuing $3 billion new currency
2. Lower gold content by international agreement
3. Take up to 100 million in silver because of war debts and issue new currency against it. The matter is being debated in Congress. The Democratic majority support and the Republican minority oppose. Personally I am with the Republican minority.

APRIL 22, 1933

It now seems that the "inflation bill" asked by the President is much broader than first anticipated. It really authorizes him to use almost every form of inflation. If he decided to use his full authority he could issue about $20 billion new currency (three times the present amount) as follows:

1. $3 billion thru purchase of U.S. Bonds by Federal Reserve and issue of new currency against them.
2. $3 billion in new greenbacks as authorized.
3. Cut gold content in half and issue $6 billion in currency against this additional gold.

4. $100 million in silver certificates.

5. The government has received almost $2 billion additional gold since the new law was passed penalizing gold hoarding. If gold content of dollar is lowered they could legally issue about $8 billion new currency against this new gold.

Everything depends on the President. It is a terrific responsibility.

CHAPTER 4

APRIL 26, 1933–DECEMBER 28, 1933

"The Depression has been broken."

EDITOR'S NOTE

In June 1933 Congress passed one of the centerpieces of the New Deal legislation, the National Industrial Recovery Act. This law profoundly changed the way business and work were conducted in America. It organized businesses into industries that would volunteer to adhere to codes designed to eliminate unfair competitive practices and to standardize wages paid and hours worked. In return for this cooperation, industries were exempt from antitrust provisions. Consumers were then asked to do business only with companies that adhered to the National Recovery Act (NRA) policies, as signified by a blue eagle logo. The act also, as Roth notes, granted for the first time the permanent right of American workers to organize into labor unions. As a result, union membership expanded dramatically—it tripled over the course of the 1930s—but strikes also became more frequent as unions began to assert their power. Many industries vital to the region around Youngstown—autos, coal, and steel—were adamantly opposed to unions in their plants. Roth notes in particular a series of violent coal miner strikes in Pennsylvania that preceded that industry's acceptance of an NRA code.

In fairly short order, it became clear that the NRA was too sweeping, and government enforcement too weak, for the NRA to make any sustained improvement in the overall economy. Roth himself was skeptical of the NRA from the very beginning yet, in what is clearly a transforming moment in his life, agrees to give multiple speeches on its behalf, all around the Youngstown area. It was, he wrote, "the only patriotic thing to do." Roth's diary from mid-1933 is filled with indications (including rising stock prices and increased steel production) that the worst of the Depression had ended. And indeed, after forty-three punishing months, the U.S. economy did stop contracting in March 1933, but the impact for nearly all Americans was minimal and the NRA—much of which would be struck down in 1935 as unconstitutional—did not live up to the administration's predictions.

Another critical aspect of Roosevelt's economic policy—and one that vexed Roth for years—was the desire to inflate the currency. This was in large part an attempt to revive the depressed commodities markets, which were particularly hurting American farmers. In order to achieve this, Roosevelt by early 1933 saw the need to take the U.S. dollar off the gold standard, on which it had operated since 1900; as Roth notes in earlier entries, many major global economies—including the U.K. and much of western Europe—had already taken this step. Many in Congress favored a policy of bimetalism, which would have fixed the value of the dollar at a certain weight of gold and a certain weight of silver, a policy Roosevelt opposed. The Emergency Banking Act of 1933, which passed in March and allowed 90 percent of the banks to reopen by June, temporarily took the dollar off the gold standard. A later act of Congress—which Roth refers to as the "inflation bill"—allowed the president to revalue the dollar-gold ratio from $20.67 an ounce to $30 an ounce.

APRIL 26, 1933

Excitement about inflation is dying down. Better public opinion seems to be veering against inflation now. It is beginning to be realized that only the speculator will profit and the consumer will lose. Already food prices have gone up although there is no reason for it except speculation. Corporation reports for 1st quarter of 1933 are worst of the whole depression.

APRIL 27, 1933

Banking troubles begin again. The biggest bank in Cleveland—The Cleveland Trust—has a record run affecting its 54 branches. Caused by rumors. In midst of run Mr. Creech, the president, stands on desk in lobby and announces the bank will remain open until 5 P.M. and all depositors will be paid in full without question. The Federal Reserve announces full support.

Bank depositors, holders of liberty bonds and other high grade bonds are just beginning to waken to dangers of inflation. They ask where they can put their money with safety. There appears to be no answer to this as long as the dollar can be tampered with.

The inflation bill is being bitterly contested in Congress. All kinds of amendments are being tacked on by special groups. The latest involve the free coinage of silver at a rate to be fixed by the President and also payment in full of the soldiers bonus with printing press money. Shades of Grover

Cleveland and William Jennings Bryan. It looks like the greenback era all over again.

In the meanwhile business is stagnant and all we do is talk about money. There is none of it in sight.

One of the woman clerks at McKelveys says she works on a commission basis of 4% of sales. One day last week she earned 8¢ for the entire day.

Chain dress shops in town are selling sweat-shop products at ridiculously low prices.

APRIL 30, 1933

A miniature "Shay's Rebellion" is taking place in Iowa. Enraged farmers in one place fought 50 deputy sheriffs to prevent a foreclosure sale. In another place they pulled the Judge off the bench during the trial, tied a rope around his neck, abused him, threatened hanging. Finally removed his pants and left him on the highway. These places and several others are now under military control and prompt punishment will be meted out to the wrong-doers. The situation illustrates the attitude of farmers who are losing farms because of deflated dollars and corn selling at 10¢ a bushel. Yesterday we drove to Ravenna and along the road eggs were selling at 11¢ per dozen.

The enormous inflation bill was approved by the Senate yesterday and the stock market took another big spurt. The bill will probably pass the House today.

MAY 5, 1933

The inflation bill has been approved by both houses of Congress and now awaits the signature of the President. The mere prospect of inflation has caused considerable speculation in commodities which are bought and placed in storage for higher prices. Already prices of all commodities are up 15% and common stock prices have doubled and trebled. The consumer is the loser because wages do not go up and there are 20 men available for every job.

Yesterday Judge David Jenkins our local Judge gave a farmer a six month respite from a foreclose decree.

At a social gathering last night the greater part of the evening was devoted to a discussion of inflation and national affairs. Every person present—both men and women—had a pretty good understanding of the subject. In the past two years there has been an amazing change in American thought from cards and golf to national politics and public matters. Life has become simple. Women's styles resemble the 1890s and even the bicycle is coming back into favor as a means of transportation.

Real estate is still a liability and a cause of vexation to the owner. Income is not enough to pay water and rent and taxes. Foreclosures are moving at a slower pace because of an aroused public opinion.

The National Surety Co.—a national insurance and casualty co.—went broke today. This is about the 10th of its kind this year.

MAY 19, 1933

General business improves both because of inflation talk and for natural causes. Steel operations have improved from 17% to 35%; stock market averages from 45 to 75; commodities have gone up about 25%. Everybody is waiting now for the conference in Europe which will try to iron out currency problems, tariffs, etc. Roosevelt continues to suggest plan after plan for the control of industry and labor by the government. No actual inflation in currency has yet taken place. Locally the situation is much the same except that steel mills are operating at 35%. Law practice shows no improvement but we are already paying more for food, etc.

MAY 24, 1933

Conditions continue to improve and sentiment grows stronger that the depression has been broken and we are on the way out. Steel mills running about 40% and for first time in 3 years are on the profit side. Many steel workers in Youngstown will tomorrow draw their first pay check in 3 years.

Investigations are the order of the day. The Senate is investigating private banking and in particular J. P. Morgan & Co. Mr. Morgan was on the witness stand all day yesterday and today. The evidence shows that his firm made loans to many men now prominent in public affairs.

First step is taken toward real inflation where Federal Reserve Bank starts today to buy back (with new money) $3 billion in government bonds. Also effort will be made to stabilize the dollar on foreign exchange at about 80¢.

The U.S. is being drawn more and more into European affairs and the present administration seems ready to abandon our policy of isolation. Personally and under present conditions I am opposed to this and believe that isolation is still our best policy. Europe is now again on the verge of war and I see no reason why we should inter-meddle with her quarrels.

After moving upward for a month since the inflation announcement, the stock market is hesitating. I believe it has over-discounted the possibilities.

MAY 29, 1933

Roosevelt asks Congress to repeal the Gold Standard Act of 1900. On the mere announcement of his request the stock market went up 10 points in the busiest Saturday of all time. As a matter of fact the U.S. has already refused to pay gold for currency, gov't bonds and other obligations, so this merely legalizes what has already been done. It leaves paper currency, bonds, etc. without gold backing as the only legal money in U.S. and acceptable for all obligations including contracts, leases, etc. calling for gold. In so far as this new law affects old contracts and nullifies them, I believe it is unconstitutional. A lower court in N.Y. however holds it is constitutional and justified because of the emergency and because there is not enough gold in the world to meet the contract demand. In the meanwhile industry is still on the upgrade and optimism continues unchecked.

Gold mining stocks (like Homestake) have been the leaders in the market. Homestake went up 17 points on Saturday A.M. In past 60 days Sheet & Tube has gone from 6 to 30.

JUNE 1, 1933

In looking back over the 3 months since Roosevelt became President it seems that the U.S. has traveled a long way toward some form of socialism or managed economy.

1. The President has been given the powers of a dictator and Congress is a mere rubber stamp.
2. We are off gold standard and will probably have inflation and a managed economy.
3. The industrial control bill is very far-reaching. It puts the government in business so that wages, prices, quantity of production etc. will be managed and controlled.
4. The greatest power producing area in the U.S. (Muscle Shoals) will be owned and operated by the gov't.
5. We are becoming "internationally minded" by promising to lower tariffs and participate in European wars of aggression.

All these things were once considered radical but in light of present conditions are being accepted calmly. Pres. Roosevelt's advisers are a group of college professors called the "brain trust."

Personally I am opposed to going off the gold standard, mixing in European affairs, lowering tariffs, etc. I think the day of reckoning will come when we will pay dearly for these experiments and then we will return to the gold standard, to a reasonable protective tariff, to individualism instead of collectivism and also obey George Washington's advice to avoid foreign entanglements.

For the present Roosevelt with his new deal and upsetting of tradition is the man of the hour because for 2 months now prices and industry have been advancing. It will be for the future to determine whether his course was a wise one.

So far the gov't has taken no action against gold hoarders. This is unfair to the citizens who turned in their gold because the gold dollar is now worth about $1.20 in currency. There is not yet however any domestic market for gold and the foreign exportation is still prohibited.

JUNE 6, 1933

For the first time in my recollection we have "sweat shops" in Youngstown. A government investigation is under way involving Moyer Manufacturing Co.; G.M. McKelvey Co.; and numerous dry cleaners and raincoat manufacturers. At Moyer's the girls claim they work long hours on piece work and get about $2.75 a week. At McKelvey's the girls worked at straight 4% commission and often did not make even car fare.

Stock market still on the upgrade. Average is 82. Sheet & Tube 31; Republic 15; U.S. Steel 52; Radio 9; Truscon 8.

I am afraid the opportunity to buy a fortune in stocks at about 10¢ on the dollar is past and so far I have been unable to take advantage of it.

It is my conclusion that the successful investor must cultivate the habit of "patience." He must be able to hold his money and wait until it is really the time to buy. In this panic it meant waiting over 3 years until stocks were really at rock bottom and selling at less than 1/10 of their normal value. I suppose the real investor would then have the patience and courage to wait until normal times returned before selling. *Patience* to wait for the right moment—*courage* to buy or sell when that time arrives—and *liquid capital*—these are the 3 essentials as I see it now. When stocks reached their all-time low in July of 1932 (when Sheet & Tube sold at 6; Republic 1 1/2;

Truscon 2; U.S. Steel 20, etc.) it would have taken plenty of courage to buy because receiverships and bankruptcies threatened the largest companies and most of the banks in the country were closed or refusing to permit withdrawals.

Steel mills are now operating at 63% as contrasted to 17% in March.

JUNE 7, 1933

In the face of opposition of almost the whole world Pres. Roosevelt refuses to stabilize the dollar and goes forward with his inflation plan of raising domestic prices. Briefly he says he will let the dollar fluctuate on foreign exchange until domestic prices are raised to a point where industry can show a profit and debts can be paid. Then he will stabilize the dollar at its then rate to foreign currencies.

Skepticism and doubt and criticism of his plan are becoming more outspoken daily. When U.S. went off gold standard we got some foreign trade with our depreciated money but we are fast losing this because of rising domestic prices and increasing foreign trade barriers.

JUNE 11, 1933

The stock market boom is completing 4 months of upward soaring without a halt. Stock averages are about 96. New brokerage offices are opening everywhere and the public is rushing in as they did in 1928. American dollar at 69¢ on foreign exchange. Steel mills are operating at 65%. Stock prices: Truscon 13; Sheet & Tube 32; U.S. Steel 65; Bethlehem 46; General Elec. 25; Penn. R.R. 43; Republic 2.

As far as professional men are concerned business continues steadily worse. People are using their new earnings to pay bills, buy food and in some cases automobiles. Sales of automobiles have doubled and trebled. The reiterated promise of Pres. Roosevelt that he will raise prices to the 1924 level is cited by brokers as a guarantee that stock prices will go up. Seems to me it is about time for a bad break.

EDITOR'S NOTE

A Senate investigation of the most powerful institutions on Wall Street in determining the cause of the stock market collapse of 1929 was well under way by June 1933. The probe would continue into

1934 under the direction of Ferdinand Pecora, an assistant district attorney from New York who would eventually go on to become chairman of the Securities and Exchange Commission. The vigorous interrogation of the most powerful bankers and brokers of the era, from J. P. Morgan Jr. to Charles Mitchell of National City Bank, revealed an embarrassing breadth of underhanded financial practices by the nation's wealthiest financiers, from skipping out on paying income taxes on bonuses to tampering with stock market pools so only friends would profit. The information disclosed in these hearings proved deeply damaging to the image of Wall Street in the eyes of the public.

JUNE 20, 1933

National affairs are very confusing. Roosevelt sticks to his inflation idea and so far has resisted attempts of the Economic Conference in Europe to stabilize currency or peg the dollar. As a result brokers' offices are crowded and stocks still go up after 2 months of unbroken progress. Market average is 87.5.

Prices of commodities are going up and stores and factories are buying large quantities of merchandise for fear prices will go still higher. The steel mills operate at 50% and a great many men have been called back to work. Wages, however, have not increased with prices. Also all the lawyers and other professional men complain of lack of business. People must be optimistic because automobile sales for past 60 days reached record proportions.

The more conservative judgment is that we are on the upgrade and on the way out provided the government will let business alone.

The Industrial Control Bill which will practically dominate business thru its trade associations is just beginning to take form. It is a radical excursion into the field of a "controlled economy."

I talked to Atty. Andrew Rheuban today. He says: "I have $35,000 equity in a 6 family brick apartment and have been fighting 3 long years to hold it against the mortgage. I would never again invest in real estate. The net income is never above 5% and the personal attention and worry is not worth the effort. I would have been better off and happier if I had put my money in government bonds." He echoes the feeling today of almost all real estate owners. I fear his view-point will change when real estate again becomes the medium of speculation.

Investigation and criminal indictment of bankers and big business men is still the order of the day. A great deal of rotten-ness in high finance has been discovered. For the present at least the lawyers as a group are not in the limelight. The banker and financiers hold the limelight as the evil genius.

JUNE 24, 1933

The upturn continues without interruption. Steel mills operate at 55% today and Youngstown sees the 3rd largest pay-day in past 3 years. The streets are crowded with Saturday shoppers. Stock market for 60 days moves slowly up and average stands at 88.

European economic conference so far has accomplished nothing. U.S. fights monetary stabilization and return to gold standard because it won't stop inflation and rising prices at home. U.S. may talk stabilization etc. when price recovery has gone a little further.

Professional men all claim that they have not so far been benefited by the mild boom we are enjoying. We will probably be among the last to feel the effect.

JUNE 27, 1933

The boom continues and prices soar upward in the most spectacular recovery the world has ever seen. I still cannot believe it is permanent. Yesterday saw the return of $1 wheat and 10¢ cotton for the first time since the depression. Inflation and control bills started the price up on March 15 but a severe drought and continued hot weather did the rest. It is now estimated that the wheat crop this year will be the smallest since 1890. The 2 main causes are (1.) Drought and (2.) Small acreage planted by discouraged farmers who had been selling at a loss.

I think the next 4 months will tell the story. The European conference is still fighting for monetary stabilization. This conflicts with Roosevelt's plan for inflation and higher prices. What happens as to money stabilization will considerably affect the near future. Personally I favor stabilization and a slower recovery—but it is anybody's guess as to what will happen.

JUNE 29, 1933

Only France, Holland, Switzerland and a few smaller countries remain on gold standard. They are fighting desperately at economic conference for stabilization but U.S. refuses. France now says that she will be forced off gold if this continues and that she and other gold nations will withdraw from conference. This would mean the whole world off gold and a race for world trade by depreciating currency—and would result in destructive world-wide inflation. Interest in real estate has picked up since inflation talk started because in Germany it proved to be the best investment at the time.

Labor unions are busy in Youngstown trying to unionize the steel industry. They claim they have broader authority under the Industrial Control Bill. This may be the fore-runner of labor difficulties.

JULY 1, 1933

I read an article a few days ago in the *Saturday Evening Post* describing the German inflation period. It is enough to strike fear into the heart of the most brave and explains why European nations are demanding stabilization of the U.S. dollar. The German inflation was a huge fraud which benefited the debtors and speculators at the expense of the large, prudent middle class. The following things happened in Germany:

a. Bonds (including governments), real estate mortgages, life insurance, bank savings and all fixed value investments became worthless because they were redeemed by debtors with depreciated money.
b. Common stocks of industrial concerns soared to fantastic heights and paid huge dividends. When stabilization came these stocks crashed and only the strongest companies survived. In spite of this common stocks proved to be the best investment.
c. Real estate owners who paid off their mortgages with depreciated currency *and held on to it* until stabilization came, still had something of value. The same applied to purchasers of commodities such as diamonds, etc.
d. Industries expanded, built huge additions to their plants and paid in worthless currency. Of all classes, the industrialists fared best.
e. Professional men were badly off.

The American dollar is now worth about 75¢ on foreign exchange and to the extent of this depreciation, we are seeing here a changed outlook on the part of the investor. Bonds are being exchanged for common stocks and commodities because prices are rising fast. There is also talk that Americans of German extraction are beginning to put their money into real estate.

Inflation is a terrible thing and I hope it will never come to America. It penalizes saving and changes the entire outlook of the prudent investor from government bonds, life insurance, etc. to speculative stocks and commodities. The German Mark before the war was worth almost 25¢ in American money. When inflation ended a dollar would buy about a billion marks. During inflation American speculators went into Germany and bought huge pieces of valuable real estate for sums as low as $50 in our money. Hunger, starvation and ruin were the results of German inflation. In no country has it ever proven to be a blessing.

JULY 6, 1933

The European Economic Conference closes today, a complete failure mainly because U.S. refused to stabilize currency and go back to gold. It looks now as tho France and the few remaining countries will be forced to leave gold and then we will have a world wide competition in depreciated currency.

I talked to Julius Kahn of Truscon last night. He said, "The depression is now a thing of the past—there is no question about it. The next 60 days will see a remarkable change for the better with thousands of additional men called back to work. Our plant is now operating at a profit."

JULY 11, 1933

Industry continues to boom and the entire public seems to be speculating in the stock market. Almost as bad as 1929. We already have 3 brokerage houses in Youngstown and another opens next week. Last Friday was a record day of the year with nine million shares changing hands. Likewise cotton and wheat markets are soaring.

In Youngstown steel mills operate at 67%. The air is again thick with smoke and hundreds of men are going back to work.

The whole recovery has been so spectacular as to be almost unbelievable. Because so much of it is based on inflation theories I have doubted its permanency. The next few months ought to tell the story.

In the meanwhile lawyers and other professional groups have failed so far to share in the boom.

The economic conference in Europe adjourns—a complete failure.

The following shows a few typical examples of increases in stock prices in past 4 months:

Amer T&T 85 to 132; Nat'l Distillers 16 to 114 (b/c of Prohibition amendment); U.S. Steel 23 to 65; Western Union 17 to 71; G.M. 10 to 33; N.Y.C. 14–56.

Again and again during this depression it is driven home to me that opportunity is a stern goddess who passes up those who are unprepared with liquid capital.

JULY 18, 1933

Col. Ayres of the Cleveland Trust Bank says in his bulletin that he is convinced that the depression definitely turned the corner between the 1st and 2nd quarter of 1933. He thinks recovery would have proceeded without inflation but that inflation has made it spectacular and abrupt. He fears that the recovery has been too rapid and may be followed by a set-back. General opinion, however, seems to be that we will move forward now in spite of occasional set-backs.

JULY 19, 1933

The stock market broke badly today. Pres. Roosevelt is alarmed and threatens to take charge of the security exchange if it threatens to interfere with his recovery progress. Stock market average drops from 102.1 to 96.3. Losses run as high as $25 per share. Wheat sold from $1.25 bu. down to $1.12. 7 1/2 million shares changed hands during the day. The U.S. dollar reaches a record low of 68¢ on foreign exchange. This brings the pound sterling about back to its old par of $4.86.

JULY 20, 1933

The stock market collapse continues for a second day and share losses range from 1 to 20. Turnover is over 8 million shares. Pres. Roosevelt again threatens to take control of the stock market. The decline has been the most drastic in years. Average stock loss is $8 per share.

According to today's *Plain Dealer* Pres. Roosevelt today ordered the grain and commodity markets to close. It seems to me ridiculous. As long as prices are going up the administration is satisfied but if they go down—they want to control the exchanges. It just can't be done.

Some of the things that happened yesterday are: Stock averages drop 96.3 to 87. Dollar jumps 17¢ on foreign exchange; wheat loses 16¢ bu. (25¢

2 days ago); cotton loses $4 per bale. Stock losses: AT&T drops 130 to 122; Bethlehem 43 to 35; U.S. Steel 64 to 56; Western Union 72 to 68.

In Cleveland the collapse of the Guardian and Union Trust Banks is under investigation and criminal action will probably follow. The investigation shows that the banks were run for the benefit of officers and directors; juggling of figures in financial reports; no examination by State Banking Board or Clearing House for 8 years; immense loans to officers and directors for speculative purposes without collateral; speculation by the bank in common stocks thru subsidiaries formed for the business; hiding of losses on bad loans by methods of accounting. Actually the bank was financing a ring of hotels, coal mines, etc. for the benefit of officers and directors.

JULY 22, 1933

The stock market crash continues for the 3rd day and with greater intensity. Losses as high as $20 per share. Stock average drops 87 to 80. Ten million shares change hands in one day. Thousands of new speculators are wiped out. Grain markets continue closed. Radio now at 5; Republic 13; Sheet & Tube 18; U.S. Steel 49; Gen. Elec. 22; Truscon 8. The following shows some of the losses in past two days: AT&T from 134 to 114; Steel 67 to 49; Union Pacific 132–108; Nat'l Distillers 124–64; Amer. Com. 89–29; Int'l Harv. 46–29; Amer. Smelting 42 to 28; West. Un. 77–49; Gen. Motr. 34–22.

Pres. Roosevelt is not satisfied with progress to raise wages under Industrial Recovery Act. Prices have gone up—not wages. Each employer will now have to be asked to sign agreements to raise wages and cut hours. He will then be permitted to mark his goods with N.R.A. label (Nat'l Recovery Act). Consumers will then be asked to buy only products bearing this label. Pres. Roosevelt will speak over radio Monday and this will be followed by a national campaign by speakers, advertising, etc. to arouse the people. It will go hard with any employer who refuses to go along—will virtually boycott him. Roosevelt thinks this plan will put five million unemployed back to working Sept. 1st and will supply additional buying power to catch up with rising prices.

I fail to see how many department stores and other businesses now on the verge of bankruptcy after 3 years of losses can now raise wages, cut hours of employment and still be prevented from exploiting the consumer by raising prices too high. Again the professional groups seem to be left out.

JULY 22, 1933, 10:30 A.M.

According to the morning newspaper Roosevelt ordered the stock exchange closed this morning (Sat.) until Monday noon. He probably figures that his speech Monday night on the radio will instill confidence and prevent further drastic decline.

JULY 24, 1933

My last statement about the closing of the stock exchange was incorrect. It will be open only three hours each day—from noon to 3. The grain market will re-open today but with restrictions including a minimum price for wheat at 90¢ bu. Likewise a maximum fluctuation in one day will be prevented. The drop in commodity markets and the rise of the dollar are interfering with the President's plan for higher prices. He may be forced soon to go further along the road to inflation.

JULY 25, 1933

Stocks made a rapid recovery today and gained 1 to 10 points. Stock average jumps from 80 to 87.

Pres. Roosevelt talked on radio yesterday and explained his new plan of asking employers to raise wages and cut hours. He asks the public to help by buying only merchandise bearing the national insignia.

JULY 29, 1933

The stock market drifts for past few days with an average of about 88. Beginning next week the stock market will be open regular hours although the Chicago commodity markets are still under restriction.

Employers are beginning to protest because beginning next week they will have to raise wages, shorten hours and employ more help. The average department store clerk gets $7.50 a week or less. Under the new law the minimum will be $14 per week. Employers will comply with the law because they fear a boycott.

Strikes are getting more numerous around the country. I fear we may hear more about this in the near future.

AUGUST 1, 1933

The NRA (Nat'l Recovery Act) goes into effect today with higher pay and lower hours. It is hailed as a remarkable experiment that may change the future of U.S. business. It gives government almost complete control of business, wages, labor, hours, etc. Opinion as to its ultimate success is about evenly divided.

Co-incident with the first day of NRA control the stock market broke badly and losses averaged 1 to 10 points. Average is 83. Higher wages and shorter hours will mean smaller earnings for corporations in the near future. This may affect the prices of stocks. Talk of inflation has died down again and nothing radical has yet been done.

AUGUST 2, 1933

The coal strike situation in Western Pennsylvania gets steadily worse. 10,000 striking miners were added to the list yesterday. State troops are on the scene and several violent deaths are reported.

Law practice gets steadily worse instead of better. It is unbelievably bad. Days go by without a single fee. The few people who do come in are of no value.

Almost all the stores in town now have NRA signs pasted on their windows. In a great many cases they are juggling hours and wages so as to minimize the benefits of the act. So far there has been no boycotting.

It is interesting to note that up to the present time the government has taken no action against gold hoarders who refused to turn in their gold.

AUGUST 3, 1933

A good many "chiselers" are doing business under the N.R.A. sign. For instance one restaurant in town boosted wages of waitresses from $8 per week (plus meals) to $14 per week and then charged back $1 per day for meals. The government promises to prosecute such violations.

Since Roosevelt became President a war-time hysteria of public opinion has been created which makes it unpopular to criticize what he does. Even newspaper editorials have unanimously supported him so and refrained from honest criticism. I believe the honeymoon will soon be over.

The stock market lays down stringent rules to curb the small speculator. Hereafter accounts under $5000 must be margined at least 50%. Pools must be reported, customers now are under closer control, etc. It is probable that the government "suggested" these rules.

It is notable that in the working out of this "new deal" the banker has dropped out of the picture as a leader. The reverse was true before 1929.

A woman hangs a government-issued National Recovery Administration Blue Eagle poster in her restaurant window in 1934, identifying the establishment as a participant in the N.R.A. codes. (Franklin Delano Roosevelt Library)

Shortage of coal caused by coal strikes may curtail steel mill operations and also work an additional hardship on the small consumer next winter.

EDITOR'S NOTE

Political activist Eugene S. Daniell Jr., who later served as a nine-term state representative in New Hampshire, set off two tear-gas bombs near the ventilation system of the New York Stock Exchange in August 1933 to protest the imbalance of wealth between those on Wall Street and the rest of the country during the Depression. Daniell served thirty days in jail for the disruption.

AUGUST 5, 1933

The federal gov't calls a truce in the coal strike until a code for the coal industry is approved. It remains to be seen if the government can prevent strikes. If it fails then the entire NRA program is endangered.

Youngstown (and all other communities) is preparing a big publicity campaign to enlist public support for NRA. Dr. Philo has been made chairman of "minute-men" speakers who will address luncheon clubs, etc. It will be similar to the Liberty Loan campaign during the war. The word "boycott" will probably not be used but it will be a mark of patriotism to patronize only NRA merchants. This is the only feature I don't like.

Tear gas bombs thrown into the stock exchange yesterday cause it to close in middle of day.

Prices of food and other necessities still go up like a sky-rocket. It is becoming a serious problem for everybody—even those with jobs. All advertising warns people to buy before Sept. 1st. Already the increase ranges 40 to 100%.

Barbers boosted haircuts from 25¢ to 35¢ and now to 50¢.

Under the NRA all forms of workers are organizing for higher pay and shorter hours. Even the house-maids are beginning to organize.

AUGUST 9, 1933

It has always been interesting to know whether *in the long run* the speculator in stocks who bought and sold frequently made more money than the plodder who bought stocks and held on. The story is told of a young couple who used the following plan:

1. Starting in 1915 they regularly saved 10% of earnings and little by little bought sound common stocks.
2. They never speculated or sold and knew nothing about the stock market. In 15 years an original investment of $5000 was worth $100,000 because of dividends, split-ups etc. of the original stock.

This seems to be the sound rule for obtaining wealth but it requires patience which few possess:

1. Live on less than you earn—save at least 10%.
2. Invest, don't speculate so that none of the principal is lost. Re-invest the earnings.
3. Never sell a good stock unless the price is above its intrinsic value (as in 1929).

It is said that George F. Baker, the New York Banker, will always buy sound common stocks when they are being offered below intrinsic value and then he will never sell them except for very good reasons. He looks for his profit in the growth of the company rather than in the speculative increase of the market quotation.

The story cited about the young couple would not happen in ordinary time—the period from 1915 to 1930 covers a very unusual boom period. If this same couple had invested in Sheet & Tube stock from 1919 to 1929 they would have had about 125 shares in 1929 for an original investment of $5,000. If they had sold in 1929 at boom prices they would have received about $17,000. *But* if they had held on for 3 or 4 years more the stock market reached a low point of $6 per share or a total value of $725. Ordinarily an investment in good sound common stocks over a period of years will show an average dividend return of 5 or 6% with possibly a doubling or trebling of the original investment if the company is young and showed growth. Only the dividend would be received and no great growth in the original capital if the investment had been made in an old established company such as the Pennsylvania R.R. In the long run the return from a conservative common stock will probably be no greater than from a good bond. The growth comes only in the young companies and here the speculative element is always present. A great number of Youngstown families grew wealthy thru steady investment in the Y. Sheet & Tube thru its early years of growth. They were fortunate however because they picked a good one.

AUGUST 21, 1933

I have been so busy making speeches lately for the NRA that I have little time for anything else. I have been named a committee member of the Mahoning County Bar Association to help the NRA and so far I have been sent out to explain the law to the various trade associations that are being formed. Last week I appeared before the Ohio Hairdressers Association and also before the Sheet Metal Association. Wednesday I speak before the Mahoning Valley Garage Owners Association. The publicity campaign for NRA is getting warm and I will probably be called on every night for awhile. I had some misgivings about the NRA plan but decided that the only patriotic thing to do was to put aside these doubts and try to put the plan across.

Business with me continues stagnant altho there is considerable activity and the streets are crowded with shoppers. Two members of our family got jobs again (the 2 Joes), so apparently the NRA is getting results.

Inflation and the stock market have been temporarily shoved in the background altho I think we will hear from them again in the fall.

The NRA ballyhoo is in full swing. Flag-raising, caravans, speeches, radio, etc. Sunday I am scheduled to give 5 short talks before audiences in downtown movie theaters. Next week I will participate in a sketch over the radio to be given by the bar committee.

It is interesting to follow the course of "controlled inflation" which began in Chile about 18 months ago. For about a year after inflation started business boomed and everybody had money. Then the government started to pay off its huge indebtedness with printing press money and trouble started. Prices began to sky-rocket, strikes broke out because wages did not keep pace and now business seems at the verge of breakdown. It is the history of Germany over again.

The U.S. Agricultural program begins with the slaughtering of millions of hogs so that pork production will be curtailed and prices go up. Also 20% of all cotton, wheat, etc. is being plowed under to prevent overproduction. The U.S. gov't pays the farmer for his loss. I don't see how the destruction of basic food supplies can bring back prosperity when so many people are hungry. If inflation comes and there is a food shortage, it won't be very pleasant.

AUGUST 31, 1933

I just came back from an automobile trip to Wheeling, W.Va. I was amazed at the commercial activity in all the river towns from Steubenville down to Wheeling. Steel mills and coal mines are all humming and the streets of Wheeling were crowded with people. I saw very few vacant homes or stores. I could also see the advantage of a steel plant having its own coal mine on one side and Ohio River transportation on the other. Between Youngstown and Wheeling, however, the small pottery towns were in bad shape. Empty stores and homes and in some places grass growing in the streets.

Labor unions have added over a million members in past few months. Under NRA protection it seems as tho even such industries as steel, automobile and coal will be unionized. The possibilities for labor trouble are enormous.

I talked to an accountant today who has been out of work for 3 1/2 years. In spite of the NRA ballyhoo there are about eleven million unemployed men in the country today.

Roosevelt permits newly mined gold to be exported. The world market rate is about 35% above our currency rate.

The stock market has made very little progress for several weeks. Average at 95.

SEPTEMBER 1, 1933

Times are certainly exciting. The air is full of talk about NRA, codes and labor trouble. The hosiery mills near Philadelphia are on strike and yesterday two strikers are killed and 18 injured. Last night I was sent to Struthers to help organize their NRA drive. Talked to the heads of about 20 organizations and helped them with their plans. In Youngstown last night about 10,000 people attended a huge outdoor mass meeting. Military drills preceded the NRA talk.

It looks now as tho all labor will be unionized under the NRA. So far Henry Ford is the only large manufacturer to refuse to come in. Already Ford cars are being boycotted. One Ford car in Detroit bore the placard "Don't blame me. I was bought before the NRA."

I am still skeptical about the ultimate success of the plan.

SEPTEMBER 5, 1933

Yesterday was Labor Day and all over the U.S. huge gatherings of union labor groups hailed the "new deal." The Democratic Party is now hailed as the Party of the Laboring Man.

SEPTEMBER 13, 1933

I spoke on the NRA to the business men of Campbell last night and helped them organize. Dave Marwick also spoke. As time goes on I am getting more skeptical as to the ultimate success of the NRA. There is too much "chiseling" going on.

Considering the fact that the dollar is worth only about 65¢ in gold, prices of stocks and commodities are still down to bottom if quoted in price of gold. The difficulty is that this cheaper money is harder to get than ever before and does not benefit the ordinary consumer.

I am again forced to the conclusion that this depression will run its full course like every other depression. We have had 4 years of it so far—and that means another year or two of slow uphill progress. I don't believe NRA or inflation will hasten the process.

SEPTEMBER 16, 1933

The picture of the "New Deal" grows clearer each day. In this picture it seems that the labor group and the farmer group are the best organized and are getting the most benefits. Every decision so far seems to indicate that labor unions will soon include every industry and the open shop will be a thing of the past. In such a situation I believe a strong government agency should be maintained to see that no injustice is done to either labor or capital. The farm group has received many benefits so far but are now clamoring for direct inflation because prices of things they buy have increased faster than their income. Credit inflation is now proceeding in a rapid pace. Also a billion dollars will be loaned to employers under NRA. I believe the issue of more direct inflation will come to a head soon. In the meanwhile my law practice remains stagnant while commodity prices go up at a dizzying pace.

I am still talking for NRA. I spoke the other night to 150 Campbell business and professional men. Talked yesterday to about 1200 high school children and teachers at Campbell Memorial High School.

SEPTEMBER 25, 1933

The demand for direct currency inflation becomes more pronounced each day. It is led by the cotton growers and farmers. They threaten an "inflation" march to Washington. They admit that farm prices are bringing them more money but claim that the increase in the price of things they buy has left them worse off than ever. This is true. I find dollars harder to get than ever before in the depression and prices are up 40 to 100%. So far Roosevelt sticks to credit inflation thru purchase of U.S. Bonds by Federal Reserve Bank.

When inflation talk first started, the stock market boomed every time the word was mentioned. This is no longer true. Both the stock market, industry and the value of the dollar have been receding for several weeks. Last week the value of the dollar went to a low of 63¢.

Personally I am more concerned than ever that prosperity will return only when we stop tampering with the dollar. Business is afraid of all this uncertainty.

SEPTEMBER 28, 1933

More than 70,000 men are on strike in the coal fields of Western Pennsylvania and West Virginia. The movement is spreading rapidly to the steel mills which also own independent coal mines.

OCTOBER 7, 1933

I spoke yesterday to an audience of almost 3000 people on the NRA at an open-air meeting in Struthers Yellow Creek Park. Altogether I have so far addressed over 20,000 people on the subject. It has been mighty fine experience for me. In spite of this, as time goes on I grow more skeptical about the ultimate outcome of the program.

The strike situation grows worse and spreads from the coal fields to the steel industry.

The government starts a huge program of "credit inflation." Millions of dollars are being loaned to industry, banks, slum elimination, etc. In France this credit inflation preceded direct currency inflation.

In the meanwhile business is flat again after 2 months of hectic buying on fear of inflation and higher prices. The average citizen earning $16 per week finds he can buy less now than before. Prices are so high as to bring on a buyer's strike.

The stock market has been drifting aimlessly for several weeks with a downward tendency.

In the last 6 weeks (under NRA) the American Federation of Labor has increased its membership from 500,000 to over four million. It is now demanding a 30-hour week and higher wages instead of the 40 hour week mentioned in most of the codes.

OCTOBER 11, 1933

Strikes continue to hold the center of attention. 75,000 coal miners are still on strike in Pennsylvania and Illinois. Violence has appeared and state militia have been called out. Also thousands of steel workers are on strike in Wheeling-Steubenville district. Here also militia have been called out. So far the Youngstown area has been clear but this morning pickets appeared at Republic Steel. Police are watching the pickets. Technical recognition of the unions is the cause for striking rather than wages or hours. It is hard to believe that men can be reduced to strike after 3 years of idleness.

In the meanwhile business remains flat and dull with no fall pick-up. The NRA starts a 12 week "buy now" campaign with a lot of ballyhoo. Most people don't have to be urged to buy—but haven't the money.

The stock market has been stagnant for about 6 weeks with an average of 90. Bonds continue strong.

The monetary question is quiet while the government continues its credit expansion program by buying U.S. bonds and lending huge sums for public works and private industry. The NRA has failed to produce promised results.

OCTOBER 12, 1933

Two years ago tomorrow the 3 large local banks closed their doors. The money on deposit there is still frozen tight even tho the banks are open.

A good many Youngstown people doubled their money recently by a speculation in Central Loan Co. pass books. They bought at about 22 and are selling today at 45. The rise in price caused by receiver filing application in court to be permitted to exchange mortgages and real estate for pass books. Here again we have proof that it is wise for the investor to have liquid assets on hand so he can take advantage of these opportunities. A small fund could be kept for this special purpose.

I am still talking on NRA. Tonight I speak at a banquet of auto accessory dealers and Sunday afternoon I speak before a group of bakers.

OCTOBER 13, 1933

I just finished reading a book called *Mellon's Millions*. In all their business ventures they conservatively built up huge cash surpluses during time of prosperity. When a panic came they were able to absorb competitors for a song. During prosperous days their corporations advanced steadily but during depression they advanced by leaps and bounds. They showed rare business judgment. For instance they sold their ship-building company for an enormous price in 1917 at the height of the war boom—but the market for ships was gutted by time war ended. In 1930 they sold McClintic-Marshall Steel Co. to Bethlehem for an enormous price and on top of that Bethlehem assumed 12 million of McClintic Bonds. Since 1930 no steel co. has ever earned interest on bonds.

OCTOBER 18, 1933

On Monday the stock market fell in one day from an average of 89 to 74. Yesterday it climbed back again to 81. Wall Street seems to have concluded that there will be no radical printing-press inflation in the next few weeks. In the meanwhile business continues stagnant and no fall rise.

I am still delivering speeches for NRA. Talked last night in Sebring at an open-air meeting before more than 5000 people. The speaking program was preceded by a parade with over 100 floats, 16 bands, a flag-raising by Legionnaires, singing of patriotic songs, etc. It was an inspiring demonstration. Other speakers included Congressman John J. Cooper and Dave Marwick, the local NRA leader.

OCTOBER 25, 1933

Two big announcements were made last week:

1. U.S. takes steps to recognize Russia. It is thought this will help our foreign trade.
2. U.S. will establish a gold market and the gov't will buy and sell gold in order to raise prices. Some think it means a "rubber dollar." Others think it means inflation. In theory, if government pays $40 per ounce as contrasted to old price of $20 per ounce, the dollar becomes worth 50¢ and prices should rise accordingly. It is too complex for me and I have my doubts. In meanwhile stock market goes up on these two items of news.

OCTOBER 27, 1933

The first 4 days of the experiment tend to disprove the government theory that raising the price of gold will raise the price of commodities. On the first day, both stock and commodity prices went up but in last 3 days they went down—even tho the price of gold was boosted daily to almost $32 per ounce.

The government buys only domestic gold as yet and pays for it in short term debentures.

On Foreign Exchange the dollar goes up. This can be controlled by buying gold on the international markets.

The whole subject is very confusing and for this reason seems to retard business more than help it.

For the first time since the depression Republic Steel showed small profit last quarter. Sheet & Tube lost over a million as compared to a 3 million loss the preceding quarter.

Law and other professions are still hard hit. Most lawyers and doctors do not take in enough cash to pay office rent. I think the large offices with big pay-rolls are hit the hardest.

I am going to speak on NRA next Friday at a mass meeting in Columbiana.

Since the government has gone into the business of buying gold, a great many old abandoned gold mines are now bustling with activity.

OCTOBER 31, 1933

U.S. announces she will now buy gold on international markets. Stocks and prices go down. Adverse criticism against the President's plan is being openly expressed for the first time. I think we will hear more of this in near future. France is being forced to point of going off gold. If U.S. intends to further depress the dollar it will hurt England and France and may result in a money war because neither country wants to lose its gold. If U.S. merely proposed to stabilize the dollar then probably the other countries will cooperate and no harm will be done.

I handled a small case yesterday involving violation of the NRA rules by a local merchant. Many of these matters are now ending up in court.

NOVEMBER 4, 1933

I talked at a Columbiana NRA mass meeting last night. It was preceded by a parade, bands, torch lights and all the trimmings of a patriotic demonstration.

Groups are being formed all over the country to oppose the President's monetary policy and to demand a return to the gold standard. Yesterday the New York Chamber of Commerce passed a resolution to this effect.

In five Western states the farmers are on a "holiday strike" again. By picketing they will prevent the sale of wheat etc. at present prices. They demand inflation and a guaranteed level of prices high enough to absorb the increased cost of the things they buy.

In Cleveland over 200 lawyers have had their office phones disconnected because of inability to pay the bills.

In spite of all the excitement, business is again on the downgrade. There has been no fall upturn. My own business is at a complete standstill. The attitude of the public toward NRA has become very cynical.

NOVEMBER 7, 1933

Business has slumped so badly this fall that we seem to be in another "panic." Steel mills in Youngstown are down to 25% production; men hired under NRA are being laid off; farmers are on strike in 5 states; buyers won't buy on account of high prices; the dollar depreciates to almost 60¢ and makes the pound worth 4.92; a currency war threatens with Great Britain; France threatens to go off gold. All in all it seems as tho the President's plan is facing a crisis. He is fighting back over the radio and by sending speakers to the troubled farm areas. Both public opinion and the Republican Party are voicing criticism of the monetary policy and of the NRA. The constant threat of possible inflation keeps the stock average up to 84. Truscon sells at 4 1/2; Sheet & Tube at 17; Republic 10, etc.

A client came in this morning who is being sued for balance on a "financial service" he subscribed to in 1931. Refuses to pay because they gave him bad advice. Told him to sell good stocks and switched him into more speculative issues now in receivership.

NOVEMBER 8, 1933

In yesterday's election the 18th Amendment (Prohibition) was repealed. It all happened in less than 18 months and the 1st 36 states voted repeal. Two—North and So. Carolina—voted dry.

Present unrest was shown by election results. In almost every city the "ins" were replaced by the dissatisfied "outs." Cleveland and New York substituted Republican mayors for Democratic and in other cities the reverse was true. Voters are dissatisfied and are ready to make any change. If this continues long it may create a Republican Congress next fall.

NOVEMBER 10, 1933

Because of the depreciating value of the dollar government bonds are beginning to slip. During the past week they went down from 100 to 96. Large investors are buying foreign bonds and stocks payable in gold. Europe seems convinced we are headed for wild inflation and says we can no longer stop it. The "new deal" will add about fifteen billion dollars to the government indebtedness.

I have been hearing "armistice day" speeches all week. They are all cynical. Sixteen years ago under Wilson we became "internationally minded." We fought in the "war to end war" and today the world is in chaos with constant threat of war. We loaned billions to Europe and now can't get it back. Time and again in this period the U.S. interfered in European affairs as a good Samaritan and every time we got a spanking. Because of these huge loans and the neglect of our internal affairs, our country is today facing one of the most serious crises in her history. With all its dangers it seems that the world is not yet ready for internationalism and our best policy for the present is to keep our fingers out of Europe. If the war debt is never paid it may stand as a monumental warning against committing a similar failing again. War veterans are most bitter because most of them were uprooted by the war and were never able to get started again. For a good many of them this depression ended all hope.

The U— family of Youngstown is following the policy of the Mellons of Pittsburgh. They are buying downtown real estate that has been foreclosed for the price of the 1st mortgage and paying even this low price in bank books which they bought as low as 50¢ on the dollar. Yesterday legal news showed the purchase of 49 feet on E. Federal St. with building (lot 181) from Home Savings & Loan for about $25,000 in pass books—or about $13,000 in cash. In normal times the property was considered valuable enough for a 1st mortgage bank loan of $25,000.

Law practice is very disagreeable. A good deal of it consists of trying to collect money from people who are helpless. Grown men and women come into the office and break into tears when they try to tell their story. So far I have been able to work out every situation without causing any harm. It is a thankless job.

A woman just came in to consult me about some government Hungarian bonds she purchased during the war. They are today entirely worthless.

The "forgotten" men of today are the doctors, lawyers, insurance men, etc. They are down and out and can do very little about it.

NOVEMBER 15, 1933

This is the 5th winter of the depression and it is blackest of all. The weather has been biting cold and thousands of families in Youngstown are suffering for lack of food and clothing. About 50,000 people in this city will have to be put on public relief.

A growing list of substantial men express the fear that U.S. is now in for bad inflation and that we have gone too far to turn about. This is because the government is pouring an endless stream of money into all kinds of pet schemes to revive business—into the NRA, agriculture, frozen banks, public works, mortgage loans, slum clearance, industrial loans, etc. Total U.S. indebtedness will soon exceed $35 billion—and in meanwhile tax collection has almost disappeared, industry is stagnant and private initiative at low ebb. Industries can't sell bond issues and turn to the government, banks won't loan money, people won't invest, expand or build b/c monetary uncertainty. People who have money buy foreign bonds or stocks. I think the time is ripe for an able leader to take up the issue for sound currency. Loyalty to the President ceases to be a virtue when he violates basic laws which may bring great harm to the country. The American dollar is listed on foreign exchange at 61¢ and the pound (without gold backing) at $5.15. A few weeks ago the pound stood at $3.40. Price of gold is over $33 an ounce. Government bonds are still going down. Stocks are stationary at 88. The threat of inflation is so imminent that many people are buying low priced common stocks—especially commodity stocks such as oil companies— where the companies have large sources of raw material which would increase in value.

NOVEMBER 16, 1933

Secretary of Treasury [William] Woodin resigns yesterday because he is not sympathetic to the President's monetary policy. So far more than a dozen resignations have taken place since March and in each case have been replaced by men who believe in the "new deal."

NOVEMBER 18, 1933

The U.S. formally recognizes Russia yesterday and this is hailed as the big news of the day. It is hoped we will be able to sell her machinery, etc. The old Russian monarchy still owes U.S. many millions for purchases before and during the war. When the Soviets took control they refused to recognize the old indebtedness and defaulted all bond issues. The Soviets now promise to "consider" these claims but probably nothing will come of it.

U.S. gov't announces it will help the relief situation this winter by paying $15 per week for 1 million jobs to unemployed. In this way Youngstown is putting about 2000 men to work cleaning streets, parks, etc. Cleveland will employ about 40,000 in the same way.

It is interesting to note that so far the raising of price of gold has failed to raise domestic prices. Not many months ago farmers claimed that raising the price of gold to $30 an ounce would restore agricultural prices. This has not happened. The price is now over $33 and the farmers are in a worse plight than ever.

It is also interesting to note that the effort to create credit by having the Federal Reserve Bank buy U.S. bonds in the open market has failed. Huge reservoirs of credit are available but banks won't make loans because business is too uncertain. It seems to prove that when business starts moving credit will expand automatically but the artificial creation of credit will not expand business.

The theory that raising gold prices will raise domestic prices and that this in turn will create prosperity also seems to be doomed to failure. Briefly the theory is as follows: When times are booming people earn more, buy more and prices go up. But is it true that raising prices will bring back prosperity by reversing the process? As it now works out, the higher prices go the less people buy because they have no earning power. It does not seem logical. Seems like putting the cart before the horse. Yet Pres. Roosevelt and his supporters insist that they will carry the experiment thru and that it is too early to judge results.

The U.S. Treasury will face the task in a few weeks of paying out a huge amount for bond interest and maturities. Where will the money come from—greenbacks?

NOVEMBER 20, 1933

Several thousand unemployed men stormed the Allied Council rooms today to get one of the government relief jobs. About 1000 will be put to work at once.

The U.S. Chamber of Commerce takes a public stand against President Roosevelt's gold policy and demands a return to sound money and the gold standard. The President strikes back by calling them a bunch of "tories." Remembering that George Washington would not accept Continental currency in his business dealings I do not quite see the parallel implied by the use of the term.

NOVEMBER 21, 1933

Prof. [O. M. W.] Sprague (formerly of Harvard) resigns from the Treasury and in a scathing letter made public criticizes the President's monetary policy and calls on the public to fight for sound money. The issue is becoming clearly defined and he may be the leader needed to crystallize public opinion. Three years ago Sprague resigned his professorship at Harvard to accept a position as monetary advisor to British gov't at $40,000 per year. When U.S. went off gold standard he accepted the call to the U.S. Treasury as a patriotic duty and at a yearly salary of $6,000. Since then his advice has been ignored and the only honorable thing left to do was to resign. Roosevelt studied economics under him at Harvard. His resignation is the big news of the day. This leaves the Treasury in full charge of men sympathetic to present monetary policy. Sprague bases his criticism on two points:

1. Raising price of gold will not raise the price of domestic articles as long as industry is stagnant and people are broke. Industrial production and wages must first increase thru normal recovery and the rest follows.
2. The new deal is bankrupting the credits of U.S. by pouring endless millions into various pet schemes. The inevitable result must be printing press money and wild inflation.

NOVEMBER 23, 1933

Sprague's resignation and criticism seem to have fired the revolt on the money question. Today's papers are full of the pros and cons of the question. It may become a bitter issue in the Congressional campaign next fall.

Business remains completely stagnant in spite of all the excitement. There is simply nothing doing and nothing you can do about it. We seem to be in the midst of another bad lull with everybody waiting for a break.

NOVEMBER 24, 1933

General opinion seems to be that Pres. Roosevelt is facing a crisis on the monetary question and that he will soon have to turn either to the left (printing press money) or to the right (stabilization and return to gold standard). In eight months of experiment the tangible improvement is slight, business on the down grade, distrust growing and huge public debt arousing fear as to the government credit. It is a very difficult time for everybody.

EDITOR'S NOTE

Despite the flurry of legislation and dramatic overhaul of the New Deal's early efforts, joblessness did not immediately improve. The American Federation of Labor estimated in April 1933 that there were 13 million Americans unemployed, up from 12 million in November 1932. To remedy this, in November 1933 Roosevelt adviser Harry Hopkins hastily assembled a plan and a $400 million budget to create the Civil Works Administration to provide federal jobs for unemployed Americans to build roads, parks, playgrounds, airports, and the like. Roth would begin to see the effects in his community almost immediately, and by Christmas some 3.5 million Americans had CWA jobs.

DECEMBER 12, 1933

Talk of inflation has died down since opposition to the President's gold policy became vocal. Very little activity in the gold market, dollar is still quoted at 60¢ and the stock-market stationary. A government bond issue of a million dollars was oversubscribed—money to be used to meet Dec. 15th interest and refunding requirements. This increased confidence. Meanwhile basic business conditions are getting better. Corporations which pared down overhead to rock bottom are now getting in a position to pay back dividends. I do not think this improvement is due to the manipulations of the new deal. The local relief problem has been solved by putting about 10,000 men to work at the government expense. They get $15 per week and dig ditches, clear parks, widen streets. None of the work is very essential. It is really a dole because local relief was unable to function. Both Morris and Joe went back to work Monday after intermittent unemployment of 3 years. Morris works as a draftsman for the city and Joe works as a book-keeper in Cleveland. Both jobs temporary.

DECEMBER 13, 1933

Col. Leonard Ayres made his annual prediction yesterday for 1934. It was not optimistic. The following are the highlights:

a. 1934 will be another depression year like 1933.
b. There will be continued manipulation of the currency but no uncontrolled inflation.
c. The NRA will fail of its purpose because it stimulates only "consumer goods"—not heavy industries.
d. Private financing is essential to recovery and this has been stopped by monetary fears and gov't regulations.
e. Prices of consumer goods will rise and these mfrs of radios, autos etc. will make money.
f. The stock market will be inactive and will move within narrow limits.

DECEMBER 27, 1933

The retail merchants report the best Christmas season since the depression started. The weather was perfect and the streets were jammed with shoppers. The situation was helped by the fact that over 12,000 people in Youngstown alone have been drawing good pay from the government on CWA projects. Also the City of Youngstown issued $450,000 in scrip to pay out about five months back pay. This scrip is redeemable in 5 years out of delinquent taxes. It is being accepted without discount by most of the stores. All in all there is more optimism this year than last year although the law business has not benefited much.

Otherwise the monetary and business situation remains unchanged. Roosevelt ordered the government to buy a limited amount of newly mined silver and boosts the price from 32¢ to 64¢ per ounce. The amount involved is too small to affect the money situation but it is giving a "hand-out" to the silver states just as he helped the farmers etc. Roosevelt is building up a tremendous following but is also building a huge government indebtedness which will someday be paid.

I just listened to a hard luck story as told by J. G. Was in liquor business in pre-Prohibition days. Came to Youngstown in 1926 with $200,000 in cash. Went into business of loaning money on 2nd mortgages and real estate and charged big bonuses. Pyramided by borrowing on these mortgages. When slump started he used all available cash to protect his 2nd mtges by buying in the properties at foreclosure. Today he has the properties but in each instance they are worth less than the 2nd mortgage. Would gladly hand them back to the bank if they would release him—but they refuse to. Is flat broke and looking for an opening in some other line. He does not think real estate will come back for several years. Also went into beer business a short time ago but lost what little he had left.

DECEMBER 28, 1933

The Secretary of the Treas. issues a new order calling in all gold in private hands. It will be paid for at the old price of 20.34 per ounce instead of the world market price of 36. This may be result of a lower court ruling that the 1st order was illegal because issued by the President instead of by the Secy of the Treasury. On the other hand it may be a preliminary step to devaluation.

Year end stock prices are about the same as during past few months.

Just finished reading a book entitled *Our Mysterious Panics* by Colman. He gives brief history of every panic from 1819 to 1929. Comes to conclusion that every panic is brought on by human greed and speculation instead of by complex economic cycles. Reasoning seems logical and as follows:

1. After a depression comes a slow return to normal.
2. A few years of "normal business," men get too optimistic and begin to over expand, speculate, etc.
3. Speculation leads to fraudulent stock issues, embezzlement, new theories such as "new era."
4. Then comes the crash or panic caused by over-expansion, fraud, embezzlement, & human greed.

It is also interesting to note the dates of these panics. They seem to recur more frequently in last 35 years:

1837–Panic caused by land craze and Western expansion
1857–California gold rush—new gold
1873–Post–Civil War. Too much R.R. expansion
1884–Gambling bankers
1893–Over-development big trusts—silver questions
1901–Too many mergers: U.S. Steel, Bethlehem; Youngstown Sheet & Tube
1907–Battling bankers—money panic

1914–Panic stopped by coming world war

1921–Primary post-war Panic

1929–New Era philosophy—fallacy that common stocks are best form of investment

The intervals between panics are 20 years—16 yrs—11 years—9 years—8 years—6 years—7 years—7 years—8 years. These periods count from the *beginning* of each preceding panic. The 1929 panic is not yet over but will end probably in 1935. On a 7 year average there should be a small depression in 1937 and a more severe depression in 1942–3. It is certainly not a pleasant picture. The only answers seems to be to keep investments fairly liquid always during "normal" times. Then even if panic comes unexpectantly you will have cash to buy bargains to the limit. Then liquidation again when "normal" times return.

The major panics came at longer intervals: 1837—1857—1873—1893—1907—1929. The intervals are 20 years—16 years—20 years—14 years—21 years. The average is about 15 years. If this is correct then the next major panic should come sometime after 1944 which gives about 10 years "normal."

CHAPTER 5
JANUARY 10, 1934–NOVEMBER 6, 1936

"It has been a long, dreary road."

While President Roosevelt initiated many dramatic new programs in his much examined, much hailed First Hundred Days, it would actually take another year or so for Roth and most white-collar Americans to experience any real, practical impact from the New Deal. Nearly twelve million Americans, for example, were still out of work by the end of 1934. It would take until the months leading up to President Roosevelt's reelection in 1936 before West Federal Street in Youngstown, as well as other main streets in America, witnessed a "boom" unmatched in post-1929 life: shopping for home furnishings and clothing, new autos on the road, and steel mills operating at 80 percent capacity. Rather, 1934 and 1935 were years in which parts of the New Deal proved successful, parts failed, and parts were overturned by the Supreme Court.

One relative success story, noted by Roth, was Roosevelt's Home Owners Loan Corporation, which saved many families from foreclosure and homelessness. The program helped rescue home owners from foreclosure and banks from bad loans. The administration offered banks the chance to trade defaulted loans for government bonds. Home owners could refinance their homes with twelve-year mortgages rather than the common five-year plan. The HOLC ended up refinancing one in five home mortgages under this plan and laid the foundation for a renewed—and more stable—mortgage-lending practice that would last for decades to come. Says Schlesinger of the HOLC, "Probably no single measure consolidated so much middle-class support for the administration."

The Federal Deposit Insurance Corporation of 1933 also counts as an almost instant success, and its continued existence has doubtlessly prevented the kind of widespread bank closures that Roth observed. By federally insuring bank deposit accounts up to five hundred dollars (via a small tax on bank deposits), the run on bank withdrawals that had paralyzed the system since the Great Crash of 1929 stopped. In fact, the number of banks that had to shutter for the remainder of the 1930s was less than 8 percent of the total that closed in just 1933. By April 1934 Roth witnessed his local Dollar and City banks remove their restrictions on withdrawals of fourteen million dollars in frozen deposits.

Other initiatives, however, sputtered. The Agricultural Administration Act passed quickly in May 1933 with a lofty aim: to return farmers to the income level and prosperity they experienced between 1909 and 1914. It also provided the secretary of agriculture with grand powers: The AAA paid farmers who agreed to cut their production output by one-third and entered into marketing agreements with processors. Much to the bewilderment of Roth and many Americans, the AAA even destroyed some existing overproduction (including the slaughter of eight and a half million piglets to boost hog farmers' income as people starved in many parts of the country) that would drive prices down if the surplus made it to the market. On one level the AAA was a success: It enabled gross farm income to increase by 50 percent between 1932 and 1936. But overall it failed: The program boosted farmers' income at the cost of taxing processors, distributors, and American households, which footed the entire bill.

In fact, by February 1935 housewives across the country picketed local butchers with signs proclaiming, "Down with high meat prices!" In Los Angeles ten thousand women boycotted meat shops until the prices dropped by five cents a pound. In New York and Chicago, similar organized protests ensued. Eventually, the courts became involved; many lawsuits were filed in 1934 claiming that the AAA's practices were unjust. In 1936 the U.S. Supreme Court ruled in *United States v. Butler* that the AAA was unconstitutional and coercive. It found, in a six-to-three decision, that the Constitution did not give the federal government the right to use its power to levy taxes on processed foods as a means to regulate the economy and subsidize farmers' profits. As a result, more than two hundred million dollars in illegal fees were returned to food-processing companies.

1934

From all reports this has been the wildest and happiest New Year in 5 years. Liquor was legal for the first time. Every hotel, theater and club was jammed New Year's Eve. The stores repeated their Christmas rush last Saturday and it was almost impossible to get thru the streets. Everybody had a little money and seemed anxious to spend it. Everywhere I met optimism for 1934. [Economic theorist Roger] Babson made a special prediction for Youngstown saying we would see a 25% improvement here on account of heavier steel production. This is contrary to [Cleveland financier Leonard] Ayres report.

All in all 1933 has been a terrible year for everybody. From January to March business was at a standstill while everybody waited for the new President to come in. Then came the closing of the banks all over the country. The balance of the year was exciting enough with talk of inflation, NRA, AAA, etc. but very little actual business. The coming year will probably see considerable debate on the currency question and on other Roosevelt measures, but all in all I feel optimistic and think there will be considerable improvement. President Roosevelt is still the idol of the great mass of people and receives over a million New Year greetings. It is almost dangerous to question any of his theories or statements.

The stock market closed the year with an average of 90 as contrasted with an average of 49 at the end of 1932.

JANUARY 10, 1934

In a recent message to Congress dealing with the Budget, Pres. Roosevelt revealed that a deficit of over six billion has been incurred by the "new deal" since March 1933 and four billion more by deficit can be expected in 1934. The government expects to float a $10 billion bond issue in the next few months to cover this.

Interesting question. Can such a huge loan be floated? Will stabilization be necessary first so the public will buy the bonds? Are we heading for inflation? This deficit will bring U.S. indebtedness to the huge total of $32 billion.

James Truslow Adams in his *March of American Democracy* points out that the 1873 panic lasted 5 full years and recovery started in the 6th year. After 1879 came fairly good business until 1884 when a short panic of a year or so took place. Then business was good until 1890. From 1890 to 1893 was a period of falling agricultural prices, grumbling about monetary

When FDR legalized beer sales within the first days of his administration in March 1933, bands played "Happy Days Are Here Again" in Times Square in New York City. The Twenty-first Amendment, repealing the Eighteenth Amendment's ban on alcohol, was fully ratified on December 5, 1933, just weeks before many New Year's parties like this one in New York City on January 1, 1934. (©Bettmann/CORBIS)

greatness, etc. strikes and finally the crash in 1893. The 1893 panic really lasted only about 3 years.

U.S. Panic Records 1873 to Date

1873–1879	Major panic. Recovery in 1879.
1880–1884	Good times.
1884–1885	Short panic.
1885–1890	Good times.
1891–1893	Falling prices and warning of panic.
1893–1896	Panic.
1897–1901	Good times.
1901–1902	Short panic.
1902–1907	Good times
1907–1908	Short panic but severe.
1908–1914	Good times.
1914	Panic threatened but stopped by war.
1914–1921	War time prosperity.
1921	Primary war panic.
1922–1929	Good times.
1929–1935	Panic.

As to the future???

1940	A short panic.
1950	A major panic.

JANUARY 15, 1934

An important monetary development took place today. President Roosevelt asked Congress:

1. To devalue the gold dollar to between 50% and 60%.
2. Permit the government to seize about $3 1/2 billion in gold now held in the vaults of the Federal Reserve Banks. The government would pay for it at the old rate of $20.67 per ounce as contrasted to the market of $34.50. Immediate results would be:
   1. Government would make an immediate profit of over $4 billion.
   2. Government could issue about $10 billion more currency using this $4 billion gold increase as a 40% backing.
   3. The possibility of rising prices has become more certain.

The entire situation has exciting possibilities and is being discussed on every street corner. Everybody is trying to figure out how it will affect them personally. The stock market is booming again.

JANUARY 20, 1934

The House of Representatives passed the 50–60 devaluation gold bill by an overwhelming vote of 360 to 40. There was almost no debate. It will now go to the Senate. The stock market went up about 7 points since the announcement and is still strong.

It seems that this is a good time to buy out a "sick business" and nurse it back to health by putting in new capital, adding new products, etc. Many businesses which were worthwhile before the depression can now be bought for a song.

My brother Joe is out of work again. Morris is still employed by the government (CWA) as a draftsman in the city engineering department. But his hours have been cut from 48 to 30. All CWA work will probably stop in a few weeks for lack of funds. This will put unemployment back where it was before.

JANUARY 24, 1934

A storm of protest is sweeping over USA over stopping CWA work by which thousands of men are employed by the government on public improvements (about 40,000 in Cleveland and 12,000 in Youngstown). The government is paying out about 75 million per week for this. To continue much longer will bankrupt the nation. On the other hand private industry has not improved and cannot absorb these men. The people have gotten used to looking to the government for help and the average man does not stop to consider where the money is coming from or how it is to be paid back.

JANUARY 30, 1934

Congress has passed the gold bill and it is believed that the President will formally devalue the dollar in the next few days. As a result, the stock market boomed yesterday and averages went up to 102.

Today however the stock market was irregular and receded. The stock market has not yet penetrated the inflation high of last July.

JANUARY 31, 1934

Big news for Youngstown. The U.S. Army Engineers have approved the canal for Youngstown. It is hoped to build it with government money as a Public Works project and thus eliminate the red tape of getting an appropriation from Congress. It will be 27 feet wide and run from the Ohio and Beaver Rivers at Rochester, Pa. to Struthers. Total cost estimated at about $40 million.

FEBRUARY 8, 1934

The past few days has seen considerable excitement on monetary questions. The President formally devalues the dollar to 59.04% of its former value, making gold worth 35 per ounce. The stock market rushes up from an average of 99 to 104. Yesterday, however, it starts down again caused mostly by the precarious continuation of the gold standard in France. In the meanwhile millions of dollars worth of gold are being rushed by the fastest ships from Europe to America. This is caused by two reasons: 1. To take advantage of the higher price of gold over here. 2. To speculate in American securities which are expected to rise with prices. In addition to this, considerable gold is coming back which was scared away at the time we went off the gold standard.

Everybody is optimistic and prospects for spring look good. Both steel and automobile trades are the best in years.

Rioting takes place in France and conditions border on revolution. This is the 8th time the government has changed in past two years. It is feared that either Communism or Fascism will gain control. In the past year France just started to feel the real depression. Inflation caused by other countries going off the gold has aggravated the situation. Her people are too excitable to take a thing like this quietly. There is no telling where it will end.

FEBRUARY 16, 1934

The European situation gets steadily worse and another war threatens. Revolution has broken out in both Austria and France and several thousands are killed. In Austria it seems to be a struggle between the Socialists, the Communists and Fascism or Nazi-ism. In the meanwhile, Italy collects troops on the Austrian border.

In the U.S. the situation is very little changed except that spring business is better. My own business remains stagnant. Even tho' the dollar has been devalued 40% it has so far made very little practical difference. It still buys

$1.29 merchandise as compared to 1923 but the income of the average man is much less.

Stocks fluctuate in a narrow range with average about 100: Truscon 8; S&T 29; U.S. Steel 56.

MARCH 5, 1934

A year has passed since Roosevelt inaugurated his "new deal." Through various agencies he created the government has poured huge amounts of money to help industry, the banks, and people in distress. It is said that today almost 1 out of every 4 people is being supported by the government. It seems impossible to stop and to continue means disastrous inflation. Private industry has so far failed to respond and for awhile even the deflated dollar is forgotten. The following are only a few of the governmental agencies created to spend money:

P.W.A.—Public Works Administration—To remedy unemployment by gov't building of canals, etc.

C.W.A.—Civil Works Administration—Hiring men on gov't pay to work on local sewer projects, etc.

A.A.A.—Agricultural Admin.—Helps farmer and pays him not to raise surplus wheat, cotton, etc.

N.R.A.—Nat'l Recovery Admin—Controls industry, wages, hours, etc. and puts blue eagle on all who obey.

Roosevelt is as popular today as a year ago. His following with the working class is tremendous. It seems he and the Democrats will be in power for some time. Socialism is now accepted calmly by ministers, professors, etc. and it is amazing to me to see how calmly most people accept drastic government regulation. Personally I am convinced this reform wave will pass and we will return to the old order with some of the abuses remedied.

None of the professional classes have benefitted from the new deal. My law practice is still at rock bottom—altho there is plenty of work but no remuneration. I believe the laboring class has benefited most of all.

Business in general is fundamentally better although with so much shouting and excitement it is difficult to know the real state of affairs. Banks are all open but not making loans. Most foreclosures have been stopped by government loans thru the Home Loan Corporation. All in all it has been an exciting and eventful year with every citizen keenly interested in government.

MARCH 16, 1934

The spring advance continues and merchants are looking for a big spring season. It also seems to me that law practice shows a few signs of awakening from its long slumber.

Within the past two months chain stores have been taking leases on Federal St. stores and very few are now available at low rentals. The tendency of landlords everywhere is to boost rentals in anticipation of better business. The only cloud in the picture is the possibility of a nationwide strike in the automobile business.

I also think we are beginning to see a reversal of trend against those policies of Roosevelt that smack of socialism.

EDITOR'S NOTE

Empowered by section 7(a) of the National Industry Recovery Act, union organizers signed up thousands of workers at plants and mills across the country. In 1934 alone more than eighteen hundred strikes ensued involving almost 1.5 million workers demanding better wages and an improved working environment. Their actions met with much violence at times, as the National Guard or local police were deployed to break up the strikes. From textile workers in Massachusetts and Georgia to autoworkers in Toledo and longshoremen in San Francisco, hundreds of union strikers were injured, some killed, in their fight for better working conditions. Roosevelt responded in June 1934 by creating the National Labor Relations Board to mediate the talks between labor unions and business leaders. But the board found it was powerless to enforce rulings. Roosevelt ultimately accepted the fact that employees and management couldn't rely on mediation to come to an agreement on their own. In 1938 Roosevelt would sign the Fair Labor Standards Act as one way to resolve some disputes, with the federal government stepping in to create a national minimum wage and maximum forty-hour workweek.

MARCH 22, 1934

The country is now threatened by huge national strikes in the auto and railroad industries. The A.F. of L. claims that the codes under the NRA give them the right to the closed shop. Industry has fostered "company unions" and refuses the demand of A.F. of L. for recognition. Industry is apparently willing to fight out the issue either with strikes or in court. A truce of 48 hours has been granted so Pres. Roosevelt can step in.

Radical socialism seems rampant in every class of society but mostly ministers and college professors. This has spread to the working class. They no longer ask for favors but "demand" government work, cancellation of mortgages, reduction of debts, etc. They feel the courts will not permit foreclosure of mortgages or ejectments, etc.

The fact that 2nd mortgages are a poor investment is now conclusively proven by the HOLC refinancing. Every time the property is appraised by government appraisers for the purpose of refinancing with government bonds, the appraisal is so low as to leave nothing for the 2nd mortgage holder. If he refuses to cancel voluntarily, he will be wiped out by foreclosure. Most of the 2nd mortgages held by my clients have proven to be worthless.

The opinion is spreading among thoughtful people that many features of the new deal are not helping recovery but retarding it. "Managed industry" under NRA has opened doors to further management and control of wages, hours, prices, unions, stock-market, etc. Managed currency has been temporarily forgotten but the 59¢ dollar has failed to help. Destruction of farm surplus is questioned. Is it really true that raising wages, cutting hours by these methods will bring prosperity? I think not. It seems to me that natural economic forces would do the job better under fair competition without too much supervision. The stock market remains stagnant at a 95 average.

MARCH 23, 1934

Another truce of 48 hours has been given in the threatened nationwide auto strike. The issue is the closed shop—not wages or hours. In the meanwhile smaller strikes are breaking out all over the country. By unionizing and striking at an important subsidiary of a large corporation the A.F. of L. is able to tie up the whole industry because it can't operate without the products of that subsidiary.

The period of early recovery in every depression of the past has been marked by big strikes. Labor wants to guarantee itself a proper share of the increased profits. The situation this time is complicated by the NRA which guarantees labor the right to collective bargaining.

APRIL 2, 1934

The auto strike has been settled by appointing an arbitration board. Steel industry raises wages 10%. Rumblings of small strikes are heard all over the country but there is nothing serious in sight.

The retail merchants have just had the best Easter season in five years. Stores were jammed for over a week. The weather was ideal.

Sentiment continues to get better. It may be due partly to the fine spring weather.

The government stops all CWA work and fires thousands of men. They are all going back on the charity list. Due to the increase of this kind of work our Joe went to work today for the Allied Council.

APRIL 11, 1934

Business continues to improve. Youngstown steel mills operate at 58%—best since 1929. Retail trade continues to boom after a fine Easter season. Storerooms on Federal St. are almost all taken—mostly by chain organizations. One of my clients took a lease last week on a store-room near the square and was offered a $5000 bonus for it by an out-of-town jewelry concern.

In spite of all this the law business continues to lag. Also about 6000 men who lost their CWA jobs with the government are again applying to the Allied Council for relief. The stock market remains stationary with an average of about 96. With increasing signs of returning prosperity, I hear less radical talk and business men appear less willing to sponsor government control of their affairs.

APRIL 14, 1934

Investigations and indictments of men high in finance are still the order of the day. Yesterday officials of the Cleveland Union Trust Bank were indicted for "window-dressing" the bank statement just before it closed. They did this by a temporary purchase and sale of ten million in government bonds and held the purchase price as a temporary deposit. No personal gain is shown by any of the men—but merely an attempt to save the bank by improper methods. Because of the change from a Republican to a Democratic administration and because of the demand by the public that somebody be punished—a great many fine men are being indicted because they permitted their good nature to overbalance their common sense. In the stress of 1931 a great many desperate things were done to save banks and corporations from failing. It is hard to see how some of these men could have refused to come to the help of a stricken bank with temporary deposits, etc. It would have been far better for them to personally have let the deflation take its course.

APRIL 20, 1934

Big news for Youngstown. The Dollar Bank and City Banks announce the removal of all restrictions on deposit withdrawals—thus releasing 14 million in bank deposits which have been tied up since the banks closed in 1931.

The banks in the past year have been getting government bonds for their frozen mortgages thru the Home Owners Loan Corporation. In addition to this the government bought 2 1/2 million of preferred shares in the Dollar Bank and 1 1/4 million in the City Bank. In the last analysis therefore the government took over the bad mortgages and loans to keep open the banks. Who will pay for this remains to be seen.

EDITOR'S NOTE

Unfortunately, Volume IV of Roth's diary was lost. It contained the entries for the second half of 1934 and all of 1935. The year 1935 saw the creation of new waves of New Deal legislation, including the Works Progress Administration—the largest of the New Deal agencies, which would employ 8.5 million Americans in a wide variety of jobs—and the National Labor Relations Act. The landmark Social Security Act was passed that year, providing federal assistance for the elderly for the first time in American history. At the same time, the Supreme Court that year declared the NRA to be an unconstitutional attempt to control commerce. Moreover, as Roth would continue to note, the overall economic situation was far from rosy, even with the unprecedented levels of government action and spending.

VOLUME V

1936

JANUARY 2, 1936

This is Volume V of a series of personal notes I have made from time to time concerning the panic which began in October 1929.

When I started these notes it never occurred to me that the depression would last more than two years. We are now in the beginning of the seventh year and the road is not yet clear—with the possibility of inflation ahead. We seem to be emerging from the panic, industry is picking up, etc.—but so much of it has been created by artificial spending that it is difficult to know just where we stand. Industrial production is only 10% below normal and the steel mills are operating at about 54%.

At this point a very brief review of events so far might clear the picture. President Hoover took office in March 1929 and the big stock market crash came a few months later in October 1929. Hoover did everything he could but to no avail. The stock market started a decline in October 1929 which continued intermittently until the summer of 1932. At that time good stocks and bonds were selling at 5% and 10% of their 1929 prices. Sheet and Tube had fallen from 175 to 6; Republic from 140 to 2; U.S. Steel from 200 to 20; Western Union sold at 13; Penn RR at 6, etc. Along with this, business was at a stand-still. Bank runs were starting; more than 40,000 people in Youngstown were in bread lines. It was a terrible time. In the meanwhile the voice of the demagog began to be heard throughout the land. Socialism, Communism, more equitable distribution of wealth, new currency and other panaceas became ordinary table talk.

8/12/46

We had very little inflation during the past ten years although it has been widely discussed. Prices are now pretty high because of post-war inflation but are being held down—especially rents—by the OPA [wartime Office of Price Administration]. Nothing very severe has happened yet government debt is now close to $300 billion and still going up.

12/1/55

The 1939 dollar is now worth about 52¢. The Dow Industrials are at 485. Business is booming and there is talk of more inflation. Lincoln and Cadillac cars sell above $5000. Fords and Chevrolets at $2500 up.

House prices of 1939 have about doubled. The government debt is still about $300 billion and the budget will be balanced because a record business year has brought in record tax collections.

7/1/73

Inflation is still raging—at rate of 6% each year. Food prices are out of sight. Apples, oranges, etc. about 10¢ each. 1939 dollar worth about 25¢. Gold sells at $12 per oz. Cadillac cars $8000 up. Dow at 880 and stock prices going down. Gold stocks and "growth" stocks have been good investments.

In November 1932 the people repudiated President Hoover and elected as President Franklin D. Roosevelt, a Democrat. He was elected on the promise of a "New Deal" for the forgotten man.

From November 1932 to March 1933 when Roosevelt took office conditions grew steadily worse. Hoover could do nothing because a Democratic Congress and the Democratic nominee refused to cooperate. The country simply waited. In the meanwhile banks began to close all over the country and an avalanche was started early in 1933 when the governor of Michigan declared a bank holiday closing every bank in Michigan. The fever spread rapidly and on the day Roosevelt took his office every bank in the country and every stock exchange was closed.

President Roosevelt inaugurated his New Deal with dramatic vigor and from that day to this the country has been dizzy with new laws and restrictions. He devalued the dollar, opened the banks under Federal restrictions, passed the NRA, the AAA, the CWA, the WPA and about twenty other recovery agencies which became known by the first letters of the name. All of these measures poured out government money to help broken down industries, to feed the poor, to restrict production and to control the economic life of the country. The entire New Deal was tinged with the color of socialism and with the idea of a managed economy.

For the first two years of his term President Roosevelt was the idol of the people and his smile and pleasant radio voice captivated everybody. Congress became his willing tool and without question passed every law he asked for even tho its constitutionality was doubtful.

During the last year Roosevelt has lost much of his popularity. For one thing, the New Deal has not worked out as he promised. For another thing he has placed the country in debt—we now owe about $35 billion—so that we will have either inflation and repudiation or perhaps many years of heavy taxation.

For another thing the Supreme Court has almost smashed the New Deal by declaring one law after the other unconstitutional. The gold devaluation act was sustained but in such a way as to be a slap at the administration. The NRA and other acts were held clearly unconstitutional and Roosevelt was told in clear terms that without an amendment to the Constitution he could not control and regulate the economic life of the country. Roosevelt then threatened to start a movement to amend the Constitution but so far it has not materialized. This is election year and the campaign has already started. The issues will be largely economic. A poll taken by the *Literary Digest* shows about 60% of the people opposed to the New Deal.

7/7/52

The debt is about $295 billion.

6/10/68

The debt is $385 billion.

7/8/72

The gov't debt is over $425 billion and going up.

In March 1935 the stock market began a steady rise which continues until the present day. It is recognized by most economists as being based on real industrial improvement which marks the end of the depression. There has not been a real break since March. It seems to me that we are about due for a set-back.

I am personally very much concerned with the question of inflation and it seems to me there is a grave possibility it will come unless the government at once balances its budget. With an election coming this seems out of the question. Every year since Roosevelt took office has seen us deeper in debt. We now owe $35 billion and 1936 seems to promise more spending than ever because it is an election year. The soldiers' bonus has an excellent chance of passing and will require a further expenditure of two billion. Relief, subsidies to farmers take additional millions and before the end of the next fiscal year the debt will probably amount to $37 billion—the greatest peace-time debt of all time. In the meanwhile taxes are not coming in and there is no effort to lay new taxes because it would be political suicide.

If the government had resorted to the printing press to get all the money spent—then the average man on the street would understand the danger and object. The difficulty is that the money is obtained in a roundabout way which has the same ultimate effect but which the man on the street does not understand. The government has been issuing bonds—these bonds are sold to the banks—the government gets the money from the banks and pays it out for relief, public works, etc. The people who get the money spend it and ultimately it flows back to the bank. This has been continued time after time until the banks are choked with excess reserves amounting to over three billion. If this money is ever withdrawn and put in circulation, we will have inflation—especially if each dollar of bank money produces $10 in credit money. The amount is fabulous and the situation is packed with dynamite which may bring a crash exceeding 1929.

Two things may happen to cause depositors to withdraw this money and spend it:

1. The depositors may lose faith in the credit of the government and withdraw their funds in order to buy real estate.
2. If business improves, business men may borrow the money for business purposes and this again means danger.

6/10/68

This has not yet happened.

7/8/72

Not yet.

The worst feature of it all is that people are no longer worried about government spending. An additional billion or two seems to mean nothing. When Coolidge was President in prosperous times he refused to pay the soldiers' bonus for fear of inflation and the people agreed with him. Today, in the face of unprecedented deficits, the people see Congress approving the bonus and there is hardly a murmur. The general indifference to increased spending seems to me to be a danger signal.

JANUARY 4, 1936

President Roosevelt delivered his annual message to Congress. He delivered it personally—at 9 P.M.—and over a national hookup. It turned out to be an emotional political plea to the people instead of a message to Congress on the State of the Nation. During the speech he was applauded by the Democrats and booed by the Republicans. It is said to be the first time in history that a President was so treated in Congress. Many people felt the President had opened himself up to such treatment by using Congress as a political hall. The speech contained very little of importance. In his budget message to Congress the next day the President was very vague. He did not know how much would be needed for relief but said there would be no new taxes in 1936.

JANUARY 6, 1936

The Supreme Court of the U.S. invalidates the Agricultural Administration Act (AAA). This is another reverse blow to the administration. Under this act the New Deal sought to raise agricultural prices by limiting and controlling production. The farmer was paid by the government for *not* raising pigs, cotton, wheat, etc. above a certain quota. A processing tax was placed on the balance which the consumer had to pay and this tax was paid to the farmer. It succeeded in raising prices of pork to 40¢ a pound (from 20) and the farmer got his money at the expense of the city worker. It also forced into bankruptcy many meat packers, cotton mills, etc. It started boycotts by housewives who refused to buy meat, etc. at such exorbitant prices. At a time when millions were starving the AAA cut down the production of wheat, hogs, etc.

By a 6 to 3 decision the Supreme Court said the AAA was unconstitutional and the government had no way to indirectly use its taxing power in order to control agriculture.

The next question is whether the government will have to pay back to the packers and producers the processing taxes which they paid under protest. Much of these taxes were impounded in the courts pending a final decision.

JANUARY 14, 1936

The U.S. Supreme Court again decides against the New Deal in the Rice Mills Case. It is held that the government must pay back the processing taxes which were illegally collected under protest. Many millions are involved. It will prevent the gov't from collecting these taxes and force the repayment of huge sums. The Steiner Provision Co. of Youngstown will get $90,000 back this way. The Standard Textile Co. has almost a million at stake. This all goes to further unbalance the budget and makes more imminent the danger of inflation.

JANUARY 21, 1936

The U.S. Senate approves the payment of the soldiers' bonus by a vote of 76 to 14. The vote is large enough to over-ride the expected presidential veto. This will add a burden of over two billion to the budget. Nobody seems to get excited over it and the general feeling is that while so much money is being spent the soldiers may as well get theirs. It is a dangerous doctrine.

JANUARY 23, 1936

I read a very able review of the entire financial situation in the annual review number of the *New York Analyst*. The writer came to the following conclusions:

1. The recovery that started last March is bona fide and will carry thru, with minor interruptions to final recovery.
2. Even tho the recovery so far and the stock market advance have been spectacular—we are still at a point in industrial production which is as low as the low points in almost all other depressions (about 12% below normal).
3. In other depressions the final recovery was spectacular and continued not only from the depth to normal but continued on far above normal. In all past depressions this spectacular recovery above normal was compressed within a space of 12 or 18 months. If this depression runs true to form—then the next year may see a continuation of spectacular recovery in a straight line upward until we are far above normal.
4. On this basis the market recovery since March is justified and stock prices are not too high. On this basis also the next two or three years offer very fine prospects for great enhancement of common stocks.
5. The near-term prospect in stocks is clouded by political uncertainty both here and abroad.

6. The writer says little about inflation. However if a general European war or other great catastrophe happened it would go hard with this country because of our precarious financial situation. Government bonds would depreciate because of higher interest rates and many banks might close because of over heavy subscription to government bonds.

12/21/37

This prediction was wrong. Stocks continued up until September 1937 and then came a worse severe era which is not yet ended. Stocks lost more than 50% and are now below 1935 prices. The 1936 boom was an inflation boom following bonus payments and was not the final recovery. Business is now 20% below normal and never exceeded normal. Steel mills now operating 30%. Much suffering.

10/15/45

Time out for WWII. The stock market takes off where it left off in 1937 and talk of inflation is heard again with renewed vigor.

10/15/45

We had a war and gov't bonds did not depreciate because interest rates were kept low.

It is curious to see how everybody is dabbling in the stock market again. The fact that they were cleaned out in 1929 seems to make them determined to make up their losses.

One client tells me how he and his brother last summer each bought 1000 shares of Warner Bros. at 3 1/2. One brother still holds his stock and the price is now 11 1/2. The other sold 500 shares for $5500 and set aside the money for his son's education. The balance of the stock he still holds.

12/21/37

Sequel. The Warner stock went up to 18 and then crashed to 7. Client held on and when stock reached 18 he started to buy on margin thinking it would go to 1929 prices. Was almost wiped out. Moral: Don't be a hog.

Dr. K. tells me that he has already made up his 1929 losses and is putting every cent he can lay aside in common stocks on the theory there will be a considerable profit over the next two or three years. None of these people seem to know the first principles of investment—how to gauge the value of a stock or how to look for accurate information. They buy and sell on tips and since the market has been rising since 1932 they are coming out ahead. They lay nothing aside in bonds. I wonder how many of them will be able to get out at the right time.

The French cabinet falls yesterday—a radical cabinet steps in and devaluation of the franc is expected soon. France has experienced severe depression in the past two years and much of her gold has been sent to America in anticipation of devaluation.

JANUARY 25, 1936

The President vetoes the soldier bonus and his veto is promptly overridden by an overwhelming vote of the House. The bill goes to the Senate Monday with prospects that it will be passed over the President's veto. It calls for payment to the soldiers of over $2 billion in gov't baby bonds bearing 3% and convertible into cash beginning next June 15th.

The following developments have again aroused a flock of inflation rumors.

1. Passage of bonus bill and publication of bad condition of gov't budget.
2. Rumors that dollar will be further devalued.
3. Rumors that silver price will be raised to par with gold.
4. Dollar breaks sharply in foreign exchange caused by European selling of dollars.

Stock market is restless and uncertain. Federal Reserve Board lays down a rule that stocks cannot be bought on a margin of less than 55%. Looks as if they are afraid of a runaway market.

JANUARY 30, 1936

It is interesting to note that United States Steel Corporation is the last to recover from the depression. This is because of its huge size and because it made mostly heavy steels. Independent companies making lighter steels did not fare so badly. In 1934 U.S. Steel lost 21 million and in 1935 it made a

profit of a million—the first since 1929. On the other hand, motor companies recovered two years ago. In 1935 General Motors showed a profit of
$129,000,000—the highest since 1929.

FEBRUARY 4, 1936

I made out my application yesterday for my soldiers' bonus which is
payable in U.S. Bonds that can be cashed after June 15, 1936. I expect to
hold the bonds as they carry 3% interest. The payment of the bonus was
rejected by the President but he was easily over-ridden in both houses of
Congress.

Inflation discussion rages in Congress. Europe thinks we are going to have
inflation and the dollar has weakened on the foreign exchange market. As a
result gold shipments are starting back to Europe. A shipment of $15 million
yesterday marked the first turn in the gold tide which has been flowing
toward the U.S. for more than 18 months. The loss of 15 million gold out of
a gold stock of $10 billion is insignificant—but the reason for the shipment is
Europe's loss of faith in U.S. currency and that may bear further fruit.

Inflation talk has been created by the need to raise cash for the bonus
and other expenditures. Because this is a presidential election year both
Roosevelt and the Congress are reluctant to levy new taxes which is the
proper thing to do. They are considering two other methods—issue and sale
of more government bonds—or printing press money. Either method is bad
but the inflation group is urging the printing press. I wonder how much
longer the government spends money without the levy of new taxes. Deficits
have been accumulating for seven years and that of this year will make a
record—over five billion deficit for this year alone. The willingness of politi-
cians to hand out bonuses and other gratuities—and their unwillingness to
levy taxes—seems to be the answer. The printing press seems to them an
ideal way to spend money without taxation. On the surface the inflationist
argument appears to be convincing but they do not seem to realize that
printing press money lays the most vicious tax of all.

The stock market continues up but slowly. There has not been a bad
break for almost 10 months.

FEBRUARY 11, 1936

Inflation talk continues to dominate the scene. A typical example of what
is going on is the court action by trustees of Leland Stanford University asking

permission to convert part of their bonds into common stock. One of the witnesses called was ex-President Hoover who testified that in his opinion there were grave prospects of inflation and that in order to preserve its assets the university should convert part of its bonds into common stocks. Institutions all over the country are doing the same thing. Some investment organizations have been liquidated and money returned to investors so they could do their own speculating. It is this persistent conversion of bond money into stocks which has sustained the long up-swing in the market. Yesterday the market advanced again and some of the steel stocks were spectacular. Sheet & Tube sold over 50—and last March was at 12.

12/21/37

Stock prices continued up until Sept. 1937 and then came a big break which is still in process. Prices are now back to 1935 level.

FEBRUARY 21, 1936

There is nothing new to report. Business is dull—Congress is quiet. In the meanwhile the stock market has continued slowly upward without a break for almost a year.

The street is full of stories of large sums of money made in the stock market. Most of these people bought stocks a year or more ago and held on grimly. Less than a year ago Sheet & Tube sold at 12 and is now 52 1/2. Many of course sold too soon and took a small profit. The speculative fever has spread just as in 1929 and all sorts of people are crowding the broker's office. Many stocks sell at 20 and 30 times earnings and a break seems overdue. Bonds pay only about 3% and because of this low return and because of fear of inflation much money has been switched to equities.

FEBRUARY 22, 1936

It is said about the wealthy banker George F. Baker of New York:

1. He always bought sound stocks and bonds when they were offered below intrinsic value.
2. He always had liquid cash for such a purpose.
3. After he bought such stocks and bonds he held on "until the cows came home." He never made a practice of speculative buying and selling and never tried to catch the market swings. He simply bought

when bargains were offered. He never sold unless the stock market was going bad or the price offered was too good to refuse.

The last three years offered just such a chance to build a fortune. How many took the opportunity I do not know. Many who understood did not have the money. Others who had money did not see the opportunity or were afraid to risk their money when things looked so black.

MARCH 3, 1936

Things move along quietly and nothing much is heard from Washington. Industrial Production in January and February fell off a little and is now about 5% below normal. The question on everybody's mind is whether the recovery which started a year ago will continue for a year or more until we are above normal or whether we have a slump this summer and full recovery in 1937. I am inclined to agree with the latter view although the vast majority are on the other side. Most financial writers tell people to hold on to stocks—that they will go higher etc. It is for this reason there has been so little selling although the market has been slightly lower and unsettled during the past week.

In *Time* magazine for 2/24/36 I found one lone financial writer who agreed with me. He said:

1. Stocks are too high. They ought to be sold now—not bought. They will be much lower next summer. Business has not carried thru.
2. Inflation will start with the 1937 Congress.
3. There will be an unprecedented boom 1937–1939.
4. This boom will be followed in 1940 by a terrific crash and prolonged depression for four or five years.
5. If Republicans are in power 1940–1944 they will become known as the depression party.

12/21/37

This prediction was more nearly right than the others. The crash came in Sept. 1937. There is no sign yet of a boom.

8/21/44

No boom yet—to the contrary, low prices all through the war.

12/15/45

. *All of these predictions proved to be wrong.*

MARCH 13, 1936

War clouds again threaten Europe. Germany sends troops and seizes the Rhine Valley which she lost after the World War. This is a violation of the Locarno Pact and France threatens military reprisal. The situation looks bad.

The stock market has been slowly heading down the past few days but nothing startling.

Business continues quiet although steel operates at 60%.

EDITOR'S NOTE

Floyd Odlum was a lawyer who accumulated wealth speculating on utility companies in New York in the 1920s and formed the Atlas Utilities Company in 1928. In 1929 Odlum sold half of his Atlas stocks and various other holdings he had acquired on Wall Street in the summer prior to the Great Crash, leaving him with fourteen million dollars in cash by October 1929. During the Depression Odlum purchased many stocks at below-market rates to become a major shareholder of such corporations as Northeast Airlines and Bonwit Teller. Howard Hughes would eventually buy RKO Studios from Odlum. By 1933 Odlum was one of the top-ten richest tycoons in the country.

APRIL 6, 1936

Business and the stock-market continue upward without a pause now for about 13 months. Steel mills operating at about 65%. In spite of all this, money continues tight and the law a difficult profession. Talk of inflation has died down and likewise there has been little political talk lately.

I read an interesting item today about Floyd Odlum and the building up of his Atlas Investment Trust. Started with $40,000 in 1924—ran it up to a million in 1929. Sold out for cash and held on to cash until bottom of depression was reached in 1932. With his cash he bought heavily in "special situations." Mostly in investment trusts hard up for cash. Stocks in these trusts were selling at less than 50% of the asset values. Since the assets were stocks quoted at depression levels—the buyer of such an investment trust bought the assets at 1/2 of depression values. He then held on and later liquidated at huge profits. He never took over the active management of a business but sold the stock to those who could run it. There were many such "special situations" during the depression. He was actually buying stocks under the hammer. The same thing happened with railroads and other companies such as Continental Shares when they went into receivership. The person who had enough money to liquidate them could have the assets for a song. Same principle as buying real estate at a foreclosure sold for price of the mortgage. Assets of the Atlas Corporation are now over $100,000,000 and they have literally become private bankers.

Like most successful bankers Odium believed that "silence" was one of the ingredients of success. Nobody knew what he planned until a thing was done—and then they got very little information directly from him.

6/18/68

Floyd Odlum went thru the wringer and Atlas sells for $6—a Uranium Holding Co.

APRIL 13, 1936

The retail merchants had a big Easter season. Yesterday in Cleveland the streets were crowded with people in new clothes and I saw more gardenias than in many years. Also the roads were filled with thousands of glittering new automobiles. It is clear that at last after a long depression the people are again spending money. In Youngstown the mills are working at 80% but in spite of this pay envelopes are small and there are many unemployed. Also in the U.S. there are still about 12 million unemployed. In spite of all this apparent prosperity the law profession lags behind. Things are better but fees are small and the work is difficult.

APRIL 28, 1936

Business continues at a high level with steel operations at over 70%.

For the last two weeks the stock market has been slowly sinking and yesterday a bad break brought losses ranging as high as 10 points. It is funny how when the stock market is rising every piece of news is regarded optimistically and bad news is ignored. Now the reverse is true.

Poland goes off the gold standard. This leaves only France, Switzerland

and Denmark and it is feared they will follow. By remaining on gold France has suffered severe deflation in past two years and has not had the gain in business felt by non-gold countries.

EDITOR'S NOTE

The Guffey Coal Act, or the Bituminous Coal Conservation Act of 1935, aimed to protect the coal industry's earnings and stabilize coal prices by fostering a coal consortium to control its prices. But on May 18, 1936, in *Carter v. Carter Coal Company*, the U.S. Supreme Court ruled that the federal government did not have the right to infringe on free enterprise in the coal industry.

MAY 19, 1936

There has been very little to add lately. Inflation talk and political has died down. The stock market suffered a number of declines but nothing serious—it has been quietly drifting for past two weeks.

General business conditions have continued good and steel mills are operating at 70 to 80%.

The U.S. Supreme Court yesterday declared the Guffey Coal Act unconstitutional. It was a small NRA.

JUNE 25, 1936

I have not had a chance to make any entries in this record for the reason that for the first time since the depression I have been busy with my law practice. Business has been better for more than a year now and is about 95% of normal but until now the professions have not felt the recovery. I hope our time has come because it has been a long, dreary road.

The gov't last week paid a soldiers' bonus of over two billion and as a result the veterans have been buying cars, clothing etc. Streets are crowded and the highways are jammed with new cars. It begins to look like old times again.

The stock market has been irregular but refuses to have a break of any size. Prices are about the same as they were in April and are actually at their highest point in 6 years. There is some fear that France may devalue her currency and halt the recovery. Barring this it seems we ought to be back at normal by Fall. Most economists think we have 2 prosperous years ahead of us and then a depression again of 1 to 4 years.

The presidential campaign is just beginning and promises to be very bitter.

JULY 15, 1936

Business continues good and there has been less than the usual summer letdown. Retail stores and most businesses are doing better than any year since 1929. Everywhere things are beginning to look like old times again. Even the legal business is showing signs of life. There is still an absence of small "bread and butter" business but this is compensated for by an occasional substantial fee for drawing a downtown lease, etc.

Steel mills are operating at about 80% and prospects are good unless a threatening strike develops.

A bad drought in the West means higher food prices this winter.

The stock market has fluctuated several months but at no time had a bad break. Averages are highest since 1930.

JULY 16, 1936

As I look back over the record of the stock market since 1932 many remarkable results can be seen. Stocks that sold at receivership prices are now selling at substantial values. Here are a few extreme examples showing quotations in 1932 and 1936. Phillips Morris Tobacco Co. 1/2 to 90; Sheet & Tube 4 to 68; Republic Steel 2 to 26; Gen. Motors 10 to 70; Chrysler 6 to 100, etc.

It is literally true that if a man had the courage to invest $5000 in 1932 and then had the courage to hold on he would be worth $100,000. Those people who did buy in 1932 sold out long ago with what they then thought was a good profit. When the depression started the "ideal" investor would have:

1. Sold out before the crash if possible; if he got caught then he would have sold anyhow at a loss.
2. He would have patiently waited until rock-bottom prices in 1932 and then bought heavily.
3. He would have then held on until prosperity returned.

Of course nobody could have foreseen these things. It might prove that long-term trading is better than short-term profits. In 1932 most people were hard put to buy food and had no money to invest. Those who had a few dollars were hoarding it in fear. Those who did invest sold quickly as soon as they saw a profit. There may be some who profited fully but I do not know of any.

JULY 24, 1936

There has been no summer letdown in business so far. Steel mils here are operating at 80%. Best since 1929. Sheet & Tube reports a profit of $3.40 per share of common for 1st 6 months of year. This is also the best since 1929. Retail trade continues good and everything points to progress. The stock market is a puzzle. It still goes steadily up without a serious break since March 1935—17 months. Sooner or later there will be a bad break but nobody knows when.

JULY 29, 1936

The *Cleveland Plain Dealer* in past few days ran a series of articles picturing Youngstown on the verge of a boom. It quoted steel operations at 80% without the usual summer let-down, bank clearings, retail sales, etc. The article was greatly exaggerated and even tho business is better than since 1929, law business is still only fair. However the next year or two look good.

It is remarkable how quickly things come back. Within the past 12 months Sheet & Tube as a money earner climbed almost from the bottom to the top of the list. Its stock which sold in 1932 for $4 a share is now selling over 70.

The stock market continues up and without a pause since March 1935. Sooner or later there will be a bad break—but when?

AUGUST 8, 1936

Nothing new except that the steel industry continues to boom and is operating in Youngstown at 80% when normally there would be a slump this time of year. In the past year it certainly came back with a vengeance. Sheet & Tube has been a spectacular performer and is now at 80 compared with 6 in 1932 and 15 about 18 months ago. Seems to be too high in spite of progress.

War again threatens in Europe.

Law business is again slow. It comes in spurts. The lawyers certainly deserve a break after the past six years.

Retail trade in Youngstown is good. Things look pretty much normal. People are traveling again and Mr. Burger tells me it is hard to get reservations.

AUGUST 14, 1936

The presidential campaign is beginning to warm up. It promises to be a close campaign but I think Roosevelt will win although personally I would like to see him defeated.

The stock market holds up well and has not had a serious set-back since March 1935. In other recovery periods it seems that after two years of rapid upturn there has always been a serious set-back because of too rapid progress. If this holds good in this depression then in spring of 1937 there may be such a set-back. This situation is also altered by possibility of inflation. The public seems to have forgotten about it but there has been no change in the basic factors. Prices are gradually rising but it is difficult to say whether this is caused by the drought or by the money situation. I am inclined to believe that the latter is a factor and that we will still see some inflation arising out of this money manipulation. In many cases for a long term investment stocks are probably still a good buy but they seem to me to have gone beyond the state warranted by present improvement.

This depression has indelibly impressed on my mind one thing—and that is the value of having on hand sufficient capital to cover emergencies. In the investment field it means the difference between success or failure to have enough capital to buy bargains when they are available or to hold on to investments thru thick and thin and not be forced to sell at a loss. My experience as a lawyer shows that a large proportion of business failures are caused by lack of capital rather than by lack of technical business knowledge. Even in domestic life there can be no happiness without sufficient surplus to cover emergencies such as illness or death. And yet knowing these things it takes infinite patience for a young man today without financial backing to lay a sound foundation. Business today requires huge amounts of capital—the small business has been crowded to the wall—and it is next to impossible for a young man working as a clerk to lay aside 10 or 20 thousand dollars in order to go into business. Either he must forget marriage or he must wait until middle years—and by that time he has lost the spirit of adventure. Even tho opportunities in business today are greater than ever, it presents an almost insurmountable wall for the young man without funds.

AUGUST 21, 1936

The European situation is again tense and it would take very little to start a war. Spain is torn by a class-war and Germany and Italy are aiding and abetting from the side-lines. It seems to be democracy vs. dictatorship with democracy losing out fast in Europe.

AUGUST 24, 1936

It is an interesting sidelight on this depression that many companies which went to receivership during the depression are now being reorganized. In most cases the common stock was wiped out but bonds or preferred are good. In 1933–4 these preferred stocks could be bought for as low as 25¢ per share ($100 par) and are now worth as high as $14 (Continental shares). Here again a man with liquid capital and courage could have made a fortune on a comparatively small investment. Some who bought at low prices did not have the courage to hold on and sold at a nice profit of $4 or $5 per share. The real winnings went to those who held onto the receivership shares through the whole reorganization. A. H. R. held 1000 shares of a tobacco (Phillip Morris) stock which sold for 50¢ a share—he sold at $16 per share and celebrated—the stock is now over $100 per share. If he had only held for a year longer instead of getting out at the beginning of the rise.

AUGUST 26, 1936

During the past 30 days there has been a very definite lull in business. My law office has been very quiet. Except for the fact that the roads are crowded with new automobiles, it would be exactly as it was 3 years ago at the bottom of the depression. Can it be possible that the rapid recovery during the past year was not normal but was caused by the distribution of the two billion dollar soldier bonds and other government expenditures? It gives me a headache to think of the possibilities.

During the past year while things boomed there has been very little talk of inflation but if anything the situation is worse than ever. It is a curious fact that all thru this depression there have been so many abnormal things to consider—such as government spending—that it has been impossible to appraise the future. It is this very uncertainty which has halted recovery so often and caused the business man to hesitate about expanding. Will the next 5 years bring an inflation boom with unexpected spurts upward and crashes down or will it bring normal recovery? I hope it will be the latter but I am inclined to believe it will be the former. I am getting very tired of the clamor and excitement and the uncertainty. I long for a return to normalcy and steady but slow growth.

SEPTEMBER 3, 1936

It is amazing to note how quickly empty store-rooms have been occupied during past 6 months. I do not believe there is one desirable location available now on West Federal St. Most of them have been taken up by chain stores at high rentals. Even the old Dome Theater is being converted into a store-room. The movement is now spreading into residential areas and new groceries, etc. are opening up on every corner.

6/10/68

There are many vacant store-rooms on Federal St. and land is cheap. Business has moved to the suburbs.

SEPTEMBER 9, 1936

With the passing of Labor Day optimism is rampant and prospects for fall business are bright. Predictions are freely made that prosperity will continue without pause for at least three or four years. In the meanwhile stocks are selling at 30 and 40 times their earnings. It is just as bad as in 1929 except that the future earnings prospects are bright. Investors feel that a stock is worth more than its present earnings indicate. Nevertheless it seems to me the stock market has already discounted future earnings for a long time ahead and that optimism will carry the market too far.

SEPTEMBER 24, 1936

General business conditions are good and almost every industrial index has reached normal. Indications are that the next year or two will move up above normal and then we will have a relapse. To date the coming National Election has been quiet and has not affected business.

In spite of this return to normal the law profession shows little or no improvement and lawyers everywhere are complaining bitterly. Streets are crowded with shoppers, new automobiles everywhere—and law offices vacant. We have between 300 and 350 lawyers in Youngstown with a population of about 185,000. This means less than 600 population per lawyer. Conditions in other cities are about the same. The situation has been aggravated by concentration of corporation legal work in large law firms. The past six years has been a nightmare for the individual practicing lawyer. The profession is clearly entitled to a break and yet in spite of this young lawyers are turned out in an increasing stream. Most of them say they do not intend to practice their profession but in the end they do because good jobs are not available and without capital they cannot go into business.

SEPTEMBER 24, 1936

I was retained today by client W to defend him in a suit by a brokerage company to recover a deficit of $5200 left after they sold him out following the 1929 crash. There is little I can do for him but a study of the record of his transactions is interesting. He started with a capital of $12000 of his own money—bought on 25% margin—and usually sold when the stocks advanced 3 or 4 points. Usually he made a profit between 1927 and 1929 but on a few occasions suffered a loss. When the crash came in 1929 he was probably a few thousand dollars ahead of the game but the broker was holding at the time $35000 of second rate stocks on a 25% margin. The broker sold him out slowly thru 1930 and 1931 always hoping the market would get better but it got steadily worse and in the end W lost his original investment of $12000 and still owes the broker $5,200. Looking back it is easy now to see that W did not have a chance to win out. He bought and sold for every few points profit. Every time he sold he bought at a higher price and his profits went back into stocks. In the end he was bound to be caught by the crash with a bag full of stocks on narrow margin. It is hard to draw any general conclusion here and this case is similar to thousands of others. Assuming that we knew the crash was coming this is what he should have done:

1. If he had bought the stocks outright instead of a 25% margin—he would at least have owned them when the crash came in 1929. If he had held them until 1936–7 he would get out almost all of his original investment.

2. The fellow who went into the market in 1927 and traded for short profits as above did not make any money and took all the risk. The fellow who really made money already owned his stocks when the boom started—held them for several years until prices were exorbitant—and then sold them because he could get more than intrinsic value.

3. Such a fellow would then hold his cash until stocks were selling at far less than intrinsic value (1932) and then buy his fill holding for 5 or 10 years until the next boom.

4. How would he know the bottom was reached in 1932? He would not

know. Most people did not realize the depression was over until a year
or more after the turn had been made. If the fellow had waited until
1933–34 when prices were shooting up he could still have bought at
bargain prices. In 1932 with stock prices at 10% of normal he could
not have gone far wrong in buying stocks with 20 or 30 years earnings
record and with a good chance to survive the depression.

However, not one man in a million succeeded in doing this and that is
why the millionaires club is still exclusive.

This case as so many others shows clearly that to build an estate it is necessary first of all to get money by saving it and secondly it is most important
to invest these savings so that they will increase and work for you without
losing the principal. Most people learn the first rule and succeed in saving
various amounts out of their earnings but very few learn the second rule—
how to invest it so it earns a profit and yet not lose the principal. It follows
then that it is most important to learn how to invest money and make it
work for you. W—above mentioned—actually saved $12000 out of his earn-
ings. Wisely invested, he might now be financially independent. Instead he
is broke. What is that one thing that leads one man to financial independ-
ence and the other to the scrap heap—when both worked hard and both
saved the same amount out of their earnings? W has a record which shows
he was avaricious and was not satisfied with a fair investment return. His
record also shows his investment judgment was bad whether he bought real
estate or stocks. He bought vacant lots in poor neighborhoods that never
developed and his equity has disappeared. Other people bought real estate
and stocks at the same time and prospered. Most of those who prospered
were not avaricious. It is all in the nature of the beast. It is probably just as
great a sin to be too conservative as too avaricious. A man who puts his
small savings in gov't bonds at 2 1/2% may have 10 to 15000 in his old age
but he never will be wealthy. Somewhere in between the ultra-conservative
man who is afraid to take even a legitimate risk and the avaricious gambler
who bets on anything—stands the ideal investor who has learned to make
his money work for him. He accumulates money first by savings—then he
carefully investigates and weighs a dozen investments before he finally
selects one to put his money in. He is willing to take a legitimate risk but is
not willing to gamble. If he invests in real estate or mortgages he first exam-
ines the property, the neighborhood, the future development and will probably have it appraised by experts. He investigates thoroughly before he
buys. Such a man with ordinary business judgment will usually make a

profit on his investment. Not much perhaps on each individual investment but in the end he will accumulate and as the pile grows he will find many bargains offered him because he has capital to invest. If he invests in stocks or bonds he will not follow blind tips or rush into a seething market with thousands of suckers—but in the quiet of his office he will carefully examine the earnings records of the company, its future prospects. He will seek advice if necessary and then buy only if he thinks the price is fair and the prospects good. He will hold on for several years and share in the growth of the company and will sell only if the company loses ground or if a stock-crazy public offers him much more for his stock than its intrinsic value.

In the last analysis it seems that if a man can develop investment sense he can build an estate even tho his savings from his earnings are small. It takes study and hard work like everything else but the fact remains that money *can* be wisely invested and *can* be made to work for you. The reward is well worth trying for but the dangers and pitfalls along the road are many.

SEPTEMBER 28, 1936

Today France went off the gold standard, put an embargo on gold and prepared to devalue the franc. She is quickly followed by Switzerland and Holland, the last remaining gold countries. The entire world is now off the gold standard. In order to prevent an international competitive cutting of the monetary standards the U.S. and England have agreed to support the franc until the change is completed. It is hoped this will pave the way to an international agreement as to the value of each currency and ultimately a return to the gold standard.

England started the movement to leave gold back in 1918. She returned to gold in 1921 and then abandoned it again in 1925. By manipulating her currency she attracted foreign trade and returned to prosperity long before other countries. But other nations found they could do the same thing, so one by one each country did the same thing for protection and profit. The U.S. abandoned gold in 1933 and our dollar is 59¢ its former value. When a country devalues, its merchandise costs less to a foreign country and hence it exports more. This advantage holds only so long as the other country does not devalue to a greater degree. Manipulation of currency and building of high tariff walls have played havoc with all foreign trade and have prolonged the crisis. France persistently refused to devalue because her people had had bitter experiences with inflation. But devaluation by other countries killed her foreign trade and while other countries were on the upgrade during the past three years France kept getting worse and worse. Within the past year France had an internal revolution and the Socialist party under Blum is now in power. He also refused to devalue but during past few months the French people hoarded their gold and sent it to U.S. and England for safety and investment. The steady out-flow of gold finally made franc devaluation inevitable.

I thought such a thing would bring a stock market crash in U.S. because it would be logical for the French to sell their U.S. stocks and take the gold home because of its increased value. As usual, however, the stock market did not follow a logical course and went up on the news instead of down. The explanation was that investors felt the way was now paved for an international agreement to return to gold and this in turn would lead to greater export trade and prosperity.

OCTOBER 13, 1936

It is exactly five years ago today since the Youngstown banks closed their doors. Fairly steady has been the recovery for almost two years now since March 1935. Mills are working over 70%; stores are busy, real estate is showing activity and it is almost impossible to find a vacant house.

In spite of all these signs of returned prosperity the law profession lags. It is a curious anomaly. Everybody seems to have money, to buy clothes, cars, etc. yet during the past 3 months I took in hardly enough to pay expenses. It would seem that after recovery people spend their first earnings to buy clothes, cars, furniture and pay off debts. After they do this and accumulate a surplus they will start buying real estate and there will be some worthwhile business for the lawyer. It is a very trying period for our profession and I heartily wish it were over.

The stock market continues slowly up without a bad break since March 1935. Sheet & Tube sells at 86. Seems too high because it is back on its preferred dividends and of course pays nothing on common. It makes me sick to think that the chance to buy stocks and real estate at depression prices has passed on without my being able to participate. It may never come again in my life-time to such a degree.

The presidential campaign seems to be getting a slow start but from present indications it will be a very close race.

OCTOBER 26, 1936

The National political campaign draws to a close. It seems to be a very close issue between Alfred M. Landon and Franklin D. Roosevelt with the betting odds 3 to 1 in favor of Roosevelt. The *Literary Digest* poll favors Landon. In Mahoning County the *Vindicator* poll favors Roosevelt. The campaign has been very bitter and unfortunately racial issues have come in the picture. President Roosevelt appointed a number of Jews to prominent positions and because of this many subversive groups have been distributing scurrilous anti-Semitic literature. I am in favor of Landon because of the basic issues involved but have been greatly disturbed by the anti-Semitic features of the campaign.

The business picture continues bright and the stock market holds its own.

OCTOBER 29, 1936

Today is the 7th anniversary of the stock market crash in 1929. On that day 16 million shares changed hands—stocks dropped 20 or 30 points and the country became panic stricken. Today the market was firm—business back to normal—people optimistic—and prospects that the next few years will be good years.

The political campaign comes to a close with the result apparently close although betting is 2 1/2 to 1 on Roosevelt. It has been a bitter campaign—full of personalities—racial issues, etc. I am glad it is over. Somehow the last few years seem to have been hectic years—lots of discussion but no business. I long for more quiet—more attention to business and less public discussions. I think that with the return of more normal business conditions many people will feel this way.

NOVEMBER 6, 1936

The National Election resulted in an unprecedented landslide for Franklin D. Roosevelt. His opponent Landon received only 8 electoral votes. Likewise both Houses of Congress are more predominantly Democratic than ever before. By a popular vote of 2 against 1, the people of the U.S. decidedly determined to follow Roosevelt and the New Deal. Unless Roosevelt becomes suddenly conservative, it seems to me we are heading for inflation. Also in state and local matters the Democrats are in charge of almost all offices. As usual the landslide swept into office some undesirable candidates along with the rest of the ticket.

The streets are crowded with people—many new 1937 automobiles are already on the road—everywhere are signs of optimism. It is reflected by a rising stock market and rising prices. In the face of all this the legal profession lags behind. It is very trying.

CHAPTER 6

DECEMBER 4, 1936–SEPTEMBER 11, 1939

"Much labor trouble lately and a great deal of violence."

EDITOR'S NOTE

"We can formally and officially announce that the depression of 1929 has ended," declares Roth on January 2, 1937. Retail stores in downtown Youngstown teemed with shoppers buying new clothes and home furnishings. Gleaming new autos crowded the roads. Youngstown steel mills operated at 80 percent capacity. The town's commercial real estate rental market was strong, and many personal and auto finance companies had sprung up again, poised to approve new loans for consumers. Plus, the stock market was bullish, enjoying a steady rise since March 1935. Even Roth's diary writing tapered off after May 1937. When he picked it up again in October, however, he described a very different picture: "I have made no entry for several months because business seemed to be normal," penned Roth on October 12, 1937. "About six weeks ago, however, the stock market had a bad break and since then it has gone steadily downward with hardly a pause."

Dubbed the "Roosevelt Recession" in the months to come, the thirteen-month period between May 1937 and June 1938 proved to be a rough ride not just for Roth and the American people but for private industry, banks, and the White House as well. Historians and economists offer various theories as to the cause of this episode of severe slowdown after the steady rise in America's economic recovery. Certainly, the simultaneous combination of unforeseen forces that fostered the new crisis quickly opened America's old wounds of 1929 that had just barely started to heal.

In January 1936 Congress finally awarded three million World War I vets (including Roth) their veterans' bonuses. The average individual sum was formidable. With amounts exceeding 30 percent of the mean household income for a man of this age group, the vets quickly cashed in their long-awaited bonuses (46 percent would be redeemed by mid-June 1936). The payout represented nearly 1 percent of the annual gross national product, and it substantially stimulated the economy, if temporarily, in 1936. Manufacturers were only too happy to step up production and hire more workers to meet demand. Consumer spending that year (thanks to veterans' bonuses, high employment, and an increase in average wages) gave the appearance of the prosperity of the Roaring Twenties.

Yet 1937 turned out very differently. President Roosevelt needed to raise taxes. Facing a $3.6 billion deficit, Roosevelt needed revenue to pay for the veterans' bonuses and offset the loss of proceeds from the AAA's agricultural processing tax that the 1936 Supreme Court had ruled unconstitutional. Although less than 5 percent of the population would actually end up paying federal income taxes in the 1930s, the perceived tax plan slowed personal spending. In addition, payrolls decreased due to a tax levied to finance the Social Security Act of 1935, one of the major parts of Roosevelt's Second New Deal. Two billion dollars was raised from the earnings of American workers in 1937. But families' spending became more cautious as they faced a smaller paycheck week after week.

The consequence of this sudden expansion and contraction resulted in an all too familiar pattern: By the end of 1938 unemployment had leaped to nearly 20 percent (compared to 14 percent the year prior). Manufacturers had to cut production levels, unload inventories, and let go workers when demand slowed. As Americans once again lost their means to maintain the consumption of goods at their 1936 levels, the economy plunged further. The notion that America was entering another "depression" crystallized in the collective mindset on "Black Tuesday," October 19, 1937. That day the stock market traded the biggest volume (7.2 million shares) since 1933, and the slump continued into 1938. By May 1938 the Federal Reserve's adjusted Index of Industrial Production had lost almost two-thirds of the gains it had made since 1933.

Many economists and historians also blame an act of the Federal Reserve Board for hurting the recovery. By late 1935 commercial banks were holding onto $5 billion in excess reserves (compared to $2.76 billion in January 1934) as large amounts of European gold poured into America, due to the escalating turmoil abroad. Banks preferred to keep the gold: The interest rates on government securities were too low to convert this surplus into bonds, plus few loan applications had good enough credit histories to accept. But the Federal Reserve Board wanted to "correct" this bank excess. They feared the reserves would ignite another overspeculative "inflationary boom." Under the 1935 Banking Act, the Federal Reserve Board doubled the necessary reserve ratio for commercial banks. The unanticipated consequence of this new requirement was dramatic and nearly instantaneous. Banks were forced to liquidate their investments, withdraw from central reserve-city banks (which also needed to meet this new reserve level), and further tighten their lending.

President Roosevelt's sudden shift in spending policy also undoubtedly contributed to the downturn. The president aimed to reduce the federal deficit upon reelection in 1936. The administration drastically and swiftly cut federal spending on his various job stimulus projects such as the WPA. The federal deficit would actually drop below $1 billion in 1937, but at a dismal cost: By September 1937 1.8 million federal jobs were wiped out. Reminiscent of 1932, Roth notes that one-quarter of the nearby Cleveland population was back on relief by April 1938.

DECEMBER 4, 1936

Since the election, business has continued to boom with the retail trade looking for the biggest Christmas since 1929. Several stores report difficulty in getting delivery of merchandise—prices are rising and threaten to increase more—everywhere are signs of the coming of a boom or collapse similar to 1929 and perhaps even worse. The 1937 automobiles came out and record sales are reported.

In the midst of all these signs of prosperity the professional men seem to be left out. Business is a little better but far below normal. Collections are bad—people seem to be buying heavily clothing—furniture—cars—amusements—but have nothing for the lawyer or doctor.

The stock market has not advanced much during the past month but in general has maintained its level.

The European situation grows worse and there is a daily danger of war.

Real estate rentals have risen rapidly and there is difficulty in finding a vacant house or apartment. New building has not gotten into full swing.

DECEMBER 9, 1936

Everybody is talking about the coming "boom." Some think it is already here and others say it will be here in 6 months or a year. At any rate business is back to normal—new cars crowd the streets—strikes are popular, etc. Prices are rising fast and merchants have a hard time getting delivery of merchandise. It may be that inflation will take hold next year. If so, then a boom for 1937–38 and then a crash.

In Europe King Edward threatens to abdicate his English throne in order to marry twice-divorced Mrs. Simpson, an ex-American. It is the topic of the day.

DECEMBER 11, 1936

King Edward of England abdicates his throne in order to marry Mrs. Simpson—the twice-divorced American. Everybody thinks he is a d— fool and many are quoting Kipling "Rag and bone" etc. The X-King delivered a farewell address over the radio last night and I heard it. Pledged his allegiance to the new King—his brother. Said he abdicated because he could not carry his burden of King without having at his side the woman he loves. He goes into exile. General prediction is that he will not find happiness with Mrs. Simpson and will be a wanderer without a country. The whole episode is amazing and revolting and seems to be just one more chapter in the crazy-quilt of world history since the world war. The ex-King is 42 (Mrs. Simpson 40) and both belong to the "lost generation" which participated in the war and became so cynical afterward.

12/24/52

The former King of England is still in exile but is still living happily with the woman of his choice.

DECEMBER 22, 1936

Xmas trade for retail stores is booming. Steel mills above 80% and every appearance of gaiety and prosperity. Prices are rapidly rising and many store-buyers report shortage of goods. Strikes are more numerous.

Talk grows about a coming boom and inflation. The present government insists that it can and will prevent boom, inflation and subsequent depression. I am skeptical. Some time ago, the government increased bank reserve requirements 50%—thereby cutting down possibility of credit inflation. Today it ordered segregated in a separate fund all newly mined gold and all the gold that is pouring in from Europe—this so that the gold could not be used as a base for further expansion of the currency.

All these steps are reminiscent of the early history of French inflation and they all failed. At the present time in U.S. there are still 8 or 10 million unemployed in spite of the prosperity—the budget is still unbalanced—and the government for political reasons hesitates to do anything that will disrupt the upward trend.

12/21/37

The business line reached normal in 1937 but did not go above. For 8 months it flattened out along normal and then in Sept. 1937 crashed straight down to 20 below. The 1st 8 months of 1937 should have been a warning that the boom was at an end.

DECEMBER 24, 1936

Talked with Al Wechsler this morning. He is manager of a ladies dress shop. Says that they have had the biggest Christmas season in their history.

It is a pretty blue Christmas for the lawyers and other professional men. Merchants and industrialists have reaped a harvest, the laboring groups have received good pay and bonuses and have promptly spent it all on consumer goods, stock market speculators have much to be thankful for, bonuses and dividends have been poured out—and yet very little of this good fortune has touched the professional group. It is hard to understand why, in the face of all this seeming prosperity, there are still about 8 million unemployed in the U.S.

Just came back thru the stores on my lunch hour. People are spending money like drunken sailors.

DECEMBER 28, 1936

Just talked with a client 63 years of age who lost everything in the late, lamented depression. He made a substantial fortune in business but all of his investments were in speculative stocks and went bad—Republic Rubber, Standard Textile, Youngstown Banks. He says now that if he had placed all his savings in gov't bonds just to preserve the principle he would have been better off. If he had it to do over again he would buy annuity insurance. At his present age a life annuity of $250 per month looks like a fortune. His story is identical to the story of many successful business men who have learned that the making of an investment is more important than the earning of the money, and that safety of principal does not go hand in hand with a high speculative profit. As he put it to build wealth you must:

1. First learn to save or accumulate money.
2. Learn how to hold these savings by avoiding speculation.
3. Learn how to make this money work for you thru conservative investments.

1937

JANUARY 2, 1937

It seems to me that the time has come where we can formally and officially announce that the depression of 1929 has ended.

> **7/19/39**
>
> *You were wrong. A new depression started Sept. 1937 and is still with us.*

Recovery started in the summer of 1932 but from 1932 until March 1935 the movement was so uncertain and there were so many set-backs that nobody dared predict very much. In March 1935 without any apparent reason the stock market began a march upward which has continued until the present day. None of the commercial indexes gave the reason for this rise and for 6 months or a year many able men predicted that it would collapse as so many other false starts had done. But it did not collapse and in its wake the automobile industry pressed forward in a spectacular fashion until now it approaches the 1929 level of production and talk of a boom is heard. Railroads and steel then picked up and have been booming during the past year. During 1936 Youngstown has changed from a depressed steel city into a booming industrial center. The roads are crowded with new cars, vacant houses and stores are at a premium and people are buying freely of consumption goods such as clothing, furniture, etc. In 1932 almost every furniture store in town was out of business—in 1936 almost 6 new furniture companies opened their doors. I generally assumed that during a depression the personal finance companies would do a big business but the reverse is true. In 1936 many new personal and automobile finance companies came here and they all appear to be doing a business. Now that people have steady jobs they are borrowing to pay old debts and are again buying on the installment plan. Along with this, prices of clothing and other necessities are rapidly rising.

Looking back now at the picture of the depression it seems to me that a student of history could have made a better prediction of when the depression would hit bottom etc. than a banker. All he had to do was to compare the chart of this depression with the charts of 1838, 1873, 1893, etc. Both 1873 and 1929 were war depressions and it follows that the charts of these two are almost identical. If an investor in 1929 had governed himself by the depression chart of 1873 he would have come close to the truth. The time of hitting bottom, the time of revival, the duration, etc. All seem identical. It is a very interesting fact that the "New Deal" with its pouring out of government funds, its managed currency, etc. did very little to change the '29 depression from that of '73. It did cause temporary and violent fluctuations but did not alter the duration of the depression or the basic structure. I realize that every depression is different and it is foolhardy to attempt to see too far into the future. Yet it seems to me that the following would be of interest to the student of history who is also an investor:

1. When the depression comes it is first most important to determine if it is a major or a minor depression. This is difficult of course and yet if we study the cause—such as war, over-speculation, etc. it may lead us in the right direction.

2. If you determine that a major depression is due in the economic cycle, then find some other depression in the U.S. history which was brought on by similar causes: e.g. 1873 was 2nd depression after Civil War and 1929 was the secondary depression after the world war. In a similar way 1837 was a bank credit and land speculation depression; 1893 resulted from over-expansion of railroads and 1907 came after over-expansion of business corporations.

3. If you can once definitely place the new depression in its proper historical background then the rest is easy. History will repeat itself and the chart of the old depression will foretell pretty accurately the course of the new. You will be told that this new depression is different because of government control, etc. but as long as human nature is the same and people like to speculate, it is probable that in the future, economic booms and depressions will come and go as in the

past. I have little faith that government can eliminate or control the economic cycle.

6/15/68

The boom after World War I lasted 10 years. The boom after World War II is now 23 years old (1945–1968) and still going strong. From about 225, the D. J. reached 1000 in 1966.

The following general conclusions can be drawn from the depression just ended:

1. The business of the lawyer did not drop off quickly in 1929 with the coming of the depression. In 1930 and 1931 the lawyer made some money out of bankruptcies, foreclosures, etc. 1932–1936 were bad depression years for the lawyer and even tho prosperity has returned for most people it has not yet returned for the lawyer. It will be a year or more before people will have enough money to buy real estate and do other things that require a lawyer. The lawyer who specialized in bankruptcies, receiverships and reorganizations reaped a harvest throughout the depression.
2. During the years 1930–1934 when people were out of work they wanted to gamble for small stakes and to play games of chance. The "bug" number game, horse and dog racing, etc. were all profitable. One Youngstown man made considerable money by inventing a marble game similar to a slot machine.
3. If you once determine that you are at the beginning of a major depression, then liquidate your investments at once even at a loss because later on you will be able to buy back at a fraction of the price. An investor who sold out at a loss in 1930 or 1931 could have bought back at 1/4 the price in 1932.
4. Cash is king in every depression. A small investment in real estate or stocks or bonds in 1932 would be worth a fortune today. Comparisons of a few 1932 stock prices with today's prices:
Sheet & Tube 4–80; Republic 2–30; Gen. Motors 8–80; Gen. Elc. 8–58; U.S. Steel 20–78; Amer. T&T 70–180, etc. Even the good stocks, bonds and real estate were selling at giveaway prices but few men had both the cash and the courage to buy when things looked the blackest.

5. When the final upturn came in 1935 it came very quietly and suddenly and kept on going up all thru 1936 and has not yet stopped although we have already passed normal. It was quiet but spectacular and the full effect cannot be appreciated unless you look back to see what progress was made in 1935–1936.

6. During the past depression prominent bankers, business men, etc. were all wrong in most of their predictions. Use your own judgment and do your own thinking.

12/1/55

The same argument still rages today. I still do not believe that gov't can wipe out cycles.

6/15/68

I still do not believe that a managed economy will work.

Inflation

I am told the managed economy of the "New Deal" has eliminated future booms and depressions but I do not believe it. I am afraid that during the next few years we will see some form of inflation. Already prices of food and commodities are going up, brokers offices are crowded again and people are just as stock crazy now as in 1929. In some respects, stock prices are as much out of line now as in 1929. Banks are piled high with deposits and do not know how to invest it because good bonds bring in only 2%. Only yesterday the Union National Bank announced it would not accept savings accounts in excess of $1000 because it could not use the money. When business really expands enough to borrow this bank surplus, there is danger that we will have pyramiding of these huge credit reserves leading to over-speculation, over-expansion, perhaps an inflationary boom and then a crash. Government officials say they can control this coming boom but I do not believe they can or for political reasons will be unwilling to restrain "good business" and expansion.

JANUARY 9, 1937

It is curious that often the boy or man who lives alone and has few friends turns out to be the greatest success. They say that as a college student Calvin

Coolidge was a red-headed boy with a poor personality and few friends—yet he became Governor and President.

Yesterday I had lunch with a lawyer of Youngstown—age 42—never had much of a practice—always poorly dressed and few friends. Yet in 1932 he had $5000 in cash accumulated out of his small earnings. He had the courage to invest it all in common stocks at bargain prices—and he had the patience or foresight to hold these stocks until the present day—they are now worth over $100,000. He asked me "what next." Hold the stocks or sell and if he sells what to do with the money. My advice was to secure for himself a life income either thru annuity insurance, good bonds or a living trust. I am curious to see how his case will turn out. He never was the possessor before of much money. He has learned the first rule for building wealth—how to accumulate—but has he learned the second step which is to hold that wealth and make it work for him so that he will have income without loss of principal?

JANUARY 9, 1937

Within the past few days President Roosevelt delivered his annual address to Congress and his budget message. It is discouraging to those who hoped he would balance the budget and drastically cut expenditures after election. He still seems in a spending mood and even tho recovery is here he continues the extravagant money spending agencies created during the depression. It seems to indicate that the present administration will not—even if it could—take the drastic steps necessary to prevent the coming of an inflation.

Former Vice Pres. [Charles G.] Dawes is writing a book on economics laying down the theory I have believed in—that each depression follows the course of former similar depressions—and that in the midst of a major depression—a study of former depressions will give us a fairly accurate glimpse into the future—as to when the depression will end—its severity etc. Each time in a depression new theories and "New Deals" are tried out but rarely do they seem to change the basic structure of the economic cycle.

MARCH 11, 1937

The march of business has continued upward now without a break for two years since March 1935. It is one of the most amazing recoveries ever witnessed and just now we seem to be entering a boom period. [Undated note added: "The market broke badly within 30 days."] Steel mills have been operating at capacity for a long time, stores are crowded, wages and prices are rapidly rising and again the common man has money to spend. Even now, however, the law profession and the building trades lag in the rear of recovery. My business is better but not normal and it comes in spurts. Real estate rentals are high, vacant houses at a premium and the banks have unloaded most of their foreclosed property—but building of new residences has lagged.

The stock market has plowed ahead also for two years and is now at a dizzy peak. Many people have made fortunes—brokers' offices are again crowded and everybody talks stocks. We have all the signs of another boom and a coming inflation.

Sheet & Tube which sold in 1932 for 6 is now over 100 and pays $3 dividend. Truscon (1932–2) now 25; Republic (1932–2) now 45; U.S. Steel (1932–25) now 125.

And so it goes. Very few people bought in 1932 and held until now. They usually sold where they could double or treble their money. If they had held on they could have gotten 20 or 30 to 1.

The greatest chance in a lifetime to build a fortune has gone and will probably not come again soon. Very few people had any surplus to invest— it was a matter of earning enough to buy the necessaries of life—and those who had a little money hoarded it and were afraid to buy stocks, bonds and real estate that nobody wanted.

Inflation? It seems to be near at hand. Rising prices, continued government spending and speculative craze all point that way.

President Roosevelt is still hell-bent for reform and his latest proposal is to pack the Supreme Court so it will hold constitutional his New Deal laws.

MAY 1, 1937

Business continues on the up-grade with very little interruption. Strikes in labor have caused an occasional slowing down but soon again the pace is accelerated. The motor and steel industries are working at capacity. Each day the newspaper contains long lists of new automobile sales. It seems as tho the roads are too crowded now. Stores are busy, real estate and building show signs of activity and people everywhere are refurnishing their homes etc.

In the face of all this prosperity the law profession continues to lag. Business has shown improvement but it is still far below normal. It seems as tho the lawyer will have to build up a back-log of pending cases before he can

Ohio steelworkers formed the Steel Workers Organizing Committee (SWOC) in April 1936 to demand higher wages and better working hours. In the "Little Steel Strike" of 1937 that followed, more than 28,000 workers halted operations at three "Little Steel" companies by late May: Inland Steel, Republic Steel, and Youngstown Sheet & Tube. Riots in Youngstown on June 9 and 10 resulted in the deaths of two strikers and the wounding of twenty-three workers. This June 23, 1937 "Labor Holiday" parade at the main gate of Republic Steel was met with National Guard troops. (Ohio Historical Society)

have a steady income again. Also it seems that the wheels of business will have to operate for awhile again before law cases will arise.

In the past few weeks the stock market has shown signs of faltering. The government continues a policy of prodigal spending—and under the surface of a seeming return to prosperity, there is the constant fear of inflation.

EDITOR'S NOTE

In the spring of 1937 a major confrontation broke out between unionized steelworkers and several of Youngstown's largest steel companies; it would come to be known as the "Little Steel Strike," because collectively the companies—including Republic Steel and Youngstown Sheet & Tube—were called "Little Steel." The steelworkers in Youngstown and South Chicago had become increasingly militant under the ascendancy of John L. Lewis and the Committee for Industrial Organization (later the Congress of Industrial Organizations). Indeed, Gus Hall, who would later become the head of the American Communist Party, was sent to Youngstown to organize during this period. Workers used sit-down strikes to keep their employers from bringing in nonunion labor. The companies, which were adamantly opposed to a unionized workforce despite the legal right to organize, at times resorted to teargassing employees to force them to leave the buildings. The state was eventually forced to call in the National Guard, and in a June clash between company guards and strikers two people were killed and almost two dozen injured. Later the companies were found to have violated federal law, and in 1942 the company recognized the steelworkers' union as the workers' representatives.

MAY 30, 1937

Business continues at a fast pace but in Youngstown it is interrupted by a steel strike—the first since 1919.

Stock prices remain about the same although there has been some recession in the past few weeks. Gen. Dawes predicts that in Sept. 1939 we will have a 2-year minor depression and then a long period of prosperity. He bases his prediction on the pattern of the 1873 depression.

As recovery proceeds a great many companies that went thru receivership are pulling out of the hole and their stocks are going up. Purchasers of these stocks are making fabulous profits. Continental Shares pfd sold at 25¢

a share while in receivership—recently as high as $25 per share with good future prospects. Standard Textile pfd sold at 50¢ and the bonds at 7. New stock now being offered and the bonds will get cash, pfd and common to the full amount. In almost all of these cases—even where they went into bankruptcy—the final payout is far in excess of the depression prices. The opportunity to buy these receivership stocks came at the tail-end of the depression. It was a fertile field for the small investor but required considerable courage because they were hopelessly in debt. This was particularly true of holding companies, railroads, etc. The quick pick-up of business and the swift rebound of stocks in the past two years changed the entire picture.

12/21/37

It now seems that when a company goes thru reorganization it is better to wait until it is reorganized and new stock issued. Holders of the new stock throw it on the market for anything it will bring. You can then buy on values and if the reorganization has been drastic there is every chance to profit in a year or two.

JUNE 22, 1937

We are having a bad steel strike in Youngstown and the mills have been closed for 3 weeks. It looks like a long drawn-out controversy. The non-union men planned to march on the mills in a body this morning and open them but the governor declared martial law and state troops kept the mills closed. There has been much labor trouble lately and a great deal of violence. The state and federal governments seem to support the labor unions and there has been a complete breakdown of law and order. Business is very quiet and everybody is hoping the strike will end soon.

OCTOBER 12, 1937

I have made no entry for several months because business seemed to be normal and it looked as tho it would continue for some time. About six weeks ago, however, the stock market had a bad break and since then it has gone steadily downward with hardly a pause until now almost all the gains for the past year have been wiped out.

There was no slump in business and no warning. Since then business has slumped and everybody is pessimistic. We have had over 2 years of recovery since March 1935. The chart of 1873 shows that after 2 years of recovery came a slump that lasted a year and then several years of good business. I wonder if we are in for that now.

During past 2 years of general recovery, the law profession lagged behind. We are still badly in debt and have not yet had a chance to recover. It has been a long, hard pull.

OCTOBER 20, 1937

The stock market break which has continued since early in September resulted in the worst break since 1929—on Monday and Tues. on each day stocks lost as high as 15 points—yesterday almost 7 1/2 million shares changed hands—ticker 22 minutes behind—talk of closing stock exchanges, etc. In last hour there was a rally which wiped out most of the losses. It is generally believed that business will be slow this winter. There is fear and pessimism in the air. Nobody seems to be able to explain why it happened. Most popular reason is that prosperity of past 2 years was a false prosperity built on government expenditures and now it has collapsed.

Needless to say stock prices look cheap today.

NOVEMBER 11, 1937

The stock market slump continues now in its 7th week. President Roosevelt calls a special session of Congress. There is talk of further devaluation of the dollar and other quack remedies to stop the slump. Russel Weisman predicts in this morning's *Plain Dealer* that this slump will develop into a major depression if the government again tinkers with the money or starts another spending spree.

NOVEMBER 19, 1937

Business continues bad—steel mills operating in the red at 50%—stock market stagnant—nobody sure whether the slump will be short or of long duration.

Congress meets in special session and all kinds of plans are urged to help business. The real need is for cessation of government spending—balanced budget—and a return to the orthodox theories of economics. I fear tho that Congress will turn to one of its numerous panaceas such as reducing the gold content of the dollar again or further government spending.

As I look over the stock market picture for the past seven years it occurs to me that next to liquid capital the investor must have patience and courage. The bad break of the past few weeks is the 7th bad break since 1930. In between each break the market arose to heights that would have permitted several hundred percent profit over the previous lows. Any investor who had the patience to wait for a bad break and then bought could have made much money. Most people do not have the patience to wait for the bad break. The average speculator is tied up in the market to the hilt when the break comes and has no liquid cash for the bargains that prevail.

There are two theories of present slump:

1. That the old depression is not yet over—we have not yet reached normal—this is the 7th set-back of the old depression.
2. The depression was over two years ago. Since March 1935 we have been going thru a boom. This is the first collapse after recovery.

I am inclined to follow the first theory! Certainly my law practice does not indicate that the depression has ended.

NOVEMBER 22, 1937

Following are some of the high and low stock prices for this year. Stocks are now at low points and most of the losses occurred in the recent recession which still proceeds.

AT&T 187–140; B&O 40 1/2–8 1/8; Gen. Elec. 64 7/8–34; G.M. 70 1/2–31 1/4; Radio 12 3/4–4 3/4; Repub. 47 1/4–12 1/2; Warner 18–4 3/4; West. U. 83 1/2–25 1/8; Yo. S &T 101 7/8–35.

There is growing belief among economists that the present recession is not an ordinary one; that the upturn since 1932 was false, based on government spending, monetary manipulation; that this recession is a liquidation of this false prosperity and that it will develop into a major depression or inflation unless the gov't balances the budget etc. Steel operations down to 40%.

If the gov't continues its spending etc. it means ultimate inflation and crash.

If the gov't stops spending, balances the budget, it means bad business during the period of adjustment but ultimately a sound recovery.

Either way the outlook is not promising.

NOVEMBER 26, 1937

The more I see of the recent stock market slump the more I am impressed with the fact that the American people look upon the stock market as a place to gamble and not to invest. In times of rising market the average American becomes over-optimistic: he invests his whole capital in common stocks of the most speculative variety; often extends himself on margin. Then when a slump comes he finds himself over-extended; no cash reserve to fall back upon; he becomes unduly pessimistic and sells at a loss. The European investor takes his capital—no matter how small—half he invests in government bonds—25% in high-grade dividend paying stocks—and the remaining 25% he will use to gamble on speculative stocks offering possibility of large gains. In the long run he comes out best. His possibility of loss is limited and in an abnormally low market like in 1932 he has capital for unusual bargains. What the American needs is not only stock exchange regulations but also an education on the investment possibilities of the stock market.

The average man who buys real estate for investment makes a careful study of the property, the location, the income, etc. and hires a lawyer to examine the title. He then expends a lot of time and energy to collect rents, make repairs, etc. At the end of 10 years if he can say that his investment shows an annual return of 6% and then a reasonable capital profit when he sells, then he will consider that investment a success. That same man when he buys stocks either will not investigate because he does not know how or because he is lazy. He bets his money as in a horse race and does not feel his venture a success unless his money is doubled in a very short time.

If the patience and care used in a real estate investment were used in making a stock investment, there would be much greater chance of success.

DECEMBER 21, 1937

The business slump continues and the stock market is stagnant although the stores are having a fair Christmas season.

Mr. R. C. S. told me another depression story today. He made $150,000 in the real estate brokerage business in the 1920s—before he was 45. Then lost $70,000 in stock of Republic Rubber Company. After that loss he put the rest of his money in 2nd mortgages bought at discount. In the foreclosure period following 1929 he bought in many properties to protect his 2nd mortgages—assumed the first mortgage expecting to pay out of rent. Then in the 1930s, he could not rent or sell the properties and lost everything.

Ended in a nervous breakdown and is just now recovering. Trying to start again as a real estate broker to earn a living. Asked what he would do with the $150,000 if he had the chance again, he said: "I would buy an annuity or government bonds. It would have made me secure for life." Is especially rabid against buying vacant lots for investment. Taxes and lack of income make them more speculative than the stock market.

The more I hear of these things the more difficult does the whole problem of investment become. Real estate is surrounded with many perils as shown during the past few years. Investment in securities is even more difficult. It requires a knowledge of intricate corporate affairs, of accounting, of business cycles and also the ability to follow the trend of national and international economic and political affairs. Even bonds are full of risk because large corporations put out so many issues that it is difficult even for the expert to determine which is a first mortgage. The recent history of corporate reorganization and bankruptcy shows that bondholders fared badly. The only solution seems to be to make a life study of it—just like any other profession—and then use your best judgment. In addition to this the investor must have a sense of business values—be conservative and yet able to act quickly when he sees opportunity. Very few can qualify and yet the rewards are great.

DECEMBER 23, 1937

I just finished reading a book by [Morrell Walker] Gaines on the *Art of Investment* (1922). I found it very instructive. Gaines first tries to show the difference between speculation and investment. He believes that certain safeguards can be built up against risk—that by study and hard work the intelligent investor can determine the business cycle we are in—can arrange to switch from common stocks to short-term bonds when speculation is rife—from short-term bonds or treasury bonds to long-term bonds after prosperity has broken and the downward swing has started—to sell the long-term bonds and switch to common stocks again when the bottom has been reached and signs of upturn begin to appear. His theory is to invest in the strongest income securities—and this return plus an occasional capital increase every two or three years in boom markets—will ultimately mean substantial profits. If the capital is not lost and if the profit is consecutive (even if not large) the fund will grow with amazing rapidity.

Defenses

To guard against loss of capital is most important.

1. Increase liquid assets when security prices are high and speculation rampant. Substitute short-time bonds for long-time bonds and common stocks. Get ready for the inevitable crash. Even if you sell too early—it is better than too late. It is sometimes wise to sell at a price you fixed when you bought the stock.
2. Deal only in well-seasoned securities with a broad market. Slow stocks may tie you up at a critical time.
3. As far as possible deal only in income bearing securities that can be held through a slump. Then if you don't sell out in time, even tho you may see low prices, you may get a reasonable return on your investment and will probably come out in the end.
4. Buy the stocks outright—not on margin. If you do borrow—borrow from banks—conservatively. If you borrow when stocks are low and money plentiful—you take less risk than when stocks are high and a crash is imminent.

Lines of Attack

1. First line of attack is accrual of income. Money doubles in 14 years at 5%—12 yrs. at 6%—and 10 yrs at 7%. 1000 for 40 years at 6% will amount to $165,000.
2. Second line of attack is to get an occasional capital increase every few years by sale of securities at higher prices. It is hard to pick a security that will go up quickly but it is less difficult to pick a security that will go up in 2 or 3 years. The difficulty diminishes with the distance. If a good security is bought below value, the investor need not be much concerned with the daily ups and downs of the market. Eventually the market will come up to him and recognize the value of the security. This means recognizing the long swings in the business cycle. It means switching to high-grade common stocks in time of depression when they sell below value—and switching again to bonds in time of prosperity when common stocks are selling at a premium and speculation is rife. When prices are high, that is the time to guard against depreciation. When prices are low that is the time for action with liquid capital. An investor who is loaded in time of depression with high

priced common stocks is rendered helpless and can only wait and hope his stocks are strong enough to carry thru.

Another source of profit is buying stocks of reorganized companies. It is best to wait until the reorganization is complete and buy the new stocks. Generally the old stockholders get tired of waiting and throw the new stock on the market for what it will bring. If the reorganization has been drastic and takes place just before an upturn in business comes then it should be a good investment.

3. There is a proper security for each phase of the business cycle—and each security—whether bonds or stocks—should bear dividends. The dividend return may vary but should be unbroken. The profit from sale of securities will be irregular and at long intervals. As the cycle changes the security should be changed. It is hard to always judge the exact place in a cycle but it is fairly easy to know whether we are in a period of great prosperity and speculation or in a period of blackness and despair. It is most difficult to know when the turn comes. It is best not to wait for the turn but to follow the simple theory of buying when a security is selling below value and to sell when above value. You will probably lose some profits but this is better than waiting too long. A conservative investor will be satisfied to increase principal to an extent that will double the dividend return. This may not sound like much but if the increase is consecutive and none of the principal lost, it will mount rapidly.

Other general points.

1. Depression is time of greatest profit. The investor who has liquid funds and the courage to act can lay the basis for great profits. The speculator is usually broke or tied up with high-priced stocks.
2. A period of railroad reorganization offers great opportunities in the stocks and bonds of the reorganized companies. If drastically reorganized, the companies will be stronger than ever. Prosperous years are ahead and the new stocks will sell below value.
3. Not too much of your capital should be risked on one particular theory. You may be wrong. You must judge the risk as well as the profit and the latter should outweigh the former.
4. Business will always come back. It will remain neither depressed nor exalted.
5. The stock market forecasts business in only a limited way. The begin-

ning of a stock market movement usually is caused by the trend of business but in the end the movement is carried too high or too low— by the extreme optimism or despair of human nature.

6. As a general rule only strong companies are worth investing in. After a severe depression this may be broadened to include 2nd grade companies which have survived the panic in good shape and have prosperous years ahead. At such times the risk is less. The risk is greatest at the top of a boom.

7. A certain amount of cash, bonds or other liquid securities should always be set aside for protection or to seize unexpected opportunities.

8. A major risk should not be taken for a minor profit. Real skill appears in appraising the risk. If it can be discovered where risks have been exaggerated by the public in lowness of price, the profit naturally follows.

9. The investor has this great advantage over the merchant or speculator—his assets are always liquid. He can switch from the treas. bonds to short or long-term bonds or to stocks with great rapidity—and he can still maintain steady dividends even tho they are lower. The investor should consider his work as a business or profession—his capital is most precious and must not be lost or tied up. He must be more interested in broad economic movements than in day by day fluctuations of the stock market. He must not let his long viewpoint be disturbed by too close contact with the stock market. He is not interested in tips. The investor must be hot in action—cold in thought.

10. Information and statistics are so voluminous that each investor must develop some simple method to make use of them. Most of the information deals with the daily ups and downs of the market—the waves and not the tides. These things are not important. The investor is interested only in that information which affects the long-time trend.

To give meaning to stock prices and values he must learn to make simple comparisons between similar things. For instance, stocks and bonds can be grouped as steels, rails, etc. Put the vital figures of U.S. Steel along side Bethlehem and compare them. General Electric vs. Westinghouse, General Motors vs. Chrysler, etc. In this way the complicated statistics have meaning and make an intelligent choice possible.

A brief comparison between similar companies as to earnings, debt, capitalization, dividends and surplus will show the true picture. Orderly knowledge can be built up out of this confusion of statistics by simple comparisons with the past and with like companies.

As to general conditions—the investor must analyze and digest general information in newspapers, business magazines and personal observation and use his own judgment as to the present state of business.

The investor must organize all the material around him so he can use it in a simple way. He must disregard the non-essential. He must discipline himself and realize that the investment of surplus funds is all-important and requires work and diligence.

1938

JANUARY 3, 1938

The year of 1937 came to a close in the midst of depression talk and after a four month's drop in the stock market which was the steepest in history. The stock market started up in the spring of 1935 and continued straight up with hardly a pause until spring 1937. A short break in August and then a long plunge which cancelled all gains of the past two years. Most economists blame it on the inflationary policies of the government. In spite of all the criticism the President appears determined to go ahead with his plans. The forecasts for 1938 are gloomy. They all say they cannot make a prediction because so much depends on what Congress will do. Most of them think 1938 will not be as good as 1937.

In Youngstown the steel mills boomed in 1936 and part of 1937 and worked as high as 80%—now down to 18%. The steel strike in May and June 1937 shut things down tight and then the market crash in August kept them down. Again it has been a disappointing year in the law profession. It is true that my 1937 earnings were about 20% above 1936 but I am still about 30% below normal.

JANUARY 24, 1938

The depression continues with increased intensity. Stocks are at a low point and business is at a standstill. It is thought now that the government will start spending money again in the spring in order to bring revival before the fall elections. If so it will be an inflation spurt. This depression seems harder for people to bear than in 1932. During the 1935–1937 spurt they bought autos, furniture etc. on the installment plan and now they cannot pay. Also most people have after 7 long years used up all their surplus and have no place to turn. Most predictions say recovery will not come until next fall or later. In the meanwhile, stores are loaded with merchandise and selling at a sacrifice. Same old story. It seems that the time is here again when good stocks can be bought cheap—to be held for the next cycle. The Erie R.R. went into bankruptcy last week. About 40% of RRs are now in receivership.

FEBRUARY 18, 1938

The "depression" continues without much change. Business continues to mark time. There has been no spring upsurge in either the stock market or in business. In past few days the government has taken steps of an "inflationary" nature and talk of inflation has started again. Once again the government remedy is toward inflation instead of correcting basic errors in policy. Again I wonder if we are heading toward a bad inflation boom and collapse. Just how long can deficit financing continue? It seems to me however that we have about reached the bottom of this bear market and the time has come again to accumulate stocks The European situation is worse than ever with a constant threat of war. Germany is now gobbling up Austria. War continues in Japan and Spain. U.S. takes steps to build up its navy. It is a crazy world.

6/1/38

Note: The low point came about when stock prices started up without warning.

MARCH 1, 1938

The depression just continues without much change. When it started last fall it was thought to be only a temporary down-turn. Now it has assumed more definite proportions and even European nations have been affected so that it is becoming international in scope. The recognized economists believe that real prosperity cannot return until Roosevelt stops trying to reform and lets business alone under fair restrictions but with a reasonable chance to earn a profit—and also no more currency manipulation and no more "white rabbits." Roosevelt does not seem the kind of a man to admit that he is wrong—especially with election coming next fall. There may be a slight spring upturn but there seems little hope of more permanent improvement until after the fall elections. 1938 will be the 9th year of bad business for me.

After 8 years of "pump priming" and other trick methods of bringing back prosperity, it is my conclusion that none of them are any good. In our capitalistic system we must let the forces of competition and demand and supply work things out in a natural way. No man or group of men is smart enough to control prices or supply and demand or currency in a nation so large as ours. I am only afraid that we have gone too far to prevent a period of inflation. After 8 years of bad business most of us are at rock bottom and are poorly prepared to weather such a storm—so what?

MARCH 15, 1938

Very little new to report. The depression continues and the stock market has been stagnant for several months. A large New York brokerage house fails. It was thought that Pres. Roosevelt would take some drastic step to break the depression but so far he has failed to act.

In Europe war becomes more imminent. Hitler seizes Austria in a bloodless coup and England and France arm rapidly to prevent the seizure of Czechoslovakia. The French Cabinet falls and Blum again becomes premier. It is a world of chaos and nobody can predict ahead. Retail stores are dumping their spring mdse at sale prices and bankruptcies are on the increase. Law practice continues bad.

MARCH 18, 1938

Fear of war caused Europe to liquidate U.S. stocks and gave a bad break to the market. Prices are now near low point of this Roosevelt depression.

Talked to J. C. R. today who is in retail merchandise business. Says his business is 70% below last year. Also says that he holds shares of stock that were worth $25,000 last year and now worth $5000.

MARCH 25, 1938

The depression deepens and yesterday the stock-market crashed thru the low point of 1937. Prices are back to 1934. It is pretty well agreed now that we are in a new cycle of depression. The old depression started in 1929 and reached bottom in June 1932. From there it climbed up until fall of 1937 and then broke again. There has been no period of "normal" business and as far as I am concerned it is the same old depression. If this continues long it will be a knock-out-blow. Most people and businesses are groggy from 1929. In 1937 they began to expand, expecting a few years of normal. They are not in a position to stand much further strain. To me it proves that the economic policies of Roosevelt did not bring a lasting recovery.

APRIL 18, 1938

The present depression is almost as bad as 1932 and continues without abatement. 1/4 of Cleveland population is on relief. Unemployment is as great as 1932. Business is stagnant and everybody is waiting for something to happen.

Pres. Roosevelt announces a new spending program to prime the business pump. He proposes to spend $3 or $4 billion. It will help him to win the November elections but we will probably have a short spurt of prosperity and then another slump. Business is afraid of his reforms and I am now afraid we will have chronic depression so long as he has control of Congress. Even with the announcement of this huge spending program there has been little inflation talk even tho it brings us nearer the abyss. People are apathetic and do not seem to care. The spending of billions seems to mean nothing. Even the stock market continues listless. If only private capital would gain confidence and go to work, the problem would be solved.

APRIL 27, 1938

The business slump continues with very little change in the picture. The index of production, consumption, bonds, etc. are still down although the decline is less abrupt.

I have been interested in trying to call the turn on the present depression. As long as the majority of the important indexes point down and the general outlook is bad, it seems to me the depression would not be over. But if stock prices go up several months in advance of business improvement— then it seems that indexes of production would go up *after* stocks have risen and would only confirm the judgment of the courageous speculator. It seems to me that all one can do is to judge the entire picture and when things are blackest—then make a guess that things will get better and buy stocks for the rise. I see the risk here because very few people knew in June 1932 that the turn had come. It seems to me that the present turn is near at hand and will come in early summer [undated note: "Right"]. It also seems easier to call the turn at the top of the boom than at bottom. At top with money rates high, speculation rampant, stocks selling far above intrinsic value, bonds falling—there are many warnings. In either case the best the investor can do is to buy and sell at approximately the right times and then not worry even if he could have made a little more by waiting.

MAY 7, 1938

France devalues the franc again yesterday for the 3rd time since the war. The history of France for the past 20 years should be a warning to the U.S. for our course here is very similar. There has been chronic depression in France all those years.

Business here continues at a standstill. Most of the important indexes still point down. In spite of this I think the upturn in the market is about due. Bonds turned up two wks. ago partly because of lowering of bank reserves and partly because of friendliness to business shown by the administration. If I had funds to invest I believe I would start accumulating stocks. Steel mills operate at 30% and the summer promises to be dull.

JUNE 7, 1938

The depression gets worse and is now down to 1933 levels without signs for a pickup in the fall. As usual, when it started in March 1937 people said it would last only a few months. They said recovery would come in fall 1937— then winter—then spring 1938—and now they say fall 1938 but I think they are wrong again. Steel mills operate at 25% and industrial production and other indexes continue to hit new lows. There is talk of a further devaluation of the dollar from 59¢ to 50¢. In the meanwhile Pres. Roosevelt is rushing his money spending program so it will take effect before the November elections. It is a dreary and uninspiring grinding depression that seems to have no end. Law business of course is at a standstill.

JUNE 24, 1938

Beginning early this week the stock market started an upward spurt which still continues. Whether it will last long and mark a major upward movement remains to be seen. It caught the commentators unprepared. There are still no signs in the industrial indexes to confirm it. For two weeks before the spurt the volume dwindled to 300,000 shares a day. It was predicted a change was coming but most predictions said it would be down. It all goes to show how difficult it is to call the turn at the bottom of a depression. Your guess is as good as anyone's. If you wait for the actual upturn to begin, it moves so rapidly that much is lost. Republic Steel for instance jumped from 12 to 17 in 2 days. Still this might be better than trying to buy on the way down.

JUNE 27, 1938

Stock prices have continued straight up for more than a week now and many gains amount to 50% or more. Just as in 1932 the rise came after a lull of several weeks and a falling down in volume of sales—but no indication of improvement in business indices. It caught the economists flat-footed.

Both 1932 and 1938 indicate there is no sure way to catch the bottom of the swing because it comes without warning. When liquidation has dried up and the situation looks hopeless—that is the turn. Your guess is as good as anybody's.

JULY 2, 1938

The market has continued straight up for two weeks and almost all commentators agree that a new major cycle has started. My own business and general business in Youngstown show no improvement. Steel mills operate 20%.

JULY 7, 1938

After pausing for a day or two over the 4th of July the market started up again and today there is another stampede of buyers to get stocks. As yet the industries' indexes show no definite improvement. At least a technical set-back seems overdue.

In looking over the past 6 months it seems clear that nobody could have guessed the bottom of the swing because nothing happened that should have caused the market to go up. The same thing happened in 1932. It is thought that Pres. Roosevelt engineered the rise in order to pave the way for November elections. All he needed was the cooperation of a few Wall St. operators. Since then the gov't has encouraged the upswing.

For several weeks before the rise the market was stagnant—sales fell to

300,000 a day—losses were small—and everybody was pessimistic. Such a sold-out market was the only sign the bottom had been reached.

JULY 11, 1938

For past few days there has been a wild reaction in the stock market with a loss of 2 or 3 points. The longer outlook is good.

JULY 20, 1938

After a pause for a week the market started up again yesterday. There has as yet been no real reaction and it seems overdue. In this depression at least the stock upturn came several weeks before business indexes showed any improvement. For the past two weeks these indexes have been turning slowly up. At the time of the stock market upsurge the indexes were very slowly moving down and some were stationary. Same with stocks. Volume was low and there were many indications of a sold-out market.

Fundamentally the whole business situation is weakened by the monetary policies of the New Deal and I do not see how we can have enduring recovery until this is rectified. This may not be until Roosevelt's term of office is over. In the meanwhile the national debt approaches $40 billion. People seem to have forgotten about the danger of inflation but it is still there just the same.

AUGUST 10, 1938

Business and the stock market have been stagnant for the past few weeks. It seems to me that stock market prices are higher than business prospects warrant. Everything is still as uncertain and clouded as when Roosevelt took office. I am beginning to believe there will be no return to normal until his term is over. A short boom and then a collapse seems to be all we can look for. Yesterday was primary election. People are slowly turning back to the Republican Party—but New Deal money with millions on W.P.A. and relief still give the Democrats the edge. It will be interesting to see how far the swing goes this fall.

AUGUST 29, 1938

Business men seem to be optimistic about fall business but there is very little in the way of statistical [evidence] to bear them out. For past two months the stock market has moved sidewise in a hesitant manner. I do not look for much during the balance of the year except a fair pick-up at best. Meanwhile it looks like war again in Europe.

OCTOBER 20, 1938

Prospects look brighter than for a long time. In September—due to war scare in Europe—stocks and business had the jitters. With the "Peace of Munich" normal recovery forces took hold of things and stocks and business forged ahead rapidly. I would not be surprised if we are now at the beginning of a cyclical upswing which may last a year or more. I also believe that the "Roosevelt Era" and the New Deal are waning—that conservatives are making progress—and that this will help business. I am optimistic for the first time in months.

1939

MARCH 6, 1939

The optimism in the last paragraph was misplaced. Once again the recovery fizzled out and since December has been down. Business is at a standstill, stocks are stagnant. At least Congress is independent but nothing is being accomplished. The New Deal has apparently been stopped but the opposing forces are not strong enough to go forward. The battle before Congress now is whether to stop pump priming. It does no good, but a lot of harm. The gov't debt is $40 billion and still increasing. Fear of inflation is always in the background. If gov't spending is stopped there may be some hope for recovery. The European situation still is badly muddled and there is always the fear of war. It is terrible to contemplate that we are in the 9th year of depression and still cannot see clearly ahead. I am afraid nothing definite will be done until Roosevelt is out of office. In meanwhile everybody is living a hand-to-mouth existence and struggling under a burden of debt accumulated in past 9 years. It is not pleasant.

MARCH 10, 1939

Talked to W. W. Z. today. He said: During the past 10 years I lost half my life savings in local banks and corporations. The directors were personal friends and they advised the investments. I thought they were high-minded men and would look after the business. When the companies were broke I found out they had protected themselves and nobody else. If I had it to do over again I would invest only in outstanding national corporations with stocks listed on N.Y. Exchange so I could sell when trouble threatened.

JULY 19, 1939

I have entered nothing on this record because there has been nothing to record. The slump which started in Sept. 1937 is still with us although in fact for days there have been some signs of recovery. Business has been rotten the past two years—mills at 60%—most millworkers earnings about $18 per week etc.—and in the background a continuous fear of war in Europe. After panic of 1893 there came a 2 year recovery—a slump of a year—then several years of good business. We had recovery 1935–37 and a slump 1937–39. Let us hope the pattern of 1873 will repeat and we have several good years ahead. Stocks are about 10% lower than last spring.

As I re-read some of the predictions made by outstanding economists in past few years, I must laugh. They were all wrong. None of them foresaw the 1937–39 collapses and many predicted inflation before this. It seems that Geo. F. Baker of New York had the right idea. He knew how to value a stock and bought when selling below value—then held on, grimly confident that in the end he would make a profit. He could with assurance buy U.S. Steel at 30—ignore all predictions—and make a profit by holding on long enough. If the country survived the stock would go up—and there was little chance of such a company going broke. Baker never tried to predict the course of business or to follow market swings. Baker's plan seems sound. It is like buying a piece of real estate or a suit of clothes below value—but you must be a good judge of values.

Let us take Yo. Sheet & Tube Co. for example:

1. Its earnings fluctuate widely and the price of its stock does also. Some years it operates at 40% capacity—other years at 80%, etc. In 1935 it operated at about 40% and stock sold for 35. In 1937 it operated at 80% and stock sold for 100.
2. Since the company survived the 1929 depression it is not likely to go broke now.
3. When it operates at 40% one year—it will likely operate at 70% or 80% in another 2 or 3 years.
4. Therefore stock bought at 35 can probably be sold at a profit in a year or two.

JULY 21, 1939

A friend of mine started to speculate on the stock market on 25% margin with $2500 in cash in May 1933. This was shortly after Pres. Roosevelt reopened the banks and devalued the dollar. For several months there was an inflation boom that trebled stock values and then a collapse. This man traded actively in public utility stocks such as Am. Super. at 8 and in steel stocks such as Republic at 19. By end of 1933, he lost his $2500 and owed the broker $7500—a total loss of $10000.

Hindsight is better than foresight. Mr. Baker would have bought outright sound stocks such as U.S. Steel—G.E.—G.M.—and he would have *held on*. In 1935–37 rises he could have had many chances to sell at treble values. Net result is that my friend is out not only the $10,000 he lost but the additional $10,000 he might have made if he followed a more conservative course. His total loss is really $20,000—a fortune to him. And this is why some men can accumulate and others cannot.

SEPTEMBER 11, 1939

On Sept. 1, 1939 war broke out in Europe. Germany marched into Poland. England and the dominions and France immediately declared war. Russia stands with Germany. Italy has declared herself neutral. Germany has during the past week occupied 1/3 of Poland and has almost surrounded Warsaw. This situation has been smoldering ever since Hitler came into power 5 years ago. It looks like a second world war of long duration.

The coming of war raises many basic questions. It seems to write finis to the New Deal and to the last 10 years of depression. In the past week the stock market boomed 20 points. What does the future hold? It is anybody's guess. A period of war prosperity—followed by a world collapse? With our huge bank reserves and a national debt of $40 billion—will the pyramiding of these huge reserves bring on the long awaited inflation? Will America enter the war? What to do to protect oneself? These are the questions in everybody's mind. Of one thing only are we certain and that is that after 10 years of depression and political uncertainty—a long war will mean troubled times ahead. I dread the prospect.

CHAPTER 7
SEPTEMBER 12, 1939–DECEMBER 31, 1941

"My children have known only blackest depression."

By his own admission, Roth hadn't anticipated he would still be writing in his diary by 1939. But by the fall of 1939 Roth determined that the impending war in Europe, and its impact on America's industry and economy, was just as dramatic and worthy of record as the Depression itself.

Indeed, the bellicose activities abroad in 1939 shifted much of America's attention away from domestic economic reforms and recovery to the preparedness of our national defense. Prior to 1939 the nation as a whole shared Roth's reluctance to get involved in overseas tensions. Between 1935 and 1939 the U.S. government passed a series of acts intended to restrict America's possibility of entering a foreign war. In April 1939 Roosevelt even sent a wire to Hitler and Mussolini suggesting a dialogue on trade and arms agreements in exchange for a guarantee of a decade of peace. He was ignored. Publicly, Roosevelt would retain the stance of U.S. neutrality even as Hitler defied the Munich agreement and invaded Poland on September 1, 1939. But domestically, Roosevelt was taking steps in Washington to bring the United States closer to war. It would also boost the American economy to heights unmatched by his New Deal.

One step, a "cash-and-carry" provision, was passed that finally loosened the grip of the U.S. arms embargo and allowed America to sell much needed arms to Great Britain. As long as the nation paid cash and ferried the ammunition on non-U.S. ships, the United States could still position itself as neutral while opening up U.S. manufacturers to new war production orders.

Second, U.S. policies moved quickly from appropriating budgets to drum up employment and public works to bulking up a national defense for both an invasion and a possible declaration of war. After Roosevelt won a third term in 1940 on a campaign platform dominated by foreign affairs rather than domestic relief programs, Congress authorized twelve billion dollars in defense spending on goods like fifty thousand new military airplanes in a year. This type of construction was a tremendous boon to the steel and rubber industries in and around Youngstown. Yet Roth continued to wonder how it was that industry could be experiencing a near-record boom without a corresponding boost in the stock market or his own law practice. His proposed explanations—the uncertainty that war produces, fears of inflation and a postwar bust, the regulatory limits to war profiteering—remain confounding factors to anyone today who tries to assess the relationship between military spending and economic growth.

VOLUME VI

SEPTEMBER 12, 1939

When I started these notes on the Depression of 1929, I expected to bring them to a close when the depression ended. I thought the depression would end in a few years in a perfectly normal way. But instead—after 10 years of depression—and New Deal politics under Roosevelt—we now see war in Europe which threatens to be of long duration and to involve the greater part of the world in its destructive effects.

The coming of war changes the whole political and economic situation. Before it broke out we still had the depression with us and it was pretty well agreed that the Democratic Party would go out of power in 1940. With this change in politics I expected to see the liquidation of the New Deal and the beginning of a normal recovery without bad inflation.

The coming war brought a hectic stock market boom with gains up to 20 points. Housewives rushed to buy groceries—sugar was scarce and doubled in price—everywhere there are signs of excitement . . . Broker's offices are crowded, prices of everything are going up—merchants and manufacturers are preparing for war time demands.

Our national debt is $40 billion—our banks have enormous reserves. If these reserves are loaned out for wartime expansion and multiplied 10 times by credit processes—it may bring on the long-awaited inflation.

England again commands the sea. Our present neutrality law forbids sale of arms to belligerent nations but Congress will meet in special session next month to change the law so that America can sell to the Allies on a cash and carry basis and help them win the war. America is neutral but American sentiment is preponderantly with the Allies.

Our banks are loaded to the gills with government bonds paying 1 1/2% interest. Last week these bonds broke badly because there is a chance to use the money to better advantage. Will depreciation in U.S. bonds affect our banking situation?

The future looks troubled. Because the situation is so interesting I have determined to continue these notes for awhile longer. If the war continues it looks like another crazy period of speculation ending in inflation and a bad crash.

Again the lawyer is on the spot. Ten years of depression has left him poorly prepared to face an inflationary period. It looks bad. The war industries will make huge profits and so will the speculator, but the lawyer faces ever diminishing returns from an inflated dollar.

For 10 years I have longed for normalcy but it does not seem so destined. My generation has already lived thru war, boom and panic but evidently we still have some excitement ahead of us.

The following shows some of the high and low averages for past 10 days: AT&T 170–148; Bethlehem Steel 100–50; Com & So. 1 5/8–1 1/4; G.E. 44–30; GM 55–36; Penn RR 25–15; U.S. St. 82–45; Repub. 28–12; Steel & Tube 56–30; United Air 46–31. The advance affected mostly steel, rails, aircrafts etc. and left other stocks almost unchanged.

OCTOBER 30, 1939

Since the war started on Sept. 1st, it has dwindled down into a siege in which England is trying to starve Germany into submission. There has been no spectacular fighting and consequently no war orders to U.S. except for a few planes. After the first spurt in "war brides" the market became stagnant. Steel and airplane and other war stocks have retained most of their gains but the other stocks are about where they were in August. Our steel mills are still operating over 90% to fill the early rush but it is predicted this will peter out and we will have a slump by spring unless the war changes. The Senate yesterday passed the "cash and carry" embargo and it is expected the House will confirm it shortly. There has been no pick-up in the law business.

NOVEMBER 13, 1939

The business picture remains much confused. So far the European war has been a phony. Very little fighting and very little buying of war supplies except airplanes. Steel mills are still above 90% but it is freely predicted we will have a slump this spring unless war orders come in. Business is much better than a year ago but the stock market is 10 points lower even after including "war babies" in the averages. Aircraft stocks and steel are higher than a year ago but the regular stocks are lower. It is a queer picture. Are we retracing the 1914 pattern when business did not pick up until the war was several years old? Part of the explanation is the orderly liquidation of stock holdings by foreign nations in order to get cash.

NOVEMBER 24, 1939

I am reading a biography of Elihu Root by [Phillip] Jessup and was interested in Root's theory and method of investing his funds. He believed—as did Geo F. Baker—that no man could predict the near future course of the market. He bought stocks that he thought were selling below intrinsic value and then held on until the market confirmed his judgment. He dealt mainly with banks and railroads with whose affairs he was familiar.

On one occasion a friend of Root's wrote asking his opinion as to the near term speculative value of a certain stock with which Root was in close contact. Root answered that he had no idea what course the market would follow and that any opinion he might express would be a guess. As for the stock itself, he was of the opinion that it was selling at an attractive price— below its value.

1940

JANUARY 5, 1940

Again we face a new year and the depression of 1929—now 10 years old is not yet completed. The year of 1939 closed without the war boom which was expected when war broke out in September. The war still rages in Europe but very little buying has been done from the U.S. except airplanes and trucks. With the outbreak of war in September the stock market rushed up and all industries prepared for a rush of war orders. It was shortly realized that very little actual fighting was taking place in Europe; that England was encircling Germany and was prepared for a long siege with as little fighting as possible and that this kind of a war meant little business for the

U.S. and it also meant a loss of much foreign trade. The stock market fell and ended the year at about the same average as January 1939 altho certain war stocks such as aviation and steels retained much of their gains.

During the last six months of 1939 Youngstown was more fortunate than many other parts of the country. With the coming of the war the steel plants were besieged with orders from domestic railroads and other industries—all rehabilitating their industries in preparation for a war boom. These orders kept the steel mills operating at a 90% capacity and it is expected that these orders will keep them going until March at about 70%. What will happen after that depends on war developments. Germany may be forced to take the aggressive to prevent strangling—this may result in much fighting and a rush of war orders. Again 1940 is a national election year and brings many uncertainties. All in all I am optimistic and hope it will be better than 1938 altho I do not look for a boom.

Due to the large payrolls—the Youngstown stores enjoyed a record-breaking Xmas season. As usual the law business trails behind. 1939 was about 10% better than 1938 but I am still about 40% below the pre-depression levels.

As I look back over the decade just closed it all seems like a bad dream. I have learned much but I hope that neither I nor my children will go thru such an experience again. None of my children—Connie 19—Bob 14—and Daniel 10—remember the pre-depression era. They have known only blackest depression—uncertainty—European wars—talk of Communism, socialism and fascism. Even their school books are filled with these subjects and with the constantly changing maps of Europe. Along with this morality and religion have been at a low ebb and the philosophy of Franklin and Lincoln are all ancient history. Even worse than this is the uncertainty of the future.

The war in Europe is rapidly spreading and even tho the U.S. may not be involved directly—we can nonetheless not escape the consequences. Our government debt is over $40 billion and constantly mounting. Will inflation come—will the war bring another unhealthy boom and subsequent deflation? Religious intolerance increases—and our country is swayed by European propaganda and subversive activities. All in all the world of 1940 is not a pleasant one. We can only hope that a better day is dawning.

JANUARY 31, 1940

Jack S— told me today: In 1937 I sold my business and I had $14,000 in cash. I went into the stock market and bought on margin. In the slump of

1938 I lost everything—in addition to which I caused losses to several relatives and friends who tried to help me out. If I had been able to hold on to these stocks I could make a handsome profit today. Several of my friends bought the same stocks on margin—but had enough surplus to carry thru the downsizing and made money. It is clear that if I had not bought on margin or could have held on just a few weeks longer I would have made money.

FEBRUARY 2, 1940

Business has been stagnant so far this year. The stock market has slowly drifted downward. It is generally predicted that prices of clothing etc. will rise this year because of the war. It is to be noticed that very few stores are pushing their January sales. The European war is not spectacular although it is thought that there will be a great deal of fighting in the spring and that this will bring in the long expected war orders.

MARCH 12, 1940

There is very little to report. There has been no spring rise so far although many expect improvement in the near future. There is some talk that the European war will become violent this spring and will bring a flood of war orders that will spell a boom here. Just now all is quiet on the western front and business is stagnant.

Stock Market Stories

Occasionally I hear a true story of the stock market which is worth recording. Had lunch with Mr. M. S. who has been manager of a branch clothing store for a growing company for about 30 years. During the 1st 20 years he accumulated stock of the company out of his savings—under employee plans, etc. Never speculated in his life. In 1929 the stock was skyhi—he had 400 shares at $130 a share—worth $50,000. On 10/10/29 he learned from his boss that the company would declare a special Xmas dividend of $5. Since the news was not made public he decided it was a good chance to speculate. Took his $50,000 stock to a bank—borrowed on it— bought more. At the end of October 1929 the crash came. He could have gotten out at 25 but he held on. It went to 14 and he lost everything but about $1000. All because he had put his stock up as collateral and had speculated with someone else's money.

His brother was the owner of an amusement park and quite prosperous. Owned a small summer home in Florida which cost him $2500 long before the Florida land boom. Sold it for $75,000 during the 1925 Florida land boom—then got land speculation fever—moved to Florida and lost everything. He knew the amusement business and made money in it. He knew nothing about real estate speculation and was playing the other man's game.

MAY 15, 1940

There has been much war hysteria in recent weeks and the tide of war has turned against the Allies. Germany has been successful in every move so far and now has control of Norway, Belgium, Holland, Poland, Hungary, and Czechoslovakia. At the present moment Germany has penetrated 12 miles into France and a critical battle is raging which may be the turning point in the conflict. As the Allies have been weak—so has the stock market weakened. The worst slump since 1937 took place Monday with the news of the Allies' danger. Stocks lost as much as 9 points on Monday and as high as 15 points yesterday. All gains of last September's war boomlet have been wiped out and stocks are lower than a year ago.

Congress is appropriating $2 1/2 billion for defense and this will raise the national debt above $47 billion. There is talk of invalidating the Johnson Act so that munitions can be sold on credit to the Allies. The U.S. has thus far received very few orders for war materials. Excitement is high and business is dull. This is typical of conditions for the past 10 years.

The following shows stock drop in past week: AT&T 171–149; B&O 4 5/8–2 3/4; Com. and So. 1 1/8–7/8; G.E. 35–28; GM 52–40; Penn RR 20 5/8–16 3/4; Radio 6 1/8–5 5/8; Republic Steel 22 1/8–15; U.S. Steel 62–48; Steel & Tube 42–31.

JUNE 10, 1940

The war in Europe continues to rage and so far the victories have gone to Germany. It looks black for the Allies. Germany has conquered Norway, Belgium and all the channel ports across from England as well as Poland and other Balkan states. Today a great battle rages on the Western Front, and Germany, with a million and a half men, is within 35 miles of Paris. Today at noon the paper announced that Italy had finally declared war on France and England. It looks bad for France with Germany attacking from the north, Italy from the south and England unable to help much. The U.S. is

Despite all of FDR's stimulus efforts in the New Deal, steel companies like Youngstown Sheet & Tube would only reach their pre-1929 production capacities as government defense contracts poured in to prepare for World War II. (The Mahoning Valley Historical Society)

sending planes etc. to the Allies and we are very near to a declaration of war ourselves. In the meanwhile very few war orders have been received so far. Business is slack and the stock market is lower than 2 years ago. Again it seems to me to be a good time to buy stocks.

JUNE 14, 1940

The European picture looks blacker than ever for the Allies. Paris falls before the invading Germans—1st time since 1870. Hitler is expected to make a triumphant entry into the city. The Maginot Line has been circled and is now being attacked from both sides. Spain enters war and with Italy is pressing from South. Germany now holds most of French and Belgium port cities and is completely segregating England.

Yesterday it was announced that England would buy for cash much needed war supplies and the market spurted up 5 points. This is the 1st change in the picture since the war started last September. Our steel mills are now operating at 70% and the picture looks pretty good for Youngstown for the immediate future.

JUNE 17, 1940

France surrenders to Germany. England faces all Europe alone. The situation seems hopeless. What will come next nobody knows. Tomorrow England will make an important announcement of her future course of action. Two months ago such a conclusion seemed impossible. Today it is a reality.

Stocks are at their lows for past two years. High and low quotations for 1940 are as follows:

AT&T 175–145; B&O 6 3/4–2 3/4; Bethlehem Steel 89–63; GE 41–26; GM 56–37; Penn RR 24–15 1/2; Radio 7 1/4–4 1/4; Republic Steel 23–14; U.S. Steel 68–42; Steel & Tube 48–26.

JULY 26, 1940

The war drags on in Europe and Germany consolidates her position as the conqueror of Europe. The threatened invasion of England by Germany has not taken place yet although the reason for the delay is unknown.

In the U.S. defense preparations go forward rapidly. It is probable that a national draft act will pass Congress in the next few weeks calling for registration of all males 21 to 64 and one year compulsory training.

Steel mills at 85% and business is active, but in spite of this, there are many misgivings for the future. The stock market is slowest since 1918—200,000 share days—and prices are stagnant.

The whole question is what will happen if Britain falls before Germany. Our export trade is already lost. Germany trades by barter—not by gold. Will the gold supply of U.S. (80% of world supply) become of no value if Germany wins and we are the only country left on the gold standard? Hitler will sell to South America and all Europe at low prices made possible by slave labor. How can we compete with him?

No matter which way the war goes—Europe faces starvation this winter while America does not know what to do with her food surpluses.

Even tho there is a gamble involved, it seems to me to be a good risk to buy stocks at present prices on the chance that Great Britain will win or that something will happen this winter to stop Hitler. Starvation in Europe may bring on revolt.

AUGUST 20, 1940

The blitzkrieg by Germany against England is now on and so far very little reliable news comes to us. Swarms of German planes cause havoc in England. This will probably be followed by a land invasion.

Our stock market shows doubt whether Britain can survive. It is at lowest point in 2 years and the volume of daily sales is lowest since 1916. In the meanwhile, domestic business is good and is feeling the stimulus of the defense program. Youngstown steel mills operate at 85%.

The national political campaign starts with Wendell Willkie opposing Franklin Roosevelt for a 3rd term. Willkie's chances look good. If Great Britain survives and Willkie wins we should experience an upsurge.

If Great Britain does go down—war orders will cease and there will be financial chaos. At present stock prices, I think it is a good gamble to buy although nobody can foresee the outcome.

AUGUST 21, 1940

The European war drags on. Air raids take place daily over London but the threatened Blitzkrieg has not yet taken place. The stock market continues to drag at low volume, waiting to see which way the battle will turn.

SEPTEMBER 10, 1940

For the past three days Germany has bombarded London unmercifully. This is supposed to be preliminary to a land invasion. If England can withstand the bombardment until then and hold back an invasion—then the crisis will be over for the winter and anything may happen before spring. The U.S. gave Britain 50 old destroyers in exchange for leases on naval bases. Co-operation between Britain and U.S. is growing closer. If the war lasts we will be in it by spring. Congress is about ready to draft all men between 21 and 45.

SEPTEMBER 25, 1940

Since Sept. 10th Germany has bombarded London incessantly and laid the city in ruins, but thus far no invasion has been possible and it seems now with the coming of fall weather that an invasion of England is out of the question until spring. The English Air Force has put up a battle that will be long remembered. Just now it looks like a long war—with starvation for Europe because of the British blockade. In the meanwhile the U.S. cooperates more closely with Britain and we may be in the war by spring. The peace-time conscription bill passed and registration takes place Oct. 16th for all men between the ages of 21 to 35.

SEPTEMBER 29, 1940

Each day the international situation grows more complicated and brings the U.S. closer to war. Yesterday Japan signs a pact with Germany and Italy agreeing on a military alliance if the U.S. enters the war. Then the Japanese proceed to march into French Indo-China. This endangers U.S. supply of tin, rubber and other essential materials. U.S. retaliated by cutting off export to Japan of scrap iron. It seems to me this will end soon in a declaration of war of U.S. and we will then see the 2 remaining democracies— U.S. and Britain—against the rest of the world, now under totalitarian domination.

In the meanwhile U.S. spends billions on defense and industry begins to hum. On Oct. 16th young men will register for the draft. The National Guard has been called to active training. Everything points to war. [Roth's wife] Marion has volunteered to help register the draftees.

Early corporation reports show about 25% of profits paid for taxes. The excess profits tax may add an additional 20 or 25%. This tax plus rising costs may result in a situation where industry works full gear but earns very little. This is one of the reasons why stocks have not increased with rising production. In spite of this I feel that stocks like Sheet & Tube at 32, Republic Steel at 18 and U.S. Steel at 58 are good buys. Higher taxes will to some extent be passed on to the consumer and these steel stocks which have not paid dividends for a long time will earn enough in spite of taxes, to pay good dividends.

War hysteria has blotted out the political campaign. Willkie delivers speeches but war headlines take precedence. Just now it looks as tho Roosevelt will get a 3rd term.

Time and again the thought of inflation comes into my mind. The national debt is $45 billion now. Defense contracts total $15 billion more and we are just getting started. In addition to this industry will borrow the huge bank surpluses for expansion. All this is borrowed money and higher taxes will not change the picture.

7/12/44
War debt is $200 billion and no inflation.

10/10/52
War debt is $270 billion and the 1939 dollar is now worth 52¢.

It seems to me we face a big headache after the war. If it follows the pattern of past wars we will have a first-post-war depression when the war ends (1921). This should last about 18 months while industry changes from war to peace time production. Then will come 6 or 8 years of hectic activity and inflation—while we feed and help to rebuild the world (1921–1929 period). At the end will come a severe crash and long depression during which currency will be placed on a normal basis and we hope for a quiet period for normalcy (1930–40).

It is a frightening picture and there is no assurance that either democracy or the capitalistic system can withstand the shock.

How to get ready to face such a world is the problem. To be conservative in investments or to be a gambler and fish in troubled waters? There will undoubtedly be violent up and down swings in the market. They will be unpredictable. Everybody will try to buy low and sell high. But what is "low" and what is "high" at a time like this? The inevitable result will be a group who will end with a profit but the vast majority broke and disillusioned.

4/2/62

I did not buy stocks because I was flat broke. Connie was in college and we had a tough time making ends meet.

OCTOBER 1, 1940

Joe R— was telling me today about Tony M—. Tony is unmarried—47—auditor for a steel company—earns about $5000. For the past 20 years has slowly accumulated the highest grade income stocks such as DuPont—G.E. etc. Buys one or two shares at a time whenever he can spare the money. Has a beautiful list of stocks today and a substantial income. Pays no attention to stock market.

Geo. F. Baker the New York banker varied this plan by buying good stocks whenever he thought they were selling below intrinsic value—and then held on. The trick is to have the cash whenever the opportunity to buy comes. During the late depression DuPont sold as high as 223 and as low as 22. Certainly the time and price of purchase were an important consideration. Seems to me Tony could have done better by holding his cash for the right buying opportunity.

EDITOR'S NOTE

In the buildup to the U.S. entry into World War II, a newfound symbiotic relationship between business and government was forged, strengthening the nation's defense while smoothing over many hindrances to corporate output and innovation. During Roosevelt's first two terms, corporate America resented many of the administration's New Deal policies—from the NRA to tax policies and tighter banking regulations—believing they sabotaged the natural need for freedom in private enterprise. But from 1940 onward, government's engagement with big business became much more cooperative as lucrative defense contracts were parceled out. In Youngstown Roth witnessed his local steel mills operating at full capacity as the nation ramped up for war. Nationally, some leaders would even leave private industry altogether to head federal agencies, such as Donald Nelson, a former vice president of Sears-Roebuck, who chaired the U.S. War Production Board from 1942 to 1945. The relationship would outlast the war as the military-industrial complex: an alliance between big business and government that would endure with mutual satisfaction for decades to come as industries finally realized the profitability of government spending and debt. Business would also finally regain its long-missed position of authority and respectability that it believed had been lost during the Great Depression.

Indeed, many historians and economists look to the relative success of the war production effort as validation of the fiscal theories of John Maynard Keynes, the British economist whose *General Theory of Employment, Interest, and Money* advocated New Deal–style government spending and "pump priming" to lift economies out of downturns. Through Roosevelt's first two terms there were always fiscal and political limits to his being able to enact a full Keynesian program, but the war created a mandate for massive government spending and private-sector output and is generally believed to have finally pulled America out of the Depression.

Even in strict employment terms, the war accomplished what the New Deal alone could not. When the Selective Training and Service Act of September 1940 required all men aged twenty-one to thirty-five to register for the draft, many young men were turned away from duty, even though there were just 350,000 in the navy, army, and air corps combined, due to malnutrition. This fact only underscored some of the shortcomings of the U.S. relief efforts. While New Deal employment and relief programs helped buoy the economy for about eight years, the nation was also still grappling with a 15 percent unemployment rate. Millions of families still had barely the means to exist on a subsistence level with an adequate dietary intake. The war was a great employer, but of course it also came at a tremendous cost.

<hr />

OCTOBER 16, 1940

Today 16 million men between the ages of 21 and 30 will register for the first military conscription in U.S. history. Marion is working on one of the draft registration boards and I have been named to the advisory board.

Steel mills and all industry is working at 100%—yet the stock market lags far behind. I think it is a good time to buy. Reasons given for the lag are uncertainty over the European situation and over possible entrance into war and uncertainty over the coming election. Betting odds have been 11 to 5 on Roosevelt but yesterday they dropped to 8 to 5. A small "Willkie" boom hit the stock market as a result.

From time to time people tell me their experience in the stock market. For the most part they were within reach of large profits but did not take them. Dr. S. D. said: In 1929 I held $180,000 in stocks subject to a 40% margin. The crash caught me and I rushed in to sell but my broker strongly advised against it. Later I had to put up $10,000 additional margin. I finally sold out in 1930 and salvaged only the $10,000 margin. I put this $10,000 in the Home Savings Bank. It closed in 1931. In 1932 when the market was at low ebb I sold my pass book on the Home Savings for $4000—and bought high grade stocks at about 1/10 their real value. I determined to hold these until the market came back to normal. I did hold on until first part of 1935 but then I needed money so badly I sold these stocks for about $10,000. Six months later these stocks shot sky high and I would have made an extra $50,000 if I had been able to hold on.

OCTOBER 15, 1940

This presidential election is the most exciting in 25 years. On every street corner people argue the matter and a good deal of bitterness is beginning to appear. Present national polls show Roosevelt with a popular lead of about 55% to 45% but Willkie is gaining steadily. If this trend keeps up he may win.

In the meanwhile both business and the stock market are stagnant although industry booms. It seems to me stocks are selling below their intrinsic value based on industrial activity. For instance Sheet & Tube is operating at capacity but the stock sells at 39. In normal times it would be selling in the 80s. The uncertainty of the national election and the fear that U.S. may enter the war plus new excessive profit taxes is holding everything back.

NOVEMBER 5, 1940

Today is Election Day. It brings to a close the most bitter campaign since the days of Bryan. Even the "polls" taken by nation-wide organizations are afraid to predict the result. It may be close—it may be a landslide. Wendell Willkie, 48, public utility president and lawyer, opposes "third term candidate" Franklin D. Roosevelt. Roosevelt pictures all the social leg-islations he has sponsored and promises the millennium if given four years more to finish his "New Deal"—pensions for the aged—food and housing for the submerged—peace and security and such an America as we have never dreamed of. Willkie promises to hold on to the social gains but to put a stop to the baiting of big business; to the trend toward government own-ership and national socialism. He promises a return to simple honesty, sac-rifice, hard work. He says the nine million unemployed can be put back to work by reasonable cooperation with business and by permitting business to expand without punitive taxes, government competition, etc. The cam-paign has been a liberal education to all in the real meaning of democracy and the American way of life. I have worked hard for Willkie but am not as optimistic as I should like to be.

Business has gone thru the usual election year dullness during the past two months although steel and other industries have been booming. Stocks have been stagnant and are far below prices that would be justified by pres-ent activity. During the past few days stock prices have advanced slightly to anticipate a possible Willkie victory. In New York betting odds are 9 to 5 on Roosevelt. There has been a strong demand recently for utility equities which are selling at receivership prices because of the government fight against them. It is thought they will fare better if Willkie wins.

It is predicted that if Roosevelt wins stocks will drift down and if Willkie wins they will go up—for about a week—and then in either case will adjust themselves to the war news.

It seems to me there is a lot of latent speculative fever which has not yet expressed itself since the outbreak of war in Sept. 1939. Given a Willkie vic-tory with the long-term assurance that an end has come to the war against business—it seems to me that the stock market could go far.

NOVEMBER 6, 1940

Franklin D. Roosevelt appears to have been re-elected by a landslide. Present incomplete reports indicate 458 electoral votes against 28. In the popular vote he receives only about 4 million votes more than Willkie. In Mahoning County all Democrats win. U.S. Senate and House are both Democratic. Harold Burton, Republican, appears to have won for Senate in spite of the landslide. It seems to me he has a good chance for the presi-dency in 4 years. Ohio re-elects its Republican governor.

NOVEMBER 7, 1940

The stock-market broke yesterday on news of Roosevelt's election and leading shares lost 2 to 4 points. Utilities in particular lost 25% of their quoted values because they have been the political football of this administration. I think it is a good time to buy. For instance Sheet & Tube sells at 40—will earn about $6 per share this year and much more next year. It should go to 75 or 80 in the next 6 months.

11/18/41

Wrong. Earns about $10 and sells at 34.

1/6/43

37 1/2

10/16/43

Sells at 35

2/22/44

@ 37

10/10/52

@ 90 (old)

4/7/62

@ 200 (old)

NOVEMBER 8, 1940

The stock market did a complete turnaround yesterday and "inflation" stocks such as steels gained 4 to 8 points. Utilities which are not much affected by inflation were stationary. It was all caused by a statement by Secy of Treas. Morgenthau that the defense program had only started—that the debt limit would be raised from $45 billion to $65 billion and that new U.S. bonds would not be tax exempt. U.S. Steel gained 7 7/8; Bethlehem Steel 6 1/2; Sheet & Tube 4 3/8, etc.

Inflation always pops up unfortunately. It is forgotten for awhile but is continually hovering in the background. Added to this, stocks are selling much below prices justified by the rate of industry, and there is a great deal of speculative fever which has been suppressed since the 1936–7 boom.

It becomes increasingly clear that nobody can predict the future behavior of the stock market. One day the results of the election upset it and the next day it booms because of some chance happening. Fools rush in to buy when the market is booming—the wise investor buys on darker days when he knows stocks are selling below value—and then holds on—confident that he cannot lose his principal and that sooner or later the market will come back and raise prices above their intrinsic value. To do this an investor must have liquid capital, courage and above all *patience and ability to hold on and wait*.

It is difficult to analyze the financial picture for the next 6 or 12 months. It seems to me that there cannot be a prolonged bull market because of the war uncertainty which dominates everything. There are three possible stages:

1. We are now in pre-war armament period.
   a. Industry is at high gear but how long it will continue nobody knows. Stocks will fluctuate widely for short periods but no prolonged bull market. Every change in the war front—threats that we will be drawn in—inflation fears—fear that war will suddenly end—all of these things preclude a long drawn bull market.
   b. In view of these short-period fluctuations it would seem wise to buy stocks whenever they are selling below intrinsic value and then to sell whenever a fair profit can be obtained.
2. War Period
   a. There is great probability that USA will be drawn into war before spring.
   b. Declaration of war might bring a crash in stocks.
   c. If this war is similar to the last one there will be no prolonged bull market during the war.
3. Post-War Period
   a. Should present money-making opportunities.
   b. Post war depression—post war boom—inflation and then a big crash.

NOVEMBER 23, 1940

The financial picture defies analysis. Industry is operating at boom levels, extra dividends are being declared, armaments are building up, huge government debts—and yet the stock market is stagnant and so is the legal profession. Retail stores are already feeling the impulse of Xmas shopping and are looking for the biggest season since 1929.

In these circumstances one would look for booming stock markets but the reverse is true. The most common explanations are:

1. Fear of sudden termination of war.
2. The New Deal will continue its old policies of restricting private enterprise, profit, etc.
3. The armament program will be carried forward without the help of private capital and if private capital is used it will receive such a low return of interest that investment will not be worthwhile.

It seems to me that the whole situation carries dynamite. Banks are crammed with huge unused deposits that could be the basis for credit inflation if some spark set it off. People have money and are spending it for clothes, gifts, etc. The times are uncertain and when the break will come nobody knows. Psychology and fear on the part of the holders of government bonds may start the trouble.

NOVEMBER 28, 1940

Yesterday a seat on the stock exchange sells for $34,000—lowest since November 1914. The 1914 sale took place just after outbreak of world war #1 when stock exchanges closed and no one knew what would happen when and if they were reopened. They did reopen and the same stock exchange seat sold for $625,000 in 1929. It seems to me the present situation is very similar. All industry is booming and it seems to me that sooner or later the market will follow.

NOVEMBER 29, 1940

A stock exchange seat sells for $33,000—lowest since 1899.

DECEMBER 4, 1940

A stock broker after 40 years experience said to me today: "The only people I know who ever made money in the stock market are those who bought for cash and owned the stocks outright. I do not recall a single margin trader who did not lose sooner or later."

DECEMBER 11, 1940

Col. Ayres of Cleveland gave his annual forecast yesterday. He predicted:

1. There will be a boom in 1941–2 in steel centers and industrial areas producing armaments. This will not be a chaotic boom a la the 1st World War. Taxes will be higher, wages higher and profits lower.
2. Agricultural areas will suffer because there is no overseas outlet for their produce.
3. A moderate rise in stock prices but no bull market. Stocks are selling low today in a comparison with industrial rate.
4. A firming of money rates and, after an early peak, a reaction in bond market.
5. Strength but not marked inflation in commodities.

Stocks remain stagnant, bonds go to dizzy heights and show a return as low as 1/2%. Gov'ts about 2%. Bonds today are as high as stocks were in 1929. It looks like an unhealthy situation. Seems to me interest rates must go up and there will be a crash in the bond market similar to stocks in 1929.

Retail trade is good but not as good as expected. Professional offices are idle.

DECEMBER 20, 1940

Very little to report. Retail stores are having a record Xmas season. Stocks have been drifting downward all month. Tax selling started late in November and is still on. It looks as tho U.S. will give full aid to Britain by giving all the arms she needs as a gift. Law practice is very slow in spite of the fact that Youngstown steel mills are operating at capacity.

DECEMBER 27, 1940

I have been thinking today of the experience of my friend A. B. in the stock market. He bought 1000 Warner at 3 1/8 outright in February 1935. This was at the beginning of a long rise which culminated in a severe crash in early spring 1937. I think A bought at that time on a mere hunch and without any thought of the coming rise. He held the stock and saw it go to a top of 18 in early 1937. Instead of selling and taking his profit he used this stock as collateral to buy more stocks on margin. In 1937 just before the collapse he bought and sold many stocks on margin. At one time his equity amounted to $30,000. In March 1937 the collapse came and he was wiped out. A year later he had a heart attack and died shortly after that. I have always felt that his experience in the stock market contributed to his illness. Looking back now it is difficult to criticize him. Even the experts did not foresee the coming rise in 1935 and none of them foresaw the collapse in 1937. It came and went without rhyme or reason. When A. began to speculate on margin early in 1937 business and the market were booming. Everybody was talking about the coming boom and inflation.

One thing is clear. Every speculator gets washed out sooner or later. If A. had sold his Warner stock late in 1937 and taken a profit—he would have gone back again for more. No one can guess right every time and sooner or later he would have gotten burned.

Another thing is clear. He held Warner stock for 2 years and watched a rising market carry it from 3 to 18—and then at the top of the market he began to buy heavily on margin. This was illogical. The market cannot go up forever and a break was due.

If A. had sold Warner at 18 and then held his money until a crash came then he could have bought again with some degree of safety. In 1938 Warner was selling again at 3. Since 1930 there have been 8 or 9 booms and collapses. The only person who could have survived them all—without much guessing or risk—would be one who bought bargains in sound stocks every time a collapse came and then selling at reasonable profit when prices returned to normal. If he bought a good stock outright at a bargain he would not have to worry or guess about what the market was going to do. His stock would not go much lower—would possibly pay dividends while he held it—and in all probability would someday go back to normal. This method presupposes some way of judging the real or intrinsic value of a stock. It also requires courage and patience—and liquid capital at a time when money is usually hard to get.

DECEMBER 30, 1940

President Roosevelt delivered a radio address last night in which he urged more aid to Britain. There will be a fight in Congress this coming session but I believe in the end Britain will get our help even if it means war.

The business picture for the coming year is clouded by war. Industry (and Youngstown in particular) will boom in the making of war materials. Wages will be higher and steadier and this ought to help my law practice.

The lawyers deserve a break. Stocks however will be uncertain because of higher taxes, higher cost of production and war uncertainty.

Because American help to Britain is not yet effective it seems to me that Hitler must do something this spring or the tide will definitely turn against him. This means that the next three or four months will see much fighting and possibly an attempted invasion of Britain. If the attempt succeeds the outlook will be black and the stock market will crash. If the attempt fails it may well become the turning point of the war. With such failure should come greater confidence and a rising stock market. I think the attempt will fail and the next few months may offer the opportunity to accumulate well selected stocks. My guess (?) then is a different market until possibly May or June and then a rising market if the fortunes of war indicate that Britain can hold out until America can give her substantial aid. The chances are 50–50 but I would bet on Britain.

1941

JANUARY 2, 1941

In an unprecedented step the U.S. Federal Reserve Board makes public certain recommendations to prevent possible inflation. It points out the danger of inflation rising from the huge armament boom, huge bank reserves, etc. The Federal Reserve Board has issued very few warnings in the past but they have been right every time. For this reason, I hope the President takes their warning seriously and follows the plan suggested.

JANUARY 2, 1941

Russel Weisman the economist gives a very conservative forecast for the coming year. He feels that much of the industrial activity in the past 6 months was devoted to producing for consumption in America rather than for Europe. Huge inventories have been built up in anticipation of higher prices. Since domestic supply is ample for the next 6 months, industry will now have to turn to war orders. It will take time to convert these plants to war orders and this means a slack season just as automobile plants close down each year to re-tool for new models. After war production starts, activity will be no greater than now because plants are working at full capacity and no new plants have been built. He does not look for a stock boom. "Smart money" stayed out of the market because government taxes and restrictions made large profits impossible. The same condition will exist in 1941 unless government policy is changed. Industry is just as active now as in 1918 but it is now a profitless prosperity. Hence the low prices of stocks.

4/1/62

He was very much wrong. This was a good time to buy.

Weisman predicts for 1941:

1. Costs will increase and profits get narrower.
2. Gov't regulation will be extended.
3. Interest rates will not harden in next 6 months.
4. Non-war and luxury business will be restricted.
5. Corporations will make small profits in war orders.
6. Agriculture will be badly off on account of loss of exports.
7. Some rise in living costs—no inflation.
8. 1941 industrial production will exceed 1940 about 10%.

In Wall St. stock trading for 1940 was the smallest in 21 years, bond trading the smallest in 17 years and stock exchange seats sold at their lowest price since 1899. This in spite of industry enjoying a war boom. There is so much psychology in the picture that it seems to me that during the coming year a brighter chance for Britain to win or an inflation scare would send stocks up rapidly.

Youngstown ought to have a good year because employment is high and people have money. I hope it helps the law profession. During the past 10 years we lawyers—like investment bankers and brokers—have been shedding tears in the midst of seeming prosperity.

JANUARY 6, 1941

Russel Weisman points out today that the Federal Reserve recommendations have come too late to prevent inflation. To adopt the plan means higher interest rates and "hard money" policy. The gov't debt is now $45 billion and may rise to $80 billion in the next 5 years. The gov't must continue its easy money policy at low interest rates so it can carry this huge debt. An increase in interest would break the gov't bond market, stop further gov't loans during the war crises, create fear and bring on dreaded inflation immediately.

This means the easy-money policy must continue during the war crisis. Gov't debt and bank reserves will increase. When the war ends and interest rates return to normal then the inflation will come. The longer it is postponed—the greater the debt and bank reserves—the greater will be the inflation and the subsequent break-down.

JANUARY 29, 1941

U.S. Steel reports 1940 earnings at $7.84 per common share. The stock sells at 67. Sheet & Tube earned slightly less than $6 in 1940 and the stock sells at 40. It is this way all thru the stock list even tho it seems that 1941 and 1942 will be busy industrial years. In spite of higher taxes and other restrictions I feel that these stocks are a good buy and that one day soon the market will break out of its present lethargy. The market has been almost at a standstill so far this year and yesterday a stock exchange seat sold for $30,000—lowest in 40 years.

In Youngstown business is slow even tho the mills are at capacity. People seem to be saving their money for expected strikes or other emergencies.

FEBRUARY 1, 1941

A stock exchange seat sells today for $27,000—lowest since Spanish American War. It reflects the pessimism of the stockbroker as to the future of the brokerage business. It is a crazy picture. Industry in a war boom— stock market stagnant—gov't bonds bringing less than 1% and selling at a high premium—stocks low and selling at five times earnings. Looks to me like a good time to buy. Someday and somehow the dam will burst. [Undated note here: "Right you were—but you had no money to buy."]

FEBRUARY 18, 1941

Industry booms—people hoard their money—general business only fair—and the stock market drags at low level. Seems to be waiting for the turn of events in Europe where the spring drive is just beginning to take shape.

MARCH 1, 1941

Business and the stock market drag along at low levels while industry booms. Germany takes over Bulgaria and prepares to march into Turkey. Looks as tho the war in Europe will get active again.

Six months ago the Federal Reserve Board recommended the gov't take certain steps to avoid inflation. This advice was ignored and the gov't continues to borrow at an increasing rate. If inflation was possible 5 years ago then it must be closer now. The gov't plan seems to be to prevent price rise by decree and priority. It did not work in the French inflation and I do not think it will work here. Recently the gov't put a ceiling on scrap prices. Many dealers who had large stocks held for a speculative rise simply refuse to sell at these prices or get boot-leg prices. Defense industries complain they cannot get enough scrap. Either the gov't will have to take complete control or let prices go up in a national response to supply and demand—and this may be the beginning of inflation. Because we have pledged ourselves to huge armament production it seems to me that sooner or later prices will go up in order to get full production and I do not believe that government decree will for long halt the rise of prices.

MARCH 14, 1941

The screwy business situation continues. Steel mills operate at 100%—part of the population draws large pay envelopes—others are on relief. Retail business is only fair and law business is scarce. People hold on to their money because of fear of strikes. Congress after long debate passes the lease-lend bill which promises full aid to Britain. Congress is now passing a bill to give the President seven billion dollars to carry out the terms of the bill. This increases the debt to $53 billion with no limit in sight and yet there is no excitement or talk of inflation. People have become calloused to an increase of the debt. The stock market is at a standstill—stocks sell at 6 times earnings and pay dividends of 5% and 6% but no buyers. They are afraid of a collapse in Europe—confiscatory taxes—government control, etc. Bonds bring a return of 2%. It is truly a profitless prosperity. It seems to me a good time to buy stocks but what can one use for money? Someday—and soon I think—the bond market will collapse as stocks did in 1929 and then stocks will go up to more reasonable levels.

APRIL 5, 1941

The country is torn by huge strikes which slow up production for defense. All of the Ford plants are closed and a crisis is approaching in the steel and coal industries. So far the government has been pro-labor but it now seems to be facing a crisis with public sentiment rapidly changing against labor.

Rising wages and booming industry renew talk of inflation but the stock market remains stagnant. Retail trade, automobiles etc. are good but law practice continues slowly.

APRIL 8, 1941

Germany starts a blitz-krieg in the Balkans and for the first 3 days meets very little resistance. As a result the stock market sinks slowly.

The stores are having a busy Easter season with people buying like mad. In the midst of all this activity the law offices stand isolated and inactive.

Talk of inflation and rising prices crops up again. It is suggested that the government stop inflation by taking away increased earnings of the labor group in the following manner.

1. By increased taxes on lower incomes.
2. By selling government bonds direct to workers.

Our office girl gets a new job at a wage we cannot afford to pay. We will have to pay more now although business is not good. For the first time in many years jobs will be waiting for college graduates and they will be in demand.

APRIL 21, 1941

The gov't puts a limit on steel prices just after steel industry grants a wage increase of 10¢ per hour. More and more talk of inflation and more restrictions by government to prevent.

The war in the Balkans goes badly with the Allies and it looks as tho Hitler will have full control of the European continent. Also looks as tho U.S. will soon start to convoy ships and become involved in the war. Retail business is good and law work continues stagnant. It is nerve-wracking to sit in a quiet office while elsewhere business is booming. I don't quite know what to do about it. With increased wages there should soon be more activity in real estate and with it more legal work.

The stock market is also stagnant and drifts down to the lows of 1939.

The S.E.C. starts to break up the utility holding companies and their common stocks go to record lows. The theory is that in liquidation the common stocks will be worthless.

APRIL 24, 1941

President Roosevelt has certainly made this a "profitless" war boom for big industry. The steel industry for instance is forbidden to raise prices and yet costs including wages, taxes and materials are constantly going up. Caught between a fixed price ceiling and rising costs—the profit margin becomes less and less. Sheet & Tube Co. as an example is now operating at a theoretical 107% capacity—and the stock sells at $30 per share. Small wonder that a steady deflation of stock prices goes on and stock exchange seats sell at record lows. So far only the laboring class has profited by increased wages and steady employment.

MAY 21, 1941

There is very little to report. During the past month industry has been booming but stocks are low and the market stagnant. Brokers are being forced out of business. Priorities, price ceilings and taxes that take all the profit are making this a profitless boom. Financially I am almost as badly off as at the depth of the depression. The U.S. is constantly on the verge of a declaration of war and the situation in Europe does not look encouraging.

MAY 28, 1941

It looks very much as though the U.S. is in the world war. In a very aggressive speech last night Roosevelt warned the dictator countries that U.S. ships would deliver armaments to Great Britain—that our boats would freely sail the seven seas and if fired upon or attacked would fight back.

It is interesting to note that the President has declared a national emergency and brought the U.S. to the brink of war without first dealing with Congress. This is typical of constitutional evasions during the past 8 years.

Law business continues slack in the face of an industrial boom since Sept. 1939. One lawyer express the thought that the law profession would be busy next fall. His theory is that the public is paying old debts and filling depression-created needs with their present earnings. It is tough to see everybody on the march except your own profession.

MAY 29, 1941

I talked with Paul C— today. He says "During the past few years I have been spending most of my time in brokers' offices trying to make a little money buying and selling stocks. I am disgusted and I will sell everything I have and stop fooling with it. For four years now the market has been stagnant and the chances to make money will not come again."

I cannot quite agree with him. It is true the market has been stagnant for several years and this is why so many brokers have gone broke. High taxes etc. prevent corporations from keeping their profits and there has been no bull market in spite of a boom in industry. On the other hand many stocks are now selling below intrinsic value and pay returns from 6% to 10%. It seems to me now is a good time to buy these stocks and they will not only show a good investment return but in the next year or two may show a substantial capital gain. As examples Sheet & Tube, Inland and National Steel are all good companies; are selling at 32—69—44—pretty close to intrinsic values— they all pay dividends in excess of 6% and have a good chance for appreciation in an inflation scare or any other happening that might drive stocks up.

JULY 9, 1941

Business hums along at top speed. As an example, G.E. received orders amounting to $521 million in first 6 months of 1941 as against $212 million in first 6 months of 1940. An increase of 145%. Same is true of all industries. Profits however have not increased because of higher taxes, wages, etc. As a result stock prices have been stagnant although during the past week they have started to move up.

Germany now fights Russia—the U.S. plants troops in Iceland and we slowly draw closer to a "shooting war."

Retail trade is good, consumers load up with household equipment, new autos, etc. for fear of a shortage. There is occasionally talk about inflation because of the growing national debt (now $49 billion) and because of the failure of the government so far to fix prices.

As usual the law profession drags along in the vanguard and has reflected very little of the war boom.

AUGUST 4, 1941

Business continues at top speed but profits of most large corporations for first half of 1941 are lower on account of higher wages, material costs, etc.

The threat of war with Japan cuts off further silk supply and closes hosiery mills. Women rush to the stores and put in an advance supply. For fear of inflation and a shortage the consuming public has been buying automobiles, furniture, real estate, radio, etc.

The government fears inflation and Congress is about to pass a bill increasing taxes and freezing prices. We are fast developing a war economy and its effect is not uniform. Many small concerns are closing their doors for lack of materials. Big industries, retail trade, automobiles, etc. are very busy. Law business has not yet benefitted except by a few real estate deals. Stocks are stagnant because of low profits shown on earning reports:

OCTOBER 10, 1941

Since the war started in Sept. 1939 there has been increasing talk of inflation, priorities, freezing of prices, higher taxes, embargos etc.

All this has led to three different buying sprees on the part of the public: First came the buying of heavy goods such as automobiles and real estate; next the buying of furniture, refrigerators, radios and household equipment. The recent embargo on silk started a rush for soft goods such as silk stockings, linens and wearing apparel. Most of the American public has already prepared itself for the duration. Stores are frantically stocking up big inventories. An unexpected end of the war would bring chaos.

It is a curious fact that none of these inflation scares have caused buying of common stocks. Due to high taxes 1941 earnings are lower in many cases than 1940 and in the opinion of most people the picture is dark. Here again the public goes to the reverse extreme and I look for a rush for stocks one of these days. It seems to me many stocks today are a good buy. Likewise all these inflation scares and rising prices have not helped the law profession. In an inflation we would fare badly.

OCTOBER 10, 1941

A good many wonder why stock prices remain low while industry booms. The answer seems to be that the market is acting just as if we were actually in the war. If this is correct and if the market follows the pattern of the last war then we may expect:

1. A stagnant and lower drifting market until we get into a "shooting war."

2. A still lower market after we enter a shooting war.
3. During the war the market will rise with good war news and reverse. Business will not affect stock prices.
4. If war seems to be heading toward final victory prices will start up.
5. If victorious armistice declared—prices will go up for about a year.
6. Then comes primary war depression.
7. Then 10 years of inflation and boom.
8. Then the big collapse—2nd war depression and this will be worse than the 1929 collapse. May even end in alteration of whole capitalistic system.

NOVEMBER 18, 1941

There is very little to add. Business booms as we get closer to a shooting war—and the stock market continues depressed and stagnant. Strikes continue—wages of workmen go higher—prices rise—shortages and priorities everywhere—government debt rises rapidly—and there are many signs of approaching inflation. My law practice is only fair—and does not reflect the business boom. Taxes are increasing and there is talk of compulsory savings laws affecting 10% or 15% of income to prevent inflation. My guess is that none of these laws can prevent the working out of the economic laws or save us from punishment for the reckless spending of the past 10 years.

NOVEMBER 29, 1941

Stockbrokers are having a most difficult time making a living. Their offices are deserted. Many have closed. Some of the men who formerly earned large commissions are now earning as low as $50 or $100 per month.

DECEMBER 6, 1941

Tax selling started early this year and has driven stocks down to low levels of 1938. Most of the sales are in low-priced utility stocks.

DECEMBER 8, 1941

Yesterday—Sunday Dec. 7th—Japan without warning attacks Hawaii, Philippine Island, Guam and other points. Several hundred people killed. I just returned from lunch and heard Pres. Roosevelt ask a joint session of Congress for a declaration of war against Japan. So the U.S. enters a shooting war.

DECEMBER 9, 1941

The 2nd day of war finds the U.S. in the midst of war hysteria. Blackouts take place in New York and Los Angeles. Many false reports of invasion by Japanese planes. 1500 lives lost at Hawaii & Philippines. The stock market has another bad day today: 2 1/2 million shares.

DECEMBER 11, 1941

Germany and Italy declare war against the U.S. about an hour ago. It is expected that both houses of Congress will meet this afternoon. Stocks dropped again yesterday. AT&T dropped from 138 to 133. A stock exchange seat sells for $19,000—lowest since 1898. Roosevelt asks for 7 day week—speeding up of industry and cessation of strikes.

DECEMBER 15, 1941

The market continues stagnant about 5 points below pre-war prices and the lowest since 1938.

One financial writer thought this was a good time to buy stocks—many of which are paying over 10% dividends and selling at 4 or 5 times earnings. He said we must conclude U.S. will win the war and on this theory stocks are a good buy for the long pull because:

1. Most industries—like GM—are changing over from peace to war production—and later will reverse the process. Even tho the gov't will not permit large profits they will be permitted to keep reasonable earnings and pay a fair investment return.
2. Public utilities will suffer from rising costs against fixed rates.
3. Little business will be squeezed—some out of existence—but big business will go on.
4. Even the taxes will be raised—it is all being spent on war production and goes back into business.
5. Stocks are selling today on a 20% earning basis. Even if taxes go higher they are a good buy for long pull.

6. After war there will be a great need for peace-time production.

7. If inflation comes—it is better to own good common stocks than cash.

DECEMBER 31, 1941

This is the craziest business year I have ever been through. We are at war, steel mills have been humming, wages are high and everybody working—yet my law practice was worse in 1941 than in 1940. Because of war, high taxes, threat of inflation, government restrictions, etc. etc. business men are afraid to expand, buy real estate or do anything constructive and there is very little for the lawyer except an occasional divorce case or other domestic business. The same with the stock market. It has dragged all year—brokers are even worse off than lawyers—stock exchange seats sell at record lows, etc. Some businesses do a record business and others go broke. It is all a matter of luck. Auto dealers sold a record number of cars in 1940 and now there are no tires to sell. Tires have been rationed—so dealers in new tires are out of business while second-hand dealers and re-treaders are busy. There may be a few people who are making money but I do not know who they are. This is truly a "profitless" prosperity and it takes a strong heart to remain in business.

EDITOR'S NOTE

Benjamin Roth continued writing his diary about the national and global economies and life in Youngstown until his death in 1978 at the age of eighty-four. While World War II brought its own hardships, both Roth's family and his law practice finally began to prosper in the 1940s. Benjamin was a very active member of the Youngstown community, heading up the local draft board, serving as president of the Bar Association, holding elective office in Youngstown, and serving on many community boards of directors, including the Youngstown School Board. The law firm that he founded continues in practice today, with Daniel B. Roth as the senior partner.

FOR FURTHER READING

There are several classic books about the stock market crash that are still very valuable resources today. There is a good reason that John Kenneth Galbraith's *Great Crash of 1929* has never gone out of print since it was published in 1955; its wit and insight continue to enlighten new generations of readers. Robert Sobel's *Great Bull Market: Wall Street in the 1920s* (W. W. Norton, 1968) is a concise but detailed summary of the age that came to a close. More recent crash scholarship includes *The Speculation Economy: How Finance Triumphed over Industry* (Berrett-Koehler, 2007) by Lawrence E. Mitchell, which gives a thorough overview of the evolution of the stock market in the 1920s. Other books that were helpful in gaining a deeper understanding of the financial markets of the era include *The Banking Panics of the Great Depression* by Elmus Wicker (Cambridge University Press, 2000) and *The Crash and Its Aftermath: A History of Securities Markets in the United States, 1929–1933* by Barrie A. Wigmore (Greenwood, 1985).

No analysis of the Great Depression or the New Deal is complete without a reading of the three-volume set *The Age of Roosevelt* (Houghton Mifflin, 1957) by Arthur M. Schlesinger Jr. The first two volumes, *The Crisis of the Old Order, 1919–1933* and *The Coming of the New Deal, 1933–1935* were particularly relevant to this book. Another fine explanation for the causes of the Great Depression and a detailed overview of the FDR years is *The New Deal: The Depression Years, 1933–1940* by Anthony J. Badger (Ivan R. Dee, 1989). Two indispensable books (complete with photos) on the devastating impact of the Great Depression on the everyday life of Americans are *The Great Depression: America in the 1930s* (Little, Brown, 1993) and *Daily Life in the United States, 1920–1940* (Ivan R. Dee, 2002) by David E. Kyvig. John A. Garraty's *Great Depression: A Classic Study of the Worldwide Depression of the 1930s* (Anchor Books, 1987) provides a thorough background on the effects of the economic downturn around the world. *Radical Visions and American Dreams: Culture and Social Thought in the Depression Years* (University of Illinois Press, 1998) by Richard H. Pells offers a valuable cultural history of the era from a leftist perspective.

From the Crash to the Blitz, 1929–1939 by Cabell B. H. Phillips and

Herbert Mitgang (Fordham University Press, 2000) and sections of *The FDR Years: On Roosevelt and His Legacy* by William Edward Leuchtenburg (Columbia University Press, 1997) also provided background for this book. For a sympathetic review of the Hoover years, nothing compares to the recollections of the president himself in *The Memoirs of Herbert Hoover* (Macmillan, 1952). In addition, two general reference books were also helpful resources: *Encyclopedia of the Great Depression* by Robert S. McElvaine (Macmillan Reference, 2004) and *Encyclopedia of the Great Depression and the New Deal* (Sharp Reference, 2000), edited by James Liment.

There are also many useful and provocative works published more recently. Liaquat Ahamed's *Lords of Finance: The Bankers Who Broke the World* (Penguin Press, 2009) is a gripping, well-informed account of how financial authorities in the world's large economies bungled through the crisis of the late 1920s. For a quick single-volume read, Eric Rauchway's *Great Depression and the New Deal: A Very Short Introduction* (Oxford University Press, 2008) is hard to beat; it is a model blend of scholarship and readability. Alan Brinkley's *End of Reform: New Deal Liberalism in Recession and War* (Random House, 1996) provides an exceptional level of detail into the politics and schisms inside the Roosevelt administration. Jonathan Alter sheds important new light on FDR's actions in *The Defining Moment: FDR's Hundred Days and the Triumph of Hope* (Simon and Schuster, 2006). And Amity Shlaes makes a case for the anti–New Deal opposition in *The Forgotten Man: A New History of the Great Depression* (HarperCollins, 2007).

For details about the history of Youngstown and its steel industry, there can be no match for *Steeltown U.S.A.: Work and Memory in Youngstown* (University Press of Kansas, 2002) by Sherry Lee Linkon and John Russo, a passionate and thorough examination of how the boom and bust of the steel mills affected the city of Youngstown and its surrounding area.

ACKNOWLEDGMENTS

DANIEL B. ROTH ACKNOWLEDGES:

In August 2008, my son, Bill, phoned me from his Wall Street office and said that if I was ever going to publish the portion of my father's diary dealing with the Great Depression, now was the time to do so. I realized that he was right but told him I had no idea how to proceed. Bill spoke with friends in New York who led me to Jim Ledbetter, editor of "The Big Money," a Web magazine that is owned by the *Washington Post*. Jim became fascinated by the diary and began publishing entries on the Internet. As a result, I was contacted by a New York publishing firm that expressed an interest in a book deal. I decided at this point that I had better get a literary agent, and so once again I turned to Bill, who ultimately brought me together with Chris Calhoun of Sterling Lord Literistic, Inc. With Chris as my agent and Jim Ledbetter at my side, we ended up with an outstanding publisher, PublicAffairs, working with Clive Priddle and Niki Papadopoulos and their very professional team.

As a naïve newcomer to the publishing world, I know that I could never have fulfilled my promise to my dad without people like Jim, Chris, Clive, Niki, and their professional coworkers. Likewise, I must express my deepest gratitude to my son, Bill, who not only helped put the team together but also worked closely with me throughout the entire process. Bill, your grandfather would have appreciated all your efforts—as do I. Likewise, I owe a debt of gratitude to my nieces, Jan Deutsch Strasfeld and Jody Nudell; my daughters, Dr. Jennifer Forche and Rochelle Landy; my secretary, Mary Ann McCloskey; and my law partners and the staff at Roth, Blair, Roberts, Strasfeld & Lodge—all of whom cheered me on and helped me along the way. And most of all, thanks to my wife, JoAnn, who sacrificed a great deal of our time together so that I could maintain my law practice during the day and work on this book at night and on weekends, and who enthusiastically supported the entire project.

Well, Dad, I promised you in 1978 that I would someday publish your diary—and finally, with the help of all of these people, I fulfilled that promise!

JAMES LEDBETTER ACKNOWLEDGES:

Bill Roth would never have contacted me in the fall of 2008 but for the September launch of The Big Money, and so for the ability to originally publish diary excerpts there, I thank Jacob Weisberg and John Alderman of the Slate Group, the Washington Post Company, and TBM's fantastic staff. This is my second book with PublicAffairs, where there are some great new faces as well as some familiar ones. It is a rare pleasure in the book business to feel that you have an entire publishing house behind you. My agent, Chris Calhoun, put a lot of thinking and positioning into this project before taking it to market, which is why it has the success it has, for which I am very grateful.

The Youngstown Public Library, Ohio Historical Society, and Mahoning Valley Historical Society provided vital research material for this book. I'd particularly like to thank William Lawson of the Historical Society for his generosity with his time and insights. I am also grateful to the Library of Congress, Franklin Delano Roosevelt Library, and National Archives for providing the photographs that round out the diary.

Ultimately, the star of this book is Benjamin Roth's diary, so I thank Bill and Dan Roth for letting me work on it, and their family for their support and enthusiasm.

The biggest acknowledgment must go to my wife, Erinn Bucklan. The amount of research, writing, and organizing she put into this book cannot be overstated. She threw herself into the project on a tight deadline and came through time and again, whether with the exact right photo or one more insight into the shortcomings of the Hoover administration. This book literally would not and could not exist without her.

BENJAMIN ROTH was born in New York City in 1894 and moved shortly thereafter to Youngstown, Ohio. After serving as an Army officer during World War I, he returned to Youngstown to start a law practice which still operates today as Roth, Blair, Roberts, Strasfeld & Lodge, with his son, Daniel B. Roth, as chairman. Roth was very active in the community, including serving as president of the Mahoning County Bar Association and as a member of the Youngstown Board of Education. He continued to practice law for 59 years until his death in 1978. [Photo credit: Courtesy of Daniel B. Roth]

JAMES LEDBETTER is the editor of "The Big Money," Slate.com's Web site on business and economics. Prior to joining Slate, he was deputy managing editor of CNNMoney.com, a financial news site. His most recent book is *Dispatches for the New York Tribune: Selected Journalism of Karl Marx*. He is also the author of *Starving to Death on $200 Million: The Short, Absurd Life of the Industry Standard* and *Made Possible By...: The Death of Public Broadcasting in the United States*. He is a former senior editor of *Time* magazine and *The Industry Standard*, and former staff writer for *The Village Voice*. He lives in New York, NY. [Photo credit: Barry Marsden]

DANIEL B. ROTH is a lawyer, business executive, and venture capitalist. He is currently chairman of the Youngstown, Ohio law firm which was founded by his father, Benjamin Roth. He is also the chairman of both McDonald Steel Corporation and Torent, Inc. [Photo credit: Bob Knuff]

PUBLICAFFAIRS is a publishing house founded in 1997. It is a tribute to the standards, values, and flair of three persons who have served as mentors to countless reporters, writers, editors, and book people of all kinds, including me.

I. F. STONE, proprietor of *I. F. Stone's Weekly*, combined a commitment to the First Amendment with entrepreneurial zeal and reporting skill and became one of the great independent journalists in American history. At the age of eighty, Izzy published *The Trial of Socrates*, which was a national bestseller. He wrote the book after he taught himself ancient Greek.

BENJAMIN C. BRADLEE was for nearly thirty years the charismatic editorial leader of *The Washington Post*. It was Ben who gave the *Post* the range and courage to pursue such historic issues as Watergate. He supported his reporters with a tenacity that made them fearless, and it is no accident that so many became authors of influential, best-selling books.

ROBERT L. BERNSTEIN, the chief executive of Random House for more than a quarter century, guided one of the nation's premier publishing houses. Bob was personally responsible for many books of political dissent and argument that challenged tyranny around the globe. He is also the founder and was the longtime chair of Human Rights Watch, one of the most respected human rights organizations in the world.

    ·   ·   ·

For fifty years, the banner of Public Affairs Press was carried by its owner Morris B. Schnapper, who published Gandhi, Nasser, Toynbee, Truman, and about 1,500 other authors. In 1983 Schnapper was described by *The Washington Post* as "a redoubtable gadfly." His legacy will endure in the books to come.

Peter Osnos, *Founder and Editor-at-Large*